Wanted TO BUY

THIRD EDITION

A listing of serious buyers paying CASH
for everything collectible!

COLLECTOR BOOKS
A Division of Schroeder Publishing Co., Inc.

The current values in this book should be used only as a guide. They are not intended to set prices, which vary from one section of the country to another. Auction prices as well as dealer prices vary greatly and are affected by condition as well as demand. Neither the Editors nor the Publisher assumes responsibility for any losses that might be incurred as a result of consulting this guide.

All ink drawings are by Beth Summers.

Additional copies of this book may be ordered from:

Collector Books
P.O. Box 3009
Paducah, KY 42002-3009

@$9.95. Add $2.00 for postage and handling.

Copyright: Schroeder Publishing Co., 1992

This book or any part thereof may not be reproduced without the written consent of the Author and Publisher.

Printed by Image Graphics, Paducah, Kentucky

Introduction

This book was compiled to help put serious buyers in contact with the non-collecting sellers all over the country. Most of us have accumulated things that are not particularly valuable to us but could very well be of interest to one of the buyers in this book. Not only does this book list the prices that collectors are willing to pay on thousands of items, it also lists hundreds of interested buyers along with the type of material each is buying. *Wanted To Buy* is very easy to use. The listings are alphabetically arranged by subject, with the interested buyer's name and address preceding each group of listings. In the back of the book, we have included a special section which lists the names and addresses of over 250 buyers along with the categories that they are interested in. When you correspond with these buyers, be sure to enclose a self-addressed, stamped envelope if you want a reply. If you wish to sell your material, quote the price that you want or send a list. Ask if there are any items on the list that they might be interested in and the price that they would be willing to pay. If you want the list back, be sure to send a S.A.S.E. large enough for it to be returned.

Packing and Shipping Instructions

Special care must be exercised in shipping fragile items in the mail or U.P.S. Double-boxing is a must when shipping glass and china pieces. It is extremely important that each item be wrapped in several layers of newspaper. First, put a four-inch layer of wadded newspaper in the bottom of the box. Secondly, start placing the well-wrapped items on top of the crushed newspaper, making certain that each piece of glass or china is separated from the others. Make sure that there are at least four inches of cushioning newspaper or foam between each item. When the box is nearly full, place more cushioning material on top of the contents and then seal the box.

Finally, place this box and contents in a large box cushioned again with a at least four inches of newspaper on all four sides, top and bottom. This double-boxing is very important. Our Postal Service and United Parcel Service are efficient; however, we must pack well just in case there is undue bumping in handling.

When shipping coins and precious metals, be sure to register your shipment and request a return slip so that you will know that the buyer received the goods as well as the date that they were delivered. All material should be insured for full value. Remember always use strong boxes, lots of packing and good shipping tape.

ADDING MACHINES AND CALCULATORS

The first calculators were made by European theologians and mathematicians in the seventeenth century. It was Charles Xavier Thomas from Colmar, France, who built the first successful calculator. Between 1821 and 1878, he sold 1,500 machines. The surviving examples of these early machines, called Arithmometre, can be found all over the world.

The first simple adding machines for bookkeeping were made in the U.S. in the last quarter of the nineteenth century. None of those simple machines found a lot of buyers, and they are hard to find today. One of the most important names in the U.S. history of adding machines, Dorr E. Felt, started to produce the legendary 'Comptometer' in 1889. Successful machines which are so plentiful today (and are therefore not valuable) are: Burroughs, Victor, Remington, Golden Gem, Lightning, and others.

I am very eager to buy scarce adding machines and calculators. Especially simple machines made before 1900 and hand-held machines such as the Midget will enhance my collection. Please contact me for a complete list of machines wanted.

Peter Frei
P.O. Box 500
Brimfield, MA 01010-0500
1-800-942-8968

We Pay

Baldwin Arithmometre 1874	600.00+
Baldwin 1875	750.00+
Bouchet 1883	1,600.00+
Calcumeter, The Standard Desk Calcumeter	200.00+
Comptograph w/Wooden Frame	1,000.00+
Comptometer	20.00+
Comptometer w/Wooden Frame	450.00+
Contostyle, Arithstyle	180.00+
Diera	600.00+
Gab-Ka	700.00+
Gem w/Wooden Frame	250.00+
Golden Gem	40.00+
Grant	1,500.00+
Lightning	30.00+
Midget	1,000.00+
Millionaire	600.00+
Original Odhner	50.00+
Peerless	400.00+

Rapid Computer Adding Machine 1893 .... **200.00+**
Saxonia w/Wooden Case .... **600.00+**
Smith 1881 .... **650.00+**
Spalding .... **750.00+**
Thomas Arithmometre... **1,300.00+**
Weeb's .... **140.00+**

ADVERTISING

    Ardent collector will pay top price for **oil and gas signs, advertising clocks, neon hand-painted signs, store displays or fixtures with advertising, soda signs, whiskey signs, tip trays, beer trays and signs, farm signs, etc.** Rust, holes, and dents detract from value although the brand name may lessen the importance of damage. Please send photos as well as descriptions as they are invaluable in determining price.

Lisa Nieland
1228 W Main St.
Red Wing, MN 55066

Advertising Tins   **We Pay**

Coffee.. **15.00+**

Advertising

Tobacco	**10.00+**
Store Bins	**20.00+**

Advertising Signs   We Pay

Porcelain, single-sided	**25.00+**
Porcelain, double-sided	**40.00+**
Porcelain, hangs parallel with wall	**45.00+**
Lithographed	**45.00+**
Wooden	**30.00+**
Painted	**30.00+**

Self-framed tin signs with advertising messages were made from about 1880 to 1920. 'Self-framed' means that when the sign was made it was stamped and printed with a wood or brass pattern that looked like a frame around the sign's picture.

Like many items originally given away by companies to advertise their products, these now fetch good prices. With old tin advertising pieces, condition is very important in pricing. I buy in very good, fine, excellent, and mint condition. Here is what I mean by those terms:

MINT: No trace of handling; absolutely as it came from the printer.
EXCELLENT: Near mint, slight hairline scratches, very minor flakes off edges.
FINE: Some faint scratches, some chips at edges, possible faint stain, no rust.
VERY GOOD: Minor scratches, minor stain or fading; tiny pinhead spots of rust must not be on important part of picture.

Prices below are for fine or better signs. Please remember there are many more signs that I need than those I have listed here.

John Goetz
Box 1570
Cedar Ridge, CA 95924

	We Pay
Coca-Cola, 1917, Elaine, 20"x30"	**1,500.00**
Golden Jubilee, Hudepohl, 22"x16"	**75.00**
Buffalo Brewing, bottles, 22"x28"	**350.00**
Westminster Whiskey, 25½"x27½"	**2,300.00**
Ebbert Wagons, 25"x37"	**1,000.00**

Francisco Auto Heater, 40"x18".. **450.00**
Munsingwear, 25½"x37¾".. **1,000.00**
Owensboro, 37½"x25½" **1,200.00**
Pacific Coast Borax Co., 32¾"x23".. **950.00**
Red Raven, child on box, 19"x26½".. **500.00**
Runkel Brothers, 22¼"x28¼" **450.00**
U.S. Ammunition, 22"x28" **750.00**

I am buying **advertising signs and country store items dating from the 1880's up to the 1950's.** I will buy single items, collections, or great quantities — up to 1,000 of the same article such as might be found in a warehouse, for instance. I will pay up to $50,000.00 for just the right individual piece and more for good quality collections. Quality and condition of an item, whether it be a $25.00 sign or a $5,000.00 poster is important to me. Always of special interest are tin, paper, cardboard, and porcelain signs. Subjects desired include soda pop, Coke, Pepsi, Dr. Pepper, general store, food products, animals, veterinary and medical, automobile and gas, beer and whiskey, etc.

Gary Metz
4803 Lange Lane SW
Roanoke, VA 24018
(703) 989-0475

We Pay

Any Single Great Sign or Item....................................... **up to 500.00-25,000.00+**

I buy **pre-1920 paper items** such as beautifully illustrated receipts, billheads or letterheads showing a product or the manufacturer's building. Old, colorful cigar box labels or any tobacco-related item are wanted as are country store or other advertising items such as posters, signs, labels, cardboard boxes, trade catalogs or salesmen's kits which have been well-kept and preserved over the past seventy to one hundred years. In other words, if it is old, made of paper (or cardboard), and beautiful to look at, I'll buy it! Please ship small items (your postage reimbursed) for offer and payment. For larger items, you may either ship (insured) or send a photo.

Mr. Joseph F. Loccisano
2264 Nicholson Square Dr.
Lancaster, PA 17601

I am interested in buying advertising items marked **Wasson** from either Indiana or Illinois. Wasson is my maiden name, and I have just recently found out that advertising items from hardware and department stores do exist. I would be interested to know what is available. Please send a description with condition and price. No newspaper ads are wanted.

Janet Oberembt
16 Indi-Illi Pkwy.
Hammond, IN 46324

We Pay

Calendar Plates.. **10.00+**
Hardware or Department Store Items... **3.00+**
Calendars... **10.00+**
Paper Items... **1.00+**

I buy items such as **signs, clocks, calendars, dolls, thermometers, displays, trays, machines, toys, etc. that are associated with any number of brands and characters**. A sample listing is given below.

Aunt Jemima	Mountain Dew
Beatles	Moxie
Bludwine	Mr. Peanut
Buddy Lee	Nehi
Charlie McCarthy	Nesbitts
Chero Cola	Nu Grape
Coca-Cola	Orange Crush
Disney	Pepsi-Cola
Dr. Pepper	7-Up
Elsie Cow	Royal Crown Cola
Esso	Shell
Grapette	Sinclair
Gulf	Smokey Bear
Hopalong Cassidy	Speedy Alka Seltzer
Howdy Doody	Suncrest
Kist	Texaco
Lone Ranger	Uncle Wiggily
Mickey Mouse	Whistle
Michelin Man	Wrigley's Spearmint

Condition determines price, so please describe the item in detail. A photo is also helpful in assessing value. As many factors are considered, prices may widely vary. Listed below are some examples.

AFRICAN ART

I collect African art. Pieces must be guaranteed authentic and show signs of use. Examples of items wanted include masks, statues, and utilitarian items. Materials may include wood, ivory, metal, and fiber. History of display and past ownership of an item is helpful. Photos and reasonable prices are essential.

Scott H. Nelson
P.O. Box 6081
Santa Fe, NM 87502
(505) 986-1176

AMUSEMENT PARKS AND RIDES

The old-time amusement park and travelling show with their carny atmosphere, chute-the-chute and roller coaster rides are uniquely American. The Europeans have long had their summer gardens and watering spas, but it took the Americans to turn these quiet garden spots into loud, noisy, thrill-packed amusement parks.

The Golden Age of amusement parks and road carnivals was from 1893, the year of the World's Columbian Exposition in Chicago, until the late 1950's. By that time most of these parks found themselves somewhat old and seedy and surrounded by the city or town that had grown up around them. It was not until the modern theme parks were built that amusement parks found new life.

I am interested in material from the old parks, items relating to rides, coin-operated machines, trade stimulators, and arcade items. Another strong interest is saloon memorabilia. The list below is only a starter list, so if you have other items please let me know.

My interests in collecting have led me to author several books. Among them are *B.A. Stevens Billiard and Bar Goods, Slots 1, Pinball 1, Arcade 1,* and *Jennings Slot Machines.* You may request these books as well as others by me from The Coin Slot (4401 Zephyr St.; Wheat Ridge, CO 80033-3299; 303-420-2222).

Richard M. Bueschel
414 N Prospect Manor
(708) 253-0791

We Pay

Open Roller Coaster Car, before 1940	250.00
Penny Arcade Sign	150.00
Cast Iron Mutoscope	450.00
Penny Toss Board	125.00
Roller Coaster Drawings/Plans	75.00
Photograph of Roller Coaster, before 1910	10.00
Photograph of Roller Coaster, after 1910	5.00
Amusement Park Post Cards	50¢
Amusement Park Photographs, before 1910	7.50
Amusement Park Photographs, after 1910	3.50
1893 The Ferris Wheel Photograph	10.00
1893 The Ferris Wheel Guide Booklet	25.00
1893 The Ferris Wheel Token	12.50
1893 The Ferris Wheel Puzzle	15.00
1893 The Ferris Wheel Ticket	2.50
1983 The Ferris Wheel Drawings/Plans	50.00
Ride Entry Sign	20.00
Roller Coaster Brochure	15.00
Tilt-A-Whirl Catalog	10.00
Other Ride Catalogs	7.50
Electric Sign	125.00
Penny Arcade Machine Sign	12.50
Ferris Wheel Seat, before 1940	75.00
Fun House Mirror	65.00

ANIMALS AND STRANGE AND UNUSUAL THINGS

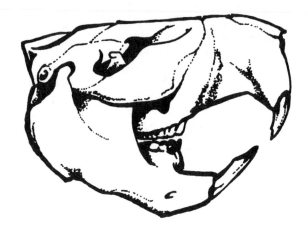

    I am buying mostly animal skulls and old skin rugs that include polar bears, lions, and tigers (only in New York State), along with strange and unusual things. Old fossils, egg collections (but not endangered species), artifacts from ancient Roman and Grecian cultures, and almost any kind of animal skulls (mostly alligator) are wanted.

David Ruschak
David's Jewelers
Auburn Plaza
Auburn, NY 13021

We Pay

Mounted Fish, small	**15.00**
Mounted Fish, large	**25.00**
Birds	**5.00**
Snakes	**5.00**
Skulls	**5.00-25.00+**
Shells	**25¢+**
Old Polar Bear Skin Rugs	**500.00+**
Old Lion Skin Rugs	**300.00+**
Old NY Tiger Skin Rugs	**500.00+**
Eggs	**100.00+**
Artifacts	**10.00+**
Fossils	**5.00+**

APOTHECARY SHOP AND DRUGSTORE ITEMS

Old apothecary shop and drugstore items and collectibles have become increasingly sought after over the past ten years. Early pharmacists concocted 'shotgun prescriptions' in a mortar and pestle, rolled pills by hand, percolated cough syrups, sold 'over-the-counter' remedies, and acted much as a country doctor. The tools, instruments, bottles, jars, fixtures, and implements of bygone apothecary shops are what we so feverently seek.

Whether you have one item or an entire drugstore, we would most likely love to have it. Whether it is an old mortar and pestle, a straw holder from an old soda fountain, syrup dispensers, Victorian window 'show globes,' or some early 'label-under-glass' apothecary bottles and jars — we are interested in buying almost anything that might have come out of an early drugstore.

We pay premium prices for early, unusual, complete, and undamaged items. We will buy one item, an entire collection, or the contents of a drugstore. The prices below are for items in mint condition. Bottles of the most

Apothecary Shop and Drugstore Items

interest are colored or clear, embossed, with or without contents, and free of cracks, chips, or any discolorations.These prices are often starting prices; your item(s) could easily be worth more to us. We prefer pictures and asking prices be sent by anyone before shipping any item.

The American Museum of Apothecary
Science & Industries
18 Smith Acres
Northport, AL 35476
1-800-445-7811
(205) 556-1188 or (502) 339-2402

We Pay

Apothecary Bottles or Jars, label-under-glass	15.00+
Apothecary Bottles, label-under-glass, cobalt	25.00+
Apothecary Jars, ceramic (old)	25.00+
Apothecary Scales	50.00+
Banana Split Dish, footed	10.00+
Bitters Bottles	25.00+
Candy Display Jar w/Ground Glass Stopper, large	50.00+
Coca-Cola Bottle Opener, early	10.00+
Coca-Cola Glass ('Drink')	5.00+
Coca-Cola Serving Tray, 1960's or earlier	15.00-1,500.00
Coca-Cola Sign, early	25.00-500.00
Coca-Cola Tip Tray, early	50.00-500.00
Crushed Fruit Jar, dispensing	50.00-500.00
Crushed Fruit Jar, w/label & contents	20.00-100.00
Decorated Vases & Jars	50.00-1,500.00
Ice Cream Chairs	25.00+
Ice Cream Cone Holder, glass, early	100.00+
Ice Cream Scoop, early	25.00+
Ice Cream Table	100.00+
Leech Jar	50.00+
Mortar & Pestle	10.00-250.00
Mortar & Pestle Sign	10.00-1,200.00
Pepsi-Cola Glass	5.00+
Pepsi-Cola Sign	25.00+
Pill Roller	75.00+
Poison Bottle	10.00+
Prescription Files	5.00+
Prescription Window (wall)	250.00-2,500.00
Quack Medical Device	25.00+
Soda Fountain, marble	250.00+
Soda Fountain Back Bar	500.00+
Soda Fountain Supply Catalog	5.00+
Scales, Street 1¢ ('Lollypop')	250.00+

Scales, counterbalance, early .... 50.00+
Show Globes (window decorations) .... 50.00+
Show Clusters w/Gas Burners .... 250.00+
Soda Glass, early .... 5.00+
Showcases, floor model .... 50.00+
Showcases, wall unit .... 100.00+
Straw Holder, clear, crystal .... 50.00+
Straw Holder, colored .... 250.00+
Syrup Dispenser 20.00-1,200.00

APPLE PEELERS

Collector is searching for unique antique mechanical apple parers. Items must be in excellent condition. Listed below are some specific apple peelers I am seeking. Please no White Mountains, Readings 78's, Lockey & Rowlands, or Goodell 1898's. Premium prices are paid for perfect parers.

Jim Sullivan
3 Rinear Dr.
Edison, NJ 08817
(201) 494-2240

We Pay

Monarch .... 150.00+
Comet .... 150.00+
Marked 'Electric 1887' .... 150.00+
Goodell 'Empire State' .... 150.00+
J.J. Parker, 1857 .... 150.00+
Lathe Style w/Tilting Coring Tube 150.00
Star, by Foster & Cotton .... 250.00+
Little Giant .... 150.00+
'Union' w/Push-Off Feature .... 150.00+
Reading 'Two Knife' .... 200.00+
Reading 'Champion' .... 200.00+
Monroe Bros. 'Eclipse' .... 200.00+
Lockey & Howland w/Table Tilted 45 Degrees .... 200.00+
Goodell 'Evaporator' .... 200.00+
Marked 'Bergner' .... 200.00+
Wooden w/Sawtooth Gears .... 200.00+
Wooden w/Spring-Tension Arms .... 200.00+

AQUARIUMS

As a serious collector, wanted are antique aquariums or terrariums, Art Deco fishbowl stands, fish-shipping cans, old aquarium equipment (i.e., heaters, filters, air pumps, ornaments), etc. Victorian or Art Deco styles such as Fiske, Adams, jeweled types, or those with metal frames are sought. Fish bowls may be made of terra cotta, depression glass, or vaseline glass and may be footed. Chalk fishbowl pieces are still another interest, as well as any related paper ephemera — magazines, books, advertisements, broadsides, etc. Please send a description and a photo of each item, if possible, along with your asking price.

Gary Bagnall
c/o Zoo Med Laboratories, Inc.
1615 E St. Gertrude
Santa Ana, CA 92705
(714) 641-3822 or FAX (714) 549-8859

ARCADE AND RELATED MUSICAL ITEMS

I am a private collector interested in buying all types of arcade and musical items. Below is a partial listing of those items I am seeking in particular.

John S. Zuk
666 Plainfield Ave.
Berkeley Heights, NJ 07922
(908) 646-0410

We Pay

Wurlitzer 1015 Jukeboxes	**5,000.00+**
Other Jukeboxes (78 rpm & 45 rpm)	**300.00+**
Pre-1940 Slot Machines	**900.00+**
Cylinder Music Boxes	**500.00+**
Disk Music Boxes	**750.00+**
Trade Stimulators	**100.00+**
Gumball Machines	**30.00+**
Player Pianos	**350.00+**
Mills Violano Virtuoso (Arcade Violin)	**1,000.00+**

16

Antique (Tube) Radios.. **50.00+**
Wind-Up Phonographs (78 RPM).. **50.00+**
Cylinder Record (Horn) Phonographs.. **100.00+**

_____

ARMS AND ARMOUR

I have been collecting arms and armour for over thirty-five years. I collect items from around the world and specialize in Russian, Islamic, Oriental, and Eastern European items. I wish to buy antique items, also military souvenirs. Wanted are the following items. Top prices paid.

Swords	Firearms
Knives	Robes
Uniforms	Helmets
Armour	Saddles
Medals	Related Objects

John Skalisky
P.O. Box 6404
San Jose, CA 95150
(408) 779-3001

_____

ART

I am interested in buying oils on canvas, charcoal or pastel art, hand-colored prints, drawings, etc. of **any military, nautical, western, or Indian subjects**. I prefer signed pieces in original frames, but this is not absolutely necessary. I am interested in all time periods. Condition, content, artist, size, and age will determine the price. Outstanding pieces will receive top dollar. I am also interested in **any early photography of these subjects**.

David L. Hartline
P.O. Box 775
Worthington, OH 43085

We Pay

Soldier in Uniform	**200.00-25,000.00**
Soldier on Horseback	**200.00-25,000.00**
Battlefield Scene	**200.00-25.000.00**
Ships in Battle	**200.00-25,000.00**
Military Ships in Port	**200.00-25,000.00**
Whaling Ships in Port	**200.00-25,000.00**
Litho Prints, pre-1890	**100.00-500.00**
Charcoal Sketches, early	**100.00-1,000.00**
Famous General or Officer Portraits	**200.00-25,000.00**
Indian Portraits, pre-1930	**200.00-25,000.00**

I will pay up to several thousand dollars for **older American and European paintings** in almost any condition. I'm especially looking for **impressionistic and expressionistic works of art from the nineteenth and twentieth centuries**. I will consider unsigned works but prefer those that are signed. Call any day of the week.

Don Johnson
3808 Grand Ave. S
Minneapolis, MN 55409
(612) 824-1111

I buy **old prints (etchings, engravings, lithographs, etc.) and original art-works (oils, watercolors, pastels, etc.), whether framed or unframed**. Being from Spartanburg, South Carolina, I am particularly interested in subject matters (maps, views, wildlife, etc.) and artists pertaining to the Carolinas and, more specifically, the Piedmont area of South Carolina. Please send a photo and description. Thank you.

Henry Barnet
516 Maverick Circle
Spartanburg, SC 29302

ART DECO AND ART NOUVEAU

I am a private collector interested in buying **all types of Art Deco items**. Below is just a partial listing of wanted items.

John S. Zuk
666 Plainfield Ave.
Berkeley Heights, NJ 07922
(908) 464-0410

	We Pay
Neon Clocks	100.00+
Frankart Castings	50.00+
Nuart Castings	40.00+
Hall China	5.00+
Red Wing China	5.00+
Fiesta China	5.00+
Russel Wright China	5.00+
Frankoma Pottery	5.00+
California Pottery Figures	100.00+
Bronze Lamps	100.00+
Bronze Statues	100.00+
Bronze Statues (nudes)	150.00+
Chase Chromeware	10.00+

Art Deco and Art Nouveau

I am interested in **Art Nouveau items** — either a single piece or many items. Listed below are some wants.

Brian Margoles
66 Waterloo St.
Winnipeg, Manitoba
Canada R3N-0S2

We Pay

Art Glass	50.00+
Tiffany	150.00+
Galle	100.00+
Art Nouveau Lamps	200.00+
Bronzes	300.00+
Marble Statues	150.00+
Bronze & Ivory Statues	500.00+
Inkwells	50.00+
Boxes	50.00+
Porcelain Statues (Goldscheider, etc.)	300.00+

Art Nouveau design is typified by women with flowing hair and gowns usually entwined with flowers — especially water lilies or flowering vines. Of special interest are pottery, glass, marble, silver, or bronze items, furniture, and paintings in the Art Nouveau style.

Steve Whysel
101 N Main
Bentonville, AR 72712

We Pay

Bronzes of Women	100.00-1,000.00
Marbles of Women	50.00-500.00
Pewter, Silver, Encased Glass, or Pottery	100.00-500.00
Hand-Painted Pottery	50.00-200.00
Furniture, carved & inlaid w/Art Nouveau designs	100.00-1,000.00
Lamps	50.00-500.00
Hand-Colored Etchings	10.00-100.00

ART GLASS

We Pay

Galle Cameo Vases, 8"..	**800.00-1,200.00**
Daum Nancy Vases, 24"..	**5,000.00-10,000.00**
Lalique Heads (mascots)...	**2,000.00-5,000.00**
Pairpoint Lamps..	**300.00-12,000.00**
Handel Lamps	**500.00-100,000**
Tiffany Lamps	**500.00-100,000.00**
Moe Bridges Lamp	**300.00-5,000.00**
Signed Lamp Bases	**100.00-1,000.00**
Jefferson Lamps...	**500.00-1,200.00**
Pittsburgh Lamps	**300.00-1,000.00**
Loetz Glass	**100.00-1,000.00**

I am interested in all etched glassware by Cambridge, Duncan Miller, Fostoria, Heisey, and Tiffin. Also wanted are New Martinsville animals as well as Lalique pieces. Crown Milano, Wave Crest, Tiffany, Cameo, and other fine quality art glass are desired. Please send a photo and your price.

Katherine Hartman
7459 Shawnee Rd.
N Tonawanda, NY 14120

AUTOMOBILIA

I am always interested in purchasing old original items related to early motoring. I only buy items that are in excellent condition. I am not interested in anything that has been repaired or has broken or missing parts. I am willing to pay premium prices for items that are in new 'old stock' condition with original boxes. I am interested in buying single pieces as well as large collections. I will respond to all letters when a complete description and asking price is given. When writing, please give a complete description noting any imperfections; please include a photo or sketch if possible. Keep in mind the listing below is only a small sample of the kinds of items I buy; there are hundreds of original and accessory items that interest me.

Joseph F. Russell
455 Ollie St.
Cottage Grove, WI 53527

**BOYCE
MOTOMETER**

We Pay

Auto Advertising Tape Measures 25.00
Auto Bud Vases 20.00
B.F. Goodrich Miniature License Plates (1938-1942) 10.00
Enameled Radiator Emblems 10.00
Ford Exposition Gearshift Knobs 35.00
Spinning Radiator Ornaments 65.00
Packard Brass Paperweights 65.00
Metal Plant Employee Badges 15.00
Motormeters 15.00
Clock Rear-View Mirrors 35.00
Leather License Plates 65.00
Dial Tire Gauges 10.00
Dial Tire Gauges w/Car Names 25.00
Marble Gearshift Knobs 15.00
Ornate Radiator Caps 50.00
License Plate Add-Ons 15.00

Automobilia

I buy and collect most any type of automobile-related item, especially sheet music, post cards, toys from early motoring days to the 1960's, and unusual items. All contacts will be answered.

Sheldon Halper
63 Cook St.
Clark, NJ 07066
(908) 272-5777

We Pay

Sheet Music	**1.00-50.00**
Post Cards	**50¢+**
Advertising Signs	**20.00+**
Radiator Ornaments	**10.00+**
Hub Caps	**2.00+**
Sales Catalogs	**1.00+**
Promotional Models	**5.00+**
Motorcycle Items	**5.00+**
Old Trophies	**5.00+**
Pocket Watches or Wristwatches	**15.00+**
Bicycles (fat-wheel type)	**25.00+**
Children's Toy Pedal Cars	**25.00+**

I am buying old pedal cars, tin oil cans, Texaco die-cast metal toy banks, gas-related porcelain signs, metal toy cars and trucks — anything old and unusual. Please send a picture and a price.

Mid City Auto Supply
409 N Hampton
De Soto, TX 75115

We Pay

Metal Pedal Cars, complete	**50.00+**
Oil Cans, tin	**5.00+**
Texaco Die-Cast Banks, #1-#6	**20.00**
Porcelain Signs	**20.00+**
Metal Toy Cars & Trucks	**25.00+**

AVIATION

I am buying **World War I (circa 1914-1918) aviation items**. I would be interested in one item or a collection. I seek both U.S. and foreign items (British, French, German, etc.). Also wanted are pilot log books, I.D. cards, books, photos, aircraft instruments, souvenir items, helmets, etc. Please get my offer before you sell.

Dennis Gordon
1246 N Ave.
Missoula, MT 59801
(406) 549-6280

We Pay

Pilot Wings & Badges	**100.00+**
Uniforms	**200.00+**
Flying Jackets & Suits	**200.00+**
Fabric Insignia (from aircraft)	**250.00+**
Medals	**50.00+**
Squadron Pins	**200.00+**

I am compiling a historical collection of **U.S. military aviation memorabilia**. Materials sought consist of WWI & WWII U.S. aviation leather flight jackets A-1, A-2, and G-1 (with or without squadron insignia). Also wanted are sterling wings by different makers, sweetheart and squadron pins, leather or cloth patches, and paper ephemera (work documents, scrapbooks, photos, etc.). Other items include WWII uniforms in near-mint condition, equipment, paratrooper helmets and jump jackets, pants patches, medals of honor, etc. Besides buying items, I'm an antique dealer who has hundreds of items to trade.

Brad C. Mann
128 Terrell Plaza
San Antonio, TX 78209
(512) 733-9941 (nights)
(512) 826-6082 (days)

We Pay

WWI Pilots Wings	**40.00-550.00**
WWI Balloon Wings	**75.00-600.00**

WWI Junior Aviators, ½-wing **35.00-300.00**
WWI Observers Wing-O-Wing, ½-wing **35.00-300.00**
WWI Officers Copper Wing & Prop Collar Insignia, pair **35.00**
WWI Pilot Log Book, Papers, Photos .... **40.00+**
WWI Flight Helmets, Goggles, Uniforms....................................... **30.00+**
1920's Leather Flight Jacket, A-1 button type **100.00-350.00**
WWI Squadron Insignia, silver or gold... **50.00-350.00**
WWI Pilots or Soldiers Medals & Documents **50.00-500.00**
WWII Pilots Wings, all types.. **20.00-150.00**
WWII Leather Flight Jackets A-2, G-1 .... **50.00-500.00**
WWII Squadron Patches, cloth or leather...................................... **20.00-125.00**
WWII Embroidered Patches on Wool **20.00-135.00**
WWII Goggles, Flight Helments **20.00-85.00**
WWII Pilot Log Books, Uniforms, Medals, Papers **50.00-500.00**

I am buying items from **passenger airline companies**. Any item from all airlines is wanted — one piece or a hangar full! I prefer examples from the 1920's through the 1960's but will consider items from other decades as well. Unusual or one-of-a-kind items are of special interest. I will travel to view large collections. Below is a sample listing of permanent wants. Highest prices are paid.

Gregory Collins
P.O. Box 610891
DFW Airport, TX 75261-08191

We Pay

Stewardess & Pilot Wings... **26.00+**
Hat Emblems .... **26.00+**
Display Models .... **60.00+**
Chrome Airplane Ash Trays... **60.00+**
Timetables... **5.00+**
Playing Cards .... **4.00+**
China & Dishes... **3.00+**
Crystal & Glassware .... **3.00+**
Silverplate Serving Pieces .... **10.00+**
Advertising Items .... **Call or Write**
Calendars... **6.00+**
Posters .... **8.00+**
Aviation Autographs... **10.00+**
Airplane Parts .... **5.00+**

Wanted: **WWII and post-war I.D. planes, promotional models, travel agency models, squadron or bomb group unit histories**, etc. Please see listing below for examples of some items wanted and the prices we will pay.

John Pochobradsky
1991 E Schodack Rd.
Castelton, NY 12033
(518) 477-9488

We Pay

I.D. Plane Models .... 25.00+
Promotional & Travel Agency Models .... 40.00+
I.D. Ship Cases .... 75.00+
I.D. Tanks .... 25.00+
Pilot Wings .... 25.00+
WWII Bomb Group or Squadron Unit Histories .... 50.00+
WWII Flight Jackets, leather .... 150.00+

BADGES

Badges

I am actively seeking **operator's badges from Pennsylvania only**. There are three different types that were issued; they are very similar — all were oval pin-backs with a keystone center.

The most common type is the 'Pennsylvania Licensed Driver,' issued from 1910 through 1919. The 1910 badge is keystone shaped; after 1911 they were oval. The second type is identical, only the wording has been changed to 'Pennsylvania Licensed Operator.' These were issued to paid employees from 1915 through 1929. The 1929 badge was round, rather than oval — about the size of a silver dollar. The third type is 'Special Licensed Driver,' issued from 1911 through 1916; they are also oval in shape. These badges were issued to residents under eighteen years of age.

Prices paid for badges are as follows. These are only guidelines; much depends on condition.

Edward Foley
227 Union Ave.
Pittsburgh, PA 15202
(412) 761-0685

Pennsylvania Licensed Driver

	We Pay
1910	60.00
1911	40.00
1912	40.00
1913	25.00
1914	25.00
1915	25.00
1916	25.00
1917	20.00
1918	20.00
1919	20.00

Pennsylvania Licensed Operator

	We Pay
1915	50.00
1916	50.00
1917	50.00
1918	50.00
1919	45.00
1920	45.00
1921	45.00
1922	45.00
1923	40.00
1924	40.00
1925	40.00
1926	40.00

1927	**35.00**
1928	**35.00**
1929	**40.00**

Pennsylvania Special Licensed Driver   We Pay

1911	**45.00**
1912	**45.00**
1913	**40.00**
1914	**40.00**
1915	**35.00**
1916	**35.00**

I collect **chauffeur's badges from all states**. Those from the northeastern states are the most common, but a few early examples are valuable. Those in nice condition warrant higher prices. Broken pins or clasps decrease a badge's value. If you have any for sale, please contact me. I am a serious buyer. For certain badges, I will pay up to $50.00

Trent Culp
P.O. Box 550
Misenheimer, NC 28109
(704) 279-6242

BANKS

I am a collector of **toy banks — both mechanical and still types**. Banks from about 1860 to 1930 are preferred. I buy broken, incomplete examples as well as those in good condition. I pay full market value and often, as a collector, a little or a lot more! Also wanted are **catalogs, trade cards, and wooden packaging boxes**.

Dr. 'Z'
1350 Kirts, Suite 160
Troy, MI 48084
(313) 642-8129

We Pay

Wooden Packaging Bank Box **100.00-500.00**
Trade Cards, multicolored **250.00-750.00**
Mechanical Banks **250.00-20,000.00**
Still Banks **50.00-1,500.00**

These tin (or tin with paper label) **miniature oil-can banks** are usually four ounces in size and represent a specialty within the collectible bank category. Beginning in the early 1940's, these banks were produced as a promotional tool for gasoline and motor oil dealers. In addition to motor oil, many specialty oils and fluids were promoted with these banks including antifreeze, top oil, and lubricants. There are well over one hundred to one hundred fifty versions known to date. Many oil companies offered five or six different banks representing most, if not all, of their oil products. Most common are Cities Service with Koolmotor tin banks for various grades of oil (HD, 5D, Premium, etc.). Another is Wolf's Head Motor Oil with a number of versions, the most desirable being Wolf's Head Light Duty and Heavy Duty Motor Oils. (The Super Duty version is the most common).

Listed below are some of the brands I seek in order to expand my collection of oil-can banks. Please drop me a card with your find and the price desired (range is from $5.00 to $20.00, based on condition and rarity). I'll respond immediately.

Peter Capell
1838 W Grace St.
Chicago, IL 60613-2724
(312) 871-8735

Banks From These Companies   **We Pay**

Bardahl Top Oil 5.00-20.00
Cross Country Motor Oil (Sears) 5.00-20.00
Conoco 'Nth' Motor Oil 5.00-20.00
Co-Op Diesel Oil 5.00-20.00
Esso Motor Oil 5.00-20.00
Lion Motor Oil 5.00-20.00
Kendall 2,000 Mile Motor Oil 5.00-20.00
Mobil Upper Lube... 5.00-20.00
Marathon Motor Oil.. 5.00-20.00
Pure/Purol Motor Oil.. 5.00-20.00
SOHIO-The Standard Lubricant... 5.00-20.00
Shell X-100 Motor Oil 5.00-20.00
Tenneco Motor Oil.. 5.00-20.00
Tiolene (Pure) Motor Oil 5.00-20.00
Triton Motor Oil 5.00-20.00
Wolf's Head Light Duty Motor Oil 5.00-20.00
Wolf's Head Heavy Duty Motor Oil 5.00-20.00
Worthmore Solvent Refined Oil... 5.00-20.00
Skelly Motor Oil, etc.. 5.00-20.00

BARBER MEMORABILIA

I am looking to buy a variety of barber items. Listed below are a few of the things I seek and prices I will pay.

Aldo Vecchio
14-57 155 St.
Whitestone, NY 11357

We Pay

Barber Pole, wooden... 500.00+
Barber Pole, other .... 100.00+
Occupational Mugs.. 100.00+

Other Mugs.. **25.00+**
Barber Chair, wooden .... **300.00+**
Barber Rack .... **300.00+**
Barber Bottles... **40.00+**
All Barber-Related Display Signs.. **50.00+**

BASEBALL CARDS AND MEMORABILIA

I am buying **old baseball cards**. Preferred are cards dating through 1987 that feature star players on the back. I will also buy common cards through the 1960's. **Football and basketball cards** through 1989 with stars on the back are wanted. I will buy common football cards through the 1960's and common basketball cards from 1986 through 1989 — Fleer or Topps. Please write about the item you want to sell. I am interested in **any older advertising that deals with baseball, football, or basketball**. The following are just a few examples of what we buy.

C.M.O. Cards
P.O. Box 2273
North Platte, NE 69103

Baseball   We Pay

1976 Dennis Eckersley 12.00
1974 Ken Griffey 8.00
1966 Fergie Jenkins 50.00
1962 Gaylord Perry 75.00

Football   We Pay

1981 Art Monk 14.00
1980 Ottis Anderson 5.00
1979 James Lofton 5.00
1973 Art Shell 12.00

Basketball   We Pay

1975 Moses Malone 30.00

Major league baseball programs have been issued by home teams since the earliest days of the sport. The teams of the present National League date from 1876. Those from the American League date back to 1901. A predecessor league, the National Association, dates from 1871 until 1875. Programs were issued for all regular and post-season league playoffs.

Post-season league playoffs pitting the champions of leagues against each other began in 1882 between the American Association and the National League. After a lapse, this was resumed within the National League as the Temple Cup from 1894 through 1897. Since 1903, this tradition has continued with the meeting of National and American league champions in the World Series.

The baseball All Star game began in 1933. This annual game pits the best players of the National League against those of the American League.

Since the early 1900's teams from the major leagues have intermittently issued yearbooks. These depict the pictures, records, and background information of all players on that year's team.

I am interested in buying specific **World Series, All Star, and other early programs, and team yearbooks**. Sample prices are shown in the following list. Depending on condition, prices may be higher or lower than those shown. I am also interested in **other early paper items from baseball and other sports — this includes autographs**. Please contact me for specific prices I will pay for your items.

Bud Glick
2846 Lexington Lane
Highland Park, IL 60035-1026
(708) 576-3521

Official World Series Programs   We Pay

1903	3,000.00+
1905	1,200.00+
1906	1,100.00+
1907, 1908, 1909, or 1910	1,000.00+
1911, 1912, 1913, 1914, or 1915	700.00+
1916	600.00+
1917	700.00+
1918	800.00+
1919 or 1920	700.00+
1921 through 1930	Write or Call

Official All Star Programs   We Pay

1933 Chicago	500.00+
1934 New York	600.00+
1935 Cleveland	200.00+
1936 Boston	800.00+
1937 Washington	250.00+
1938 Cincinnati	350.00+
1939 New York	600.00+
1940 St. Louis	300.00+
1941 Detroit	250.00+
1942 New York	1,200.00+
1946 Boston	500.00+
Other Years, pre-1974	Write or Call
Yearbooks, any year	Write or Call

I am interested in purchasing **baseball memorabilia — especially from the New York Yankees, New York Mets, New York Giants, Brooklyn Dodgers, and the St. Louis Browns**. I will buy World Series programs, All Star programs, pennants, autographed pictures and baseballs, bats, pins, uniforms, etc. A partial listing is given below. Depending on condition, prices may be higher or lower. I am also interested in **early items (especially paper) from hockey, golf, boxing, auto racing, and other sports**. I will buy or make offers on items in average or above condition. Again, condition will determine price. I am looking for all pre-1920 items.

Phil Glatz
164 N Garfield Ave.
Mundelein, IL 60060
(708) 949-4280

Official World Series Programs   We Pay

1903 Boston American League 5,000.00
1903 Pittsburgh National League 5,000.00
1905 Philadelphia American League 3,000.00
1905 New York National League.. 3,000.00
1906 Chicago American or National League........................ 2,000.00
1907–1947 .... Call or Write

Other Memorabilia   We Pay

Store-Made Bats 10.00-100.00
Game Bats.. 100.00-500.00
Official All Star Programs .... Call or Write
Uniforms 50.00-500.00

I am buying **baseball, football, basketball, and other sports cards, as well as non-sport trading cards, and sporting memorabilia**. My main interests are better rookie and star cards from before 1980, old sporting magazines, posters, programs, etc.

The market for cards is so volatile that it is difficult to give a fixed buying price. However, I've listed some sample percentages of current book price. (I use the Beckett monthly and yearly price guides for card values.) I'm also looking for **unusual sports items**. Please write before sending large shipments.

Winfred Partin
414 Oak St.
Morristown, TN 37813

Baseball Cards and Memorabilia

Common Baseball Cards, near mint/mint, all years, per 1,000 .... **5.00+**
Common Football Cards, near mint/mint, all years, per 1,000 .... **5.00**
Common Basketball Cards, near mint/mint, all years, per 1,000................ **6.00**
Pre-1980 Rookie & Star Cards, near mint/mint .... **50%+**
Pre-1980 Rookie & Star Cards, very good/excellent.................................. **30%+**
1981 to Present Rookie & Star Cards, near mint/mint............................... **50%+**
Pre-1980 College Football or Basketball Programs, excellent+................. **3.00+**
Pre-1980 Pro-Baseball, Football, or Basketball Programs, excellent+ .... **3.50+**
First Issue *Sports Illustrated*, near mint/mint **125.00**
First Issue *Beckett Baseball Monthly*, near mint/mint.............................. **75.00**
Non-Sports Cards, all series, all years, commons, near mint/mint
    per 1,000.. **3.00+**
1990 Andy Griffith Show Set (Pacific Trading Cards), near mint/mint **7.00**
1966 Get Smart Set (Topps), near mint/mint... **65.00**
1978 Elvis Wax Box of 36 (Donruss), unopened **30.00**

We are buying **baseball cards, all sports cards, and sports memorabilia from 1890 through 1991**. We would be especially interested in older **wax boxes and cases** which might be found in old candy warehouses and drugstores, or Mom & Pop grocery stores no longer in business. Also wanted are **non-sport cards** relating to movies, movie stars, TV sitcoms, musicians, and singers.

Al Cobb
417 Whitaker St.
Savannah, GA 31401
(912) 234-1582

Baseball, Basketball, Football, or Hockey Card Cases............................ **200.00+**
Golf, Boxing, Racing Cards, or Non-Sports Card Cases........................ **150.000+**
Signed Baseballs .... **10.00+**
Photographs.. **2.00+**
Posters .... **3.00+**
Tickets .... **1.00+**
Press Pins .... **15.00+**
Championship Rings.. **500.00+**
All Star Rings .... **400.00+**
Yearbooks... **1.00+**
Any Other Item .... **Write**

As a private collector, I seek **complete sets of baseball, football, or basketball cards**. Unopened packages of cards as well as some single cards are purchased. I will pay up to 80% of price guide values. Your list should include a complete description and condition of the cards along with your asking price. I will respond to all letters. No collect calls please.

Greg Wade
1320 Ethel
Okemos, MI 48864-3009
(517) 349-8688

I can use **baseball, hockey, football, soccer, tennis, and golf memorabilia**. No loose cards, posters, or paper goods, please. I am not interested in autographed or game-played items. Items are wanted in excellent condition only. Please send all information with your price.

Judd Wildman
175 E Chick Rd.
Camano Island, WA 98292

We Pay

U.S.A. Baseball Mitts	10.00+
Soccer Awards, Ribbons, Etc.	5.00+
Sports Illustrated, older magazines	2.00-5.00+
Other Older Magazines w/Baseball Players on Covers	5.00+
Jim Beam Golf or Baseball Decanters	6.00+
Golf Memorabilia, Trophies, Etc.	5.00+
B18 Baseball Blankets	5.00+
S74 Baseball Silks	5.00+
Wooden Shaft Golf Clubs	6.00+

I am a major buyer of **baseball memorabilia and autographs**. I am especially interested in purchasing material relating to Hall of Famers, New York Baseball teams (NY Yankees, NY Mets, NY Giants, and Brooklyn Dodgers) and the 1919 Black Sox. I buy autographs, yearbooks, programs, ticket stubs, pins, advertising pieces, and other interesting and unusual baseball items. Please contact me if you have any quality baseball material for sale. I am also a buyer of **football and boxing material**.

Richard Simon Sports, Inc.
Sports Memorabilia & Autographs
215 E 8th St.
New York, NY 10021
(212) 988-1349
FAX (212) 288-1445

BILLIARDS

I am buying pool tables, accessories, billiard equipment, and anything related made prior to 1930. I am also buying custom-made pool cues from any year. These items must be reasonably complete and original for me to be interested. Listed below are some of the things I am seeking.

Alan D. Conway
1696 W Morton Ave.
Porterville, CA 93257

We Pay

Pool Tables	500.00+
Custom Cues	10.00+
Brunswick Cue Rack	20.00+
Billiard Cards	10.00+
Coin-Operated Chalk Dispenser	40.00+
Lights	20.00+
Advertising Signs	4.00+
Books	2.00+
Leather Cue Cases	10.00+
Pool Novelty Items	1.00+

BLACK CATS

I am interested in buying Shafford Black Cats. These figural novelty and kitchen ware cats are made of red clay, glazed in a high gloss black, and wear painted-on red bows at the neck. Their eyes are green lined in white, and they have white whiskers and eyelashes, although the white has often been washed away over the years. You'll also find similar cats with yellow or white eyes, and I may be interested in some of these as well. Please write and tell me what you have! I am also looking for serving pieces to go with my Red wing dinnerware in the Normandie (apple) pattern. It comes in green and burgundy — I need the burgundy. I have all the plates, cups and saucers, and dessert bowls I need.

Sharon Huxford
1202 7th St.
Covington, IN 47932
(317) 793-2392

BLACK MEMORABILIA

During the past nineteen years I have enjoyed searching for many types of Black items. Since thousands were commercially produced and hundreds more were one-of-a-kind folk art, the search is endless. Several of my favorite categories are: rag dolls, carved walking sticks, Weller Mammy kitchen set, jigsaw puzzles, valentines, paper dolls, playing cards, skill games, sewing items, children's books, souvenir spoons, watercolors, prints, jewelry, and advertising items. These can reflect Black images from both realistic and stereotypical viewpoints. I am interested in items that represent both aspects as long as they are not common (such as Mammy/chef salt and pepper sets, Mammy shopping reminder lists, outhouse figures, and linen post cards).

Fortunately, many unusual items are available in every part of this country. I can usually buy from a photo or photocopy as long as condition is clearly described. I prefer not making offers; and if a SASE is not enclosed, I will only answer on items of interest. The following are some of the items I am buying and the prices I will pay for them in fine condition. I am interested in other items and will consider higher prices than those listed.

Jan & Bruce Thalberg
23 Mountain View Dr.
Weston, CT 06883
(203) 227-8175

We Pay

Cloth Doll, Beloved Belindy	150.00
Print, My Honey, by Gutmann	150.00
Print, Mammy's Angel Child, by Gimball	150.00
Print, Four Seasons, by Maud Humphrey	50.00
Cookie Jar, Mammy, by Pearl China	200.00
Cookie Jar, Mammy, by Weller	300.00
Bottle, Mammy, by Robj	150.00
Cup & Saucer, Coon Chicken Inn	50.00
Flatware, Coon Chicken Inn, each	10.00
Lamp, Mammy, full-figure, glass	250.00
Wall Lamp, Mammy head, ceramic	125.00
Wall Clock, Mammy, full-figure, metal	200.00
Playing Cards, pre-1930	25.00
Mechanical Valentines, pre-1920	20.00
Mechanical Valentines, 1920–1940	10.00
Greeting Cards, pre-1950	5.00
Sheet Music, by E.T. Paull	10.00
Pincushion & Emory, Mammy face	25.00
Paper Mask, Aunt Jemima	25.00
Pencil Sharpener, Our Gang	15.00
Papier-Mache Candy Container	75.00
Papier-Mache Christmas Figural Ornament	150.00
Cotton Batting Christmas Figural Ornament	100.00

Glass Christmas Figural Ornament.. **150.00**
Appliqued or Embroidered Dish Towel................................... **20.00**
Recipe Box, Mammy, green plastic **45.00**
Ronson Bartender Lighter.. **250.00**

I am interested in buying Black memorabilia items that date from before 1955 such as **cookie jars, string holders, toys, Aunt Jemima items, F&F Mold, Luzianne,** etc.

Paulette Johnson
4966 Hickory Shores Blvd.
Gulf Breeze, FL 32561-9209

We Pay

National Silver Chef Cookie Jar... **125.00+**
Aunt Jemima Camp Stove.. **100.00+**
Luzianne Original Cookie Jar .... **125.00+**
String Holders .... **40.00+**
Amos & Andy Original Toys .... **200.00+**
Mason Blacking Box .... **50.00+**

I have collected Black memorabilia for the past ten years. I'm always interested in adding different and unusual items to my collection. Especially liked are sterling souvenir spoons featuring a Black on the handle or in the bowl of the spoon. Other items of interest are advertising items: bottles (whiskey, ale, soda, salad dressing, etc.), boxes, tins, containers, signs, ads, etc. Other items include cookie jars, string holders, grocery shopping boards, dish towels, salt and pepper shakers, plates, dishes, cookbooks, children's books, matchcovers, ink blotters, etc. I am not interested in native-type items or dolls. A photo or photocopy is helpful along with a description and condition, as well as your asking price.

Joyce Wolford
1050 Spriggs Dr.
Lander, WY 82520

We Pay

Souvenir Spoons, demi or teaspoon size................................ **50.00+**

Bottles, advertising .... 20.00+
Boxes, cardboard or wooden .... 25.00+
Tins, advertising .... 20.00+
Dish Towel, printed, appliqued or embroidered.................................... 18.00+
Grocery Shopping Boards.. 20.00+
String Holders .... 45.00+
Plates .... 20.00+
Salt & Peppers, unusual sets.. 30.00+
Cookbooks or Recipe Booklets .... 15.00+
Matchcovers .... 4.00+
Ink Blotters... 6.00+
Children's Storybooks... 15.00+
Figural Toothbrush Holders .... 45.00+
Cookie Jars .... Write

THE BLUE MOON GIRL

The Blue Moon girl was the logo for Blue Moon silk stockings sold by the Largman-Gray Company. We are interested in any original item, advertising, or promotional giveaway with the Blue Moon girl logo. Photocopies or close-up photos are most helpful. I will make offers and answer all replies.

Bill Sinesky
7228 McQuaid Rd.
Wooster, OH 44691

BOHEMIAN GLASS

I am buying eighteenth and nineteenth-century Bohemian glass: goblets, beakers, and other types of drinking vessels in particular. Colored or clear glass with wheel-engraved landscape scenes, portraits, animals, spa scenes, religious themes, etc. are wanted. Cameo-type work is especially desired. In addition to wheel engraving, I'm seeking all other types of Bohemian glass from this period including pieces decorated with transparent or opaque enamels, overlays, cutting, gilt work, painting, etc. I am paying $50.00 to

$1,000.00 and up, depending on rarity, condition, size, etc. Single pieces or collections are wanted. Please indicate if you wish photos returned. I reply to all correspondence.

Tom Bradshaw
325 Carol Drive
Ventura, CA 93003

PHILIP BOILEAU

I am buying artist-signed materials by Philip Boileau. Most of his works are signed and dated with the copyright of the publisher or artist with dates from 1894 through 1917. Subject matter may be a woman, either full-length or a bust portrait, or multiple subjects such as two women, woman and child, etc. Publishers include Reinthal/Newman, Tuck, Osborne Co., National Art Co., International Art Co., T.D.M. Co., Knapp Co., F.A.S. or F.A. Schneider, Reinthal & Gross, Flood & Conklin Co., A.P. Co., Weinthal & Co., Lever Bros. Co., Wolf & Co., Taylor Platt Co., American Colortype, M.E.U., Sheahan, etc.

Gordon L. Gesner.
1800 24th St. NE
Salem, OR 97303
(503) 371-3998

We Pay

Ink Blotter, any publisher	**15.00-40.00**
Post Card, any publisher except Reinthal/Newman	**25.00-150.00**
Prints or Posters, any publisher	**50.00-300.00+**
Calendars, any publisher	**45.00-200.00+**
Minneapolis Journal Sunday Magazines	**15.00-30.00**
Portrait China Plates	**50.00+**
Portrait China Vases or Pitchers	**150.00+**
Other Philip Boileau Items	**Write**

BOOKMARKS

Bookmarks in mint condition of any material such as paper, metal, silk, wood, or celluloid are always wanted. I collect bookmarks which are old and/or unusual, pertain to old advertising, or are commemorative of world events or places. I am particularly looking for Alden Fruit Vinegar paper bookmarks for the months of June, July, October, and November. I'm also especially hunting for small paper bookmarks advertising Sozodent. If you have any out-of-the-ordinary bookmarks to sell, please contact me.

Mrs. M. Budish
2739 S Xanadu Way
Aurora, CO 80014
(303) 752-1283

 **BOOKS**

I am buying **house plans books and catalogs from the late nineteenth through mid twentieth centuries**. I am also interested in promotional materials and company records. These materials are used in historical architecture research and have been used to produce numerous articles and the book *America's Favorite Homes*. Listed below are some of the companies we are researching (please state condition and whether or not house pricing information is included). We would be happy to hear from parties with materials from other related companies and items other than those listed below. Other major companies are Aladdin, Gordon-Van Tine, Harris Bros., Lewis, Sears, Sterling, and Wards. Items such as wallpaper books, light fixtures books, furniture booklets, millworks books, etc., and anything to do with house production and sales functions are wanted.

Robert Schweitzer
3661 Waldenwood Dr.
Ann Arbor, MI 48105
(313) 668-0298

We Pay

Aladdin Homes, 1906-1945	20.00+
Aladdin Homes, 1946-1987	10.00+
Bennett Homes	20.00+
Bossert Homes	20.00+
Bowes, C.L. (Hinsdale, IL)	15.00+
Brown-Blodgett	15.00+
Economy Portable Building Co.	20.00+
Garlinghouse Homes, to 1940	20.00+
Garlinghouse Homes, after WWII	10.00+
Gordon — Van Tine Homes	25.00+
Gunnison Homes	10.00+
Harris Homes	20.00+
Hodgson Portable Homes	20.00+
Home Planners Inc.	10.00+
Keith's Co. Plans Books	20.00+
Keith's Magazine	8.00+
Lewis Homes	25.00+
Mershon & Morley Portable Homes	30.00+
National Plan Service	15.00+
Plan Service Co. (St. Paul, MN)	15.00+
Sears Modern Homes	30.00+
Standard Homes Co.	20.00+
Sterling Homes (International Mill & Timber)	25.00+
Togen — Stiles	25.00+
Ward/Wardway Homes	25.00+

I am interested in buying books written by **Jean Stratton Porter** or **Harold Bell Wright**. I will pay $2.00 to $10.00 depending on the book title and the condition of the book.

Marilyn Hammond
P.O. Box 965
Los Molinos, CA 96055

_____

All books are a fascinating blend of intrinisic and extrinsic — the book as knowledge and the book as object. Here at the shop in Redlands, California, we focus on books of lasting value, both inside and out. We carry fine and unusual books and are always interested in obtaining notable volumes in the following varied categories: Literature; Americana; Modern Art and Architecture; Signed and Inscribed Books; Early Printing (pre-1800); Limited Editions; Science and Medicine; Alcoholics Anonymous; Books with Original Art or Photographs; many others as well. Below you will find examples of prices I will pay for these books in good original condition. All your quotes will be answered, but we do ask that you describe fully the book's condition, publication information, etc., and include a SASE. Thank you in advance.

Paul Melzer Fine and Rare Books
12 E. Vine St.
Redlands, California 92373
(714) 792-7299

Alcoholics Anonymous   **We Pay**
(Wilson, Bill) Alcoholics Anonymous. NY, 1939-1955 ....**25.00-2,000**

Exploration   **We Pay**
Dixon, George. A Voyage Round the World. London, 1789......................**750.00**
Lewis & Clark. History of the Expedition. Philadelphia, 1814, 2 vols **2,000.00**

Illustrated Books   **We Pay**
Chagall, Marc. Illustrations for the Bible. NY, 1960..............................**1,200.00**
Chagall, Marc. Jerusalem Windows. NY, 1962 ....**400.00**
(Matisse) Joyce, James. Ulysses. NY, 1935, ltd. **1,000.00**

Literature   **We Pay**
Austin, Jane. Sense & Sensibility. London, 1811 or 1813, 3 vols **750.00**
Crane, Stephen. Red Badge of Courage. NY 1895.....................................**250.00**
Defoe, Daniel. Robinson Crusoe. London, 1719–20, 3 vols **3000.00**
London, Jack. The Cruise of the Dazzler. NY, 1902 ....**300.00**
Melville, Herman. Moby Dick. NY, 1851, 3 vols **2,500.00**
Melville, Herman. The Whale. London, 1851, 3 vols.............................**5,000.00**

I am interested in **1930's and 1940's Nancy Drew** books with the original dust jackets. I will pay $5.00 to $10.00 depending on the condition of the book and its jacket. Some writing in the book is alright. I am interested in other children's books, especially *Bobbsey Twins*, *Mary Poppins*, and *Trixie Belden*. All inquiries enclosing SASE will be answered.

D.F. Yates
229 Forkner Dr.
Decatur, GA 30030

I am interested in buying **folio-sized books of the Victorian era**. Of special interest are books with color plates, steel or wood engravings, atlases with hand-colored maps, and government publications. Also wanted are bound volumes of periodicals from 1830 to 1940, such as *Harper's Weekly*, *Leslie's*, *Ballue's*, *The Daily Graphic*, *Puck*, *Judge*, *Collier's*, *Illustrated London News*, *The Graphic*, and a host of others. I am interested in books in any condition, including ex-library books, those without covers or having missing pages, etc. I will also buy complete libraries, and I am willing to travel to do so. The following is a list of some prices I will pay for folio-sized books.

Hugh Passow
306 Main St.
Eau Claire, WI 54701

We Pay

Art Journal	**25.00+**
Picturesque America	**80.00+**
Gleason Pictorial	**50.00+**
American Art Review	**75.00+**
The Graphic	**35.00+**
Art Treasures of America, set	**100.00+**
Les Ideas Nouvelles (French fashion)	**75.00+**
Picturesque Europe	**100.00+**
Picturesque World	**75.00+**
French Architecture Plate Books	**50.00+**
Coulton's Atlas, 1865	**200.00+**
Mitchell's Atlas, 1851	**400.00+**
Illustrated London News	**50.00+**
Leslie's Weekly	**50.00+**
Harper's Weekly	**100.00+**
Harper's Weekly, 1873	**400.00+**
U.S. Government Survey	**35.00+**

Books

Puck ....**100.00+**
Judge Magazine .... **100.00+**
Collier's .... **50.00+**
Studer's Birds .... **100.00+**

I am buying **children's, illustrated, hunting, and fishing books**. I prefer fine first or early edition books. I will buy one or a collection. Listed below are some of the authors and illustrators I am seeking.

Illustrators	Authors
Burkert, Nancy Ekholm	Auel, Jean
Dillon, Diana & Leo	Brichehill, Paul
Egielski, Richard	Burgess, Thornton
Gag, Wanda	Brooks, Terry
Gruelle, Johnny	Donaldson, Stephen
Hauge, Michael	Field, Rachel
Hyman, Trina Schart	Forbes, Esther
Jeffers, Susan	George, Jean Craighead
Jones, Elizabeth Orton	Hill, Gene
Lenski, Lois	Hyde, Daton
Locker, Thomas	Jeffers, Susan
Milhouse, Katherine	Lewis, C.S.
Moser, Barry	Lenski, Lois
Parrish, Maxfield	Lofting, Hugh
Rackham, Arthur	Moody, Ralph
Seredy, Kate	Sendak, Maurice
Sendak, Maurice	Seredy, Kate
Tarrants, Margaret	Wilder, Laura Ingals
Tudor, Tasha	White, E.B.
Van Allsbery, Chris	

Hidden Treasures
P.O. Box 643
31580 Hwy. 97 N
Tonasket, WA 98855
(509) 486-4496

I buy **children's series** and **Limited Edition Club** books. Series books before 1960 almost all came with dust jackets; these should be present. I will not buy pictorial cover Nancy Drew or Hardy Boys series books but will buy pictorial cover Judy Bolton, Chip Hilton, Dana Girls, and Rich Brant series books. As for the Limited Edition Club books, each book was limited to 1,500 copies or less and was signed by the author, designer, and/or artist. The Limited Edition Club was Founded in 1929 by George Macy. I am particularly looking for *The Lysistrata* and *Ulysses.* In addition, I can use the thirty-seven volume Shakespeare set. All Limited Edition Club books must be with the original boxes and in fine condition. I will also buy any ephemeral material associated with the Limited Edition Club — especially long runs of monthly letters.

Lee Temares
50 Heights Rd.
Plandome, NY 11030

We are always buying books in two categories: **circus** and **Florida**. We prefer first editions, but all printings are considered. We appreciate quotes on books relating to The Ringling Brothers and Barnum & Bailey Circus; but we buy books, magazines, and ephemera on every known circus. We also buy books and other materials on every aspect of Florida, including fiction by well-known Florida authors such as Marjorie Kinnan Rawlings, Marjorie Stoneman Douglas, and John D. MacDonald. Old and unusual material is always desired, but we buy many common items for stock. Books with dust jackets and those in very good condition are our preference.

Main Bookshop O.P. Dept.
1962 Main St.
Sarasota, FL 34236

I am interested in buying old **gun-related books, hardware store books and fishing catalogs**. I am especially interested in the pre-1960 hardcover books listed below. Any softbound book will be 50% less than prices listed below. Any item published after 1960 will also be 50% less. I am not buying any magazines or paperback books. Write and describe title, author, and condition.

Robert Lappin
P.O. Box 1106
Decatur, IL 62523
(217) 428-2973

We Pay

Blacksmithing .... **10.00+**
Gunsmithing.. **10.00+**
Smith & Wesson .... **15.00+**
Colts (a book) by Sutherland .... **200.00+**
Winchester .... **15.00+**
Any Hard-Bound Book on a Specific Gun .... **15.00+**
Fishing Catalog.. **2.00+**
Hardware Store Books .... **20.00+**

I would like to buy a copy of *The Big Book of Buttons.* I am willing to pay up to $75.00 for a copy. Please send any information you may have.

Maggie's Place
682 Hudson St.
Columbus, OH 43211

I would like to purchase books entitled *Guide Book of United States Coins* by R.S. Yoeman. These books were published by Whitman Publishing in Racine, Wisconsin, starting in 1947 and have been issued every year since. The books are commonly called 'red books' because of their red covers. Each edition covers all of the known coins issued since colonial times in the United States with their current values. I am primarily interested in purchasing the first ten issues from 1947 to 1956. Other issues from 1957 to 1962 may also be purchased if in excellent condition. The price paid for each volume will be determined by year of issue and condition. Damaged books are of little or no value. Examples of value range are as follows. Please send list of books and accurate condition. Postage will be refunded on all accepted deliveries.

Doug Chaussee
5190 Hunt Club Rd.
Racine, WI 53402

We Pay

1947 First Edition **10.00-25.00**
1948 .... **5.00-10.00**

1949	**5.00-8.00**
1950-1954	**2.00-6.00**
1955-1959	**1.00-5.00**
1960-1962	**50¢-2.50**

I buy old or unusual books on food, drink and pleasurable pastimes. I prefer items from the 1950's or before, but I am also interested in newer unique titles. Subject examples are **cookbooks, books on entertaining, etiquette, parties, games, card playing, dancing, etc.** I pay a minimum of $1.00 and up for little recipe pamphlets and $3.00 and up for hardcover books. All books need to be in good condition.

Jennifer Fuller
P.O. Box 1218
Seaside, CA 93955
(408) 899-0531

This former schoolteacher is interested in buying all kinds of books and ephemera. Particular interests include **regional Americana printed prior to 1930 and early Santas in any form**. You may pass over things every day that you do not want — except that now you are reading this page, and those things may help me! I will appreciate hearing from you if you have one item or twenty! Condition is important, but things do not have to be perfect. If something is in poor condition, still tell me about it. Send a quick post card describing your item(s) and include your telephone number and asking price. An incomplete listing of subjects wanted is given below.

Books About Books
Judaica, anything
Exploration
Sporting & Wildlife
Color Plates
Minatures
Raphael Tuck, anything
Books on Papermaking

Decorative Books (pretty covers)
Tea, Coffee, or Tobacco, anything
Early Books w/Dust Jackets
Genealogy
Early Historicals
Limited Editions
First Editions
Illustrated Children's Books,
    Games, Cards, Puzzles, Etc.

C. Whitehead
2893 Westover Dr.
Danville, VA 24541

I am currently purchasing any books related to the **Arts and Crafts movement**. Items wanted include pamphlets, mottos, advertising, catalogs — particularly books published by the Roycrofters. I would also purchase **any art pottery or metalwork related to the Arts and Crafts era**.

Tim Ward
3232 #8 Denver Ave.
Merced, CA 95348

BOTTLE OPENERS

I collect figural bottle openers that are three-dimensional and stand up. Most are made of painted cast iron or aluminum. I also collect those that mount to the wall.

Charlie Reynolds
2836 Monroe St.
Falls Church, VA 22042

We Pay

Boy Winking, face, wall mount .... **400.00+**
Skull, face, wall mount .... **400.00+**
Amish Man, face, wall mount .... **400.00+**
Coyote, face, wall mount .... **500.00+**
Eagle, face, wall mount .... **400.00+**
College Girl with Books, standing .... **500.00+**
College Boy with Books, standing **1,000.00**
College Cheerleader, standing .... **400.00+**
Other College Figural .... **100.00+**
Dodo Bird, painted cast iron .... **200.00+**
Beer Drinker, apron string opener, cast iron .... **200.00+**
Girl in Swimsuit, Wave Opener Ptd. AL .... **300.00+**

BOTTLES

We are especially interested in American-made bottles from 1900 which feature embossed product names or full labels. Americans bottled countless products during the 1800's. We are interested in **any type of bottle, from food to medicine to alcoholic beverages**. These might be clear, amber, aqua, blue, green or milk glass. No machine-made bottles, please. The prices below are starting prices for the pieces we need; your bottle could easily be worth more to us. Please contact us for prices paid for specific items. Please enclose a SASE for a response.

Steve Ketcham
P.O. Box 24114
Edina, MN 55424

We Pay

Historical Flasks .... **50.00+**
Bitters .... **25.00+**
Barber Bottles .... **50.00+**
Patent Medicines .... **10.00+**
Inks .... **10.00+**
Figurals .... **25.00+**
Beers .... **5.00+**
Whiskeys .... **10.00+**
Bar Decanters .... **25.00+**
Sodas .... **10.00+**
Fruit Jars .... **25.00+**

I want to buy **pint and half-pint glass whiskey bottles with paper labels intact, dating from the 1920's through 1939**. I prefer full bottles but will consider empty or evaporated items. I will also consider buying quart, half-gallon, and gallon sizes if they are from the same circa with their labels intact. Also collected are **gift decanters (ceramic and glass) that once held cognac or Armagnac**. Some of the cognac brands I need are Martel, Larsen, Hine, Gautier, Remy Martin, Otard, and Camus. Prices are based on condition and quantity. Please write or call before shipping.

John Decker
660 Crockett
Elmhurst, IL 60126
(708) 832-1449

We Pay

Whiskey Pints or Half-Pints, full.. **20.00+**
Whiskey Pints or Half-Pints, empty .... **5.00+**
Whiskey Quarts or Half-Gallons, empty .... **9.00+**
Whiskey Gallons, empty.. **10.00+**
Cognac or Armagnac Gift Bottle, empty .... **Call or Write**

I collect **bitters bottles that are bimal or have a tooled top**. These would be pre-1900. I prefer that they are in good condition. I will pay a fair price depending on condition and rarity. Please write describing the bottle. All letters will be answered. I also collect **unusual or colored pre-1900 medicines and cures**.

Nick Merten
2811 S Blaine
Grand Island, NE 68801

I want to buy **Erie, Pennsylvania, bottles**. Embossed bottles of all kinds which say 'Erie' on them are of the most interest to me, especially medicines, beers, sodas, and mineral waters. I will also buy **other Pennsylvania bottles**.

Jim Finn
P.O. Box 7306
Erie, PA 16510

We Pay

Mizpah Cure for Weak Lungs **60.00**
Bentle & Andrews Drugs... **10.00**
H.V. Claus, beer... **10.00**
Carter's Extract of Smart Weed.. **3.00**
John J. Graney, beer... **10.00**
P. Minnig & Co., medicine **10.00**
Ackerman **25.00**
Wayne Brewery, green **40.00**
J. Kretz, beer **10.00**
Doc. P. Hall's, iron pontil **30.00**
Steven's & Co., blue **75.00**

F. Nick's Pharmacy **4.00**
Lancaster, Erie Co., NY; flask **80.00**
Cunningham & Co., Pittsburgh, fruit jar, iron pontil **100.00**
A. Stone & Co., Philadelphia, fruit jar, iron pontil **100.00**
For Pike's Peak, Pittsburgh, PA; flask **100.00**
Jas. Shaughnessy, Eric, PA **20.00**
J.H. Welsh, Erie, PA **20.00**

I am buying **colored poison and medicine bottles made before 1910,** especially cobalt blue or green bottles. Of special interest are bottles that have embossed (raised) lettering and designs and the kind of lip that would hold a cork or glass stopper (no screw tops please). I am a member of the Los Angeles Historical Bottle Club. I am also interested in go-withs, e.g., advertising items and signs. I will pay $10.00 to $500.00 for old colored poison and medicine bottles in excellent condition.

Adrienne S. Escoe
P.O. Box 342
Los Alamitos, CA 90720
(213) 430-6479 (evenings)

I am seeking to buy **miniature liquor bottles.** Two desirable criteria for a collection is that it be interesting and inexpensive. I have found that antique miniature liquor bottles fit that description perfectly. I have about two dozen that are 3½" to 6" in height. They vary greatly in shape and age. I have paid about $5.00 to $10.00 for each one. I am mostly interested in ones with visual appeal, such as an interesting shape or color. If it is sealed with the original contents, that is even better. If you have an interesting one, please contact me with a brief description and your asking price (include postage costs in your price).

Charles S. Knight
1608 Delmar Dr.
Charlottesville, VA 22901

I am buying **Japanese figural sake, wine, or liqueur bottles of porcelain or china only from 1960 through 1970** — one bottle or an entire collection.

Please see the following list of brand names and bottles below. Call or write with the name of your bottle and your price.

Al Sparacino
743 La Huerta Way
San Diego, CA 92154
(619) 690-3632

House of Koshu (Japanese)
Geishas: Cherry Blossom
       Plum Blossom
       Chrysanthemum
       Violet
       Lily
       Wisteria
       Blue
       Kneeling
       Reclining
       Orange
       Pink
       Purple
Masks: Noh
       Okame
Sake God: Colored
       White
White Lionman
Red Lionman
Two Lovers
Faithful Retainer
Playboy
Daughter
Maiden
Princess
Pagodas: White
       Green
       Gold
Lantern — Doro
Karate (Japanese)
Karate Ma

Kikukawa (Japanese)
Tsunadara (Tub):
  Large Red & Gold
  Mini Red & Gold
Royale Couple (pair)
Standing General
Sitting General
Samuari
Kokeshi Dolls: Kumiko
          Minako
          Tomiko
Kamotsuru (Japanese)
7 Gods (Set) #1 thru #7
Golden House
Treasure Tower
Gion Festival Carriage
Sedan Chair
Joan & Darby (Pair)
Kokkoman (Japanese)
Geisha
Girl Sitting
Noah Dancer
Okura Shuzo (Japanese)
Gold Sake Tub
Sasaiti Shuzo (Japanese)
Monkey Trio
Smokisan
Owl

BOXES

    I am seeking decorative celluloid glove, jewelry, collar, and dresser set boxes as well as celluloid autograph albums. These items have colorful lithographic scenes and must be in top condition. The inside condition is secondary. I will pay asking price.

Andra Behrendt
6321 Joliet Rd.
Countryside, IL 60525

BOY/GIRL SCOUT COLLECTIBLES

The Boy Scouts of America was organized in the United States in 1910. The original idea for the Boy Scouts came from the observations of General Baden-Powell during the Boer War. He found that boys were eager to learn and to do outdoor-related things in an organized manner.

Several organizations that had already been going became a part of the new movement that spread across the States in a very short time. The first Boy Scout Jamboree that was to be held in Washington D.C. was canceled due to an outbreak of polio in 1935 and was not held until 1937.

Now many of the items having to do with the history of the scout movement have become of interest to those who have been or are now active in scouting. I am interested in items that are in good condition and that help to tell a part of the history of the scout movement.

Below is a partial listing of scout items I am looking for. I am interested in buying one piece or large collections of scout and scout-related items. The variety of items issued by or about the scouts is too large to list in entirety. I have an interest in nearly everything. When writing, please describe your item, its condition, and what you want for it. I am willing to go through your collections and estimate what I would be willing to pay for them. Please write or call.

Doug Bearce
P.O. Box 4742
Salem, OR 97302
(503) 399-9872

We Pay

1935 Jamboree Patch	**45.00-60.00**
1935 Jamboree Neckerchief	**35.00-50.00**
1937 Jamboree Patch	**45.00-60.00**
1937 Jamboree Neckerchief	**35.00-50.00**
1953 Jamboree Jacket Patch	**50.00-75.00**
1924 World Jamboree Patch (good condition)	**1,000.00**
World Jamboree Patches 1929, 1937, 1947, 1933, ea	**50.00-200.00**
1950, 1953, or 1957 Jamboree Patch, ea	**5.00-15.00**
Boy Scout Handbook 1910	**50.00-250.00**
Boy Scout Handbook 1911-1925	**17.50-100.00**
Boy Scout Handbook 1925-1935	**6.00-35.00**
Boy Scout Diary	**5.00-10.00**
Pins	**No Value to 100.00**
Scout Uniforms (according to patches on it)	**No Value to 300.00**
Order of the Arrow Patches	**3.50-100.00**
Fiction Books (about scouting)	**1.00-20.00**
Baden-Powell Books	**5.00-35.00**
Seton Books	**3.00-45.00**
Daniel Beard Books	**3.00-35.00**
Patch Vests, Merit Badge Sashes	**No Value to 200.00**
Camp Patches	**50¢-5.00**
Eagle Medals	**25.00-100.00**
Senior Scout Medals	**40.00-250.00**

Wanted: boy and girl scout memorabilia, all items considered! I will buy one piece or your entire collection. The following price range will apply for all scout items. If you have any boy/girl scout items you wish to sell, please call or write.

Joseph Tucker
4725 Terrace
Kansas City, MO 64112
(816) 753-4101 or (816) 421-3355

We Pay

Patches 1.00-25.00
Uniforms 5.00-75.00
Pins.. 1.00-25.00
Medals 10.00-50.00
Books & Magazines 1.00-10.00
Jamboree Items.. 1.00-50.00
Order of the Arrow Items 1.00-50.00
Explorer Items... 1.00-25.00
Pictures.. 1.00-15.00
Neckerchiefs... 1.00-25.00
Pamphlets & Paper Items.. 1.00-15.00

I am interested in purchasing Boy Scouts of America memorabilia. I presently am seeking entire collections or single items with preference for pre-1950 items. However I am willing to discuss and advise on all materials for potential purchase. Specific wants include handbooks, manuals, older uniforms and uniform parts, patches of all types, pamphlets, flags, banners, and streamers. Of special interest are items marked with WWW and a number on a patch. I also seek **Lone Scout, Sea Scouts, Air Scouts, and Explorer Scouts memorabilia**.

I am an active collector and have been an active advertiser for over fifteen years. I answer all inquiries. I encourage collect telephone calls. The best time to telephone is after 6 P.M. Eastern Standard Time.

Bruce J. White
3 Woodfern Ave.
Trenton, NJ 08628
(609) 882-5584

BREWERIANA

We are interested in buying all types of **pre-prohibition brewery memorabilia**. These items were generally given away by breweries to advertise their products during the latter half of the 1800's and the early 1900's. The prices below are only starting prices; your item could easily be worth much more to us. Please contact us for the price we would pay for your specific item and be sure to enclose a SASE for a response.

Steve Ketcham
P.O. Box 24114
Edina, MN 55424
(612) 920-4205

We Pay

Bottles... 5.00+
Calendars.. 20.00+
Corkscrews .... 10.00+
Etched Glasses.. 35.00+
Enameled Glasses... 75.00+
Foam Scrapers.. 10.00+
Industrial Publications.. 10.00
Knives... 35.00
Match Safes .... 10.00+
Mirrors, large.. 35.00+
Pocket Mirrors.. 35.00+
Mugs w/Brand Name .... 35.00+
Steins w/Brand Name .... 35.00+
Openers .... 10.00+
Photos .... 10.00+
Pin-Backs.. 10.00+
Playing Cards .... 20.00+
Post Cards... 10.00+

Breweriana

Signs	**75.00+**
Trays	**75.00+**
Tip Trays	**25.00+**
Tokens	**10.00+**
Watch Fobs	**25.00+**

Foam scrapers were also known as beer combs. They were used to clean the foam off the top of glasses or pitchers of beer. Scrapers went out of use in the early 1960's. Rumor has it that foam scrapers were discontinued for sanitary reasons. They were usually made of plastic, celluloid, bone, ivory, or aluminum. Sizes vary, but most are about 1" wide and 9" long. The name of a beer (and/or a brewery) should be marked on them. I will buy any U.S. foam scraper. Prices will depend on condition and name of beer or brewery advertised. I also buy **Connecticut breweriana** such as signs, thermometers, trays, tap knobs, matches, or any other item with advertising for Connecticut beer or breweries on it.

Dick Purvis
15 Strong Street
Manchester, CT 06040
(203) 646-0356

As a collector, I specialize in **breweriana of New Jersey.** I am always looking for quality **pre-1940 beer advertising** in fine condition. Large lots of ball-type beer tap knobs are also desired. Listed below are a sampling of prices. Rare items, of course, are worth more.

Paul E. Brady
P.O. Box 811
Newton, NJ 07860

	We Pay
Beer Cans	**5.00+**
Calendars	**10.00+**
Novelties	**5.00+**
Signs	**10.00+**
Labels	**2.00+**
Foam Scrapers	**5.00+**

Tip Trays	**5.00+**
Trays	**5.00+**
Coasters	**2.00+**
Tap Knobs	**4.00+**

Wanted to Buy: **Hamm's Beer lighted sign** that moves horizontally and shows a wilderness camping scene with waterfall, running water, campfire with smoke, and canoe. Sign must be in excellent condition — no scratches on wilderness scene as it moves. Please call after 6 P.M. or write with your price.

Raymond L. Pratt
112 Rolling Dr.
Wilmington, DE 19713
(302) 454-7074

BRONZES

I am interested in bronzes of Art Nouveau and Art Deco styles. I will purchase one or a collection.

Brian Margolis
66 Waterloo
Winnipeg, Manitoba
Canada R3N 0S2

We Pay

Spelter & Ivorene Figures	**100.00+**
Bronze Figures	**250.00+**
Bronze & Ivory Figures	**500.00+**
Bronze & Marble	**300.00+**
Bronze & Ivorene	**200.00+**
Bronze Boxes, Inkwells	**100.00+**
Bronze Vases	**150.00+**

BUFFALO POTTERY

I am buying Deldare Ware by Buffalo Pottery. These items are hand-painted and will be marked with a figure of a buffalo and the word Deldare or Emerald Deldare on the back. Scenes of people are the most common motif, but it can also be found with stylized florals. I am only interested in mint-condition pieces. Listed below are some of the pieces I am looking to buy.

Lynn Thompson
P.O. Box 24611
Winston-Salem, NC 27114-4611

We Pay

Demitasse Cup & Saucer	**300.00**
Tea Cup & Saucer	**175.00**
Mug	**275.00**
Plate, 6" or 7"	**100.00**
Plate, 8½"	**150.00**
Plate, 9" or 10"	**250.00**

Platters & Trays **350.00**
Bowls **300.00**
Teapot **375.00**
Coffeepot **375.00**
Water Pitcher **350.00**
Candlesticks **450.00**

BUTTER BOXES

I collect one-pound butter boxes, both old and current, from all over the United States. Most boxes are printed on heavy paper. The current boxes must be in excellent shape, carefully opened on ends, and flattened to mail. If the box has a tear-tab, open the other end, and then it can be reglued. I pay according to age and condition. Please list the dairy's name and location listed on your boxes with your inquiry.

Anne E. Wachter
809 Redland Dr.
Madison, WI 53714-1722

We Pay

Current-1990's .... **10¢**
1989-1980's .... **25¢**
1979-1970's .... **50¢**
1969-1960's **1.00-3.00**
1959-1950's .... **photocopy for offer**
Earlier Boxes .... **photocopy for offer**

BUTTONS

I seek brass uniform buttons of military schools. I also have many of these for sale or trade. I am primarily interested in the uniform buttons of private military schools and colleges. I pay up to $3.00 for specific buttons for my collection. If you have brass uniform buttons but are unable to determine whether or not they are the type I need, please send a sketch or photocopy. I will try to identify the item and will make an offer.

Arthur J. Grau, Jr.
1935 Quincy Ave.
Racine, WI 53403

CALIFORNIA PERFUME COMPANY

In New York City, New York, in 1886, Mr. D.H. McConnell, Sr., founded the California Perfume Company (C.P.C.). These toiletries continued to be manufactured with the C.P.C. label until 1929 when 'Avon Products Inc.' was added. Both names appeared on the label until about 1939 when 'C.P.C.' was removed, and the labeling continued as 'Avon Products.' The name 'Perfection' was used on the household products issued by these companies.

I am interested in buying certain C.P.C. items from the circa 1900 period. I am particularly interested in the Natoma Rose fragrance and will pay good prices for such items. I do not want anything bearing the Avon name. When writing, please send a complete description, including condition and any note of importance. A large SASE is required if you are seeking information only. Please, no collect calls.

Mr. Richard G. Pardini
3107 N El Dorado St.
Stockton, CA 95204
(209) 446-5550 (7 am to 11 pm Pacific)

CAMERAS

I buy stereoscopic cameras, viewers, and supplies from the 1930's to the 1960's, including advertising and dealer displays. Look for cameras, viewers, and projectors with two lenses. Stereo Realist, Stereo Kodak, Busch Verascope, Zeiss Stereotar, and Wollensak are a few names. 3-D slides, views, viewers, and holders are of value, as are books and printed matter covering stereo photography. View Master cameras, cutters, and close-up lenses have value as well as unusual military and advertising View Master reels and three-packs. I also buy Nikon, Canon, Leitz, and Zeiss cameras. Colored Kodak, Gift Kodak, Kodak Bantam Special, Super Six-20, and Chevron cameras are wanted.

Harry Poster
P.O. Box 1883
S Hackensack, NJ 07606
(201) 794-9606

We Pay

Stereo Realist, Stereo Kodak, Revere Cameras .... **70.00+**
Wollensak, Verascope, Belplasca.. **250.00+**
Realist, Kodaslide II, Wollensak 3-D Viewers .... **40.00+**
TDC & Similar 3-D Projectors.. **150.00+**
View Master Camera w/Film Punch **200.00**
View Master Reels (advertising, military, gold, etc.).......................... **5.00-15.00**
Early Canon or Nikon Cameras .... **1,000.00+**
Kodak Colored (non-black) Folders .... **50.00+**
Kodak Bantam Special... **150.00+**
Kodak Gift Kodak w/Box.. **500.00+**
Camera in Lady's Compact .... **300.00+**

———————————

I am buying unusual antique and collectible cameras. I prefer pre-1920
items, whether a single piece or a collection, and will buy newer unusual
cameras as well. Listed below are examples of cameras I am seeking.

Steve G. Gabany
585 Woodbine Dr.
Terre Haute, IN 47903

Manufacturer & Model	We Pay
Kodak Beau Brownie, No. 2	9.00+
Ihagee Kamerawerk Exa	6.00+
Graflex Graphic '45'	44.00+
Universal Camera Corp. Iris	3.00+
Agfa Memo, Half-Frame	9.00+
Monolta Minolta Autocord	15.00+
Kodak No. 2 Bull's-Eye	8.00+
Kodak No. 2 Stereo Brownie	75.00+
Blair No. 2 Weno Hawk-Eye	5.00+
Kodak No. 4A Folding Kodak	25.00+
Yamato Pax (I)	10.00+
Kodak Petite	25.00+
Q.R.S.-DeVry Corp. Q.R.S. Kamra	15.00+
Kodak Quick-Focus Kodak Camera No. 3B	31.00+
White Stereo Realist, Model 1041	23.00+
Voigtlander Vitessa	19.00+
Voigtlander Vito	6.00+
Expo Watch Camera	25.00+
Unknown Wooden Box Camera	2.00+
Kodak World's Fair Flash	2.00+
Zeh Zeca-Flex	163.00+

Paying $1.00 to thousands for older cameras, lenses, and accessories. The condition and rarity of the item are important in determining price. Cameras from the 1800s through the 1970's such as those listed below are wanted as well as any number of other camera names and types of stereo, classic, unusual, and rare types of cameras, lenses, and accessories. Please write or call.

Bob Coyle
1006 Lincoln Ave.
Dubuque, IA 52001
(319) 588-9694

Leitz
Leica

Plaubel
Voightlander

Zeiss
Rolleiflex
Canon
Nikon Range Finder
Quality or Unusual Kodak
Alpa

Ernemann
Fed
Panon
Robot
Steinheil

CAN OPENERS

The first 'modern' kitchen collectible and the first tool to be used in the kitchen, the can opener is a metal cutter designed to open sealed cans of perishables. It was first used in the late 1850's (Napoleon's army first used tin cans in volume for military rations) in the industrialized nations of Great Britian, the United States, Germany, and France; but the can opener didn't really catch on until after the American Civil War. The 'golden age' was the 1870's through the 1890's when a wide variety of mechanical solutions were tried. By World War I the classic hooked blade form was developed. In the early 1930's and increasingly after World War II, the manual wall-mount crank opener was a common tool in the American kitchen, only to be replaced by electric can openers in the 1960's. Now, after a hundred years, the highly energy efficient hand-held hand-crank manual type is once again returning to popularity.

We are interested in unique food can openers to add to our collection, as well as images, photos, advertising, histories and articles, instructions, and packaging. We are not interested in beer can or bottle openers unless a metal cutting can opener is part of the tool. It is best to send a photo or drawing and price wanted. We are writing a history and price guide about can openers.

Richard M. Bueschel
414 N Prospect Manor Ave.
Mt. Prospect, IL 60056
(708) 253-0791

We Pay

Cast Iron Figural Can Openers	**20.00**
Cast Iron Working Mechanical (moving parts) Can Openers	**35.00**
Cast Iron Can Openers, patent date before 1890	**20.00**
Cast Iron Can Openers, patent date 1891–1920	**5.00**
Cast Iron Can Openers w/Name in Casting	**15.00**
Cast Iron Can Openers w/Name on Blade	**5.00**

Multipurpose (sharpener, glass cutter, etc.)
Cast Iron Can Openers, before 1905 .... **15.00**
Multipurpose (sharpener, glass cutter, etc.)
Cast Iron Can Openers, after 1905 .... **10.00**
Wooden-Handled Can Openers w/Advertising on Handle **8.00**
Metal Can Openers w/Advertising in Metal **5.00**
Wall-Mount Manual Openers in Original Box **10.00**
Painted Wall-Mount Can Openers w/Wall Bracket **2.50**
Old Photo of Can Opener in Use, prior to 1930 .... **10.00**
Photo of Manual Can Opener in Use, circa 1930-1985 .... **2.50**
Real Photo Post Card of Can Openers, static or in use **12.50**
Can Opener Advertising or Catalog Pages, before 1905 .... **7.50**
Can Opener Advertising or Catalog Pages, after 1905 .... **1.50**
Can Opener Instructions, before 1930 .... **5.00**
Can Opener Instructions, after 1930 .... **2.00**

CANDY CONTAINERS

I want **papier-mache and/or composition types of candy containers**. Holiday and non-holiday themes are wanted from the Victorian era to the 1940's.

William R. Strater
3720 Cannon Ave.
Las Vegas, NV 89121

We Pay

Animals .... **25.00+**
Figurines .... **25.00+**
Inanimate Themes .... **20.00+**
Holiday (depends on type, condition, etc.) .... **Write**

PEZ candy containers are wanted for my collection. I am searching for those available during the 1950's through 1980's. Also of interest are other PEZ-related items such as comics, costumes, stickers, premiums, etc.

Melody Clark
105 Ballard Hall, OSU
Corvallis, OR 97331-3608
(503) 737-1323

Dispenser	We Pay
Air Spirite	10.00+
Alpine	10.00+
Annie	5.00+
Arithmetic	10.00+
Astronaut	10.00+
Baseball Glove	10.00+
Batgirl	5.00+
Batman w/Cape	10.00+
Betsy Ross	5.00+
Bozo	5.00+
Bozo Diecut	10.00+
Bride	5.00+
Brutus	5.00+
Bullwinkle	5.00+
Candy Shooter	10.00+
Captain	5.00+
Captain America	5.00+
Casper	5.00+
Casper Diecut	10.00+
Clown	5.00+
Cockatoo	5.00+
Cow	5.00+
Cowboy	10.00+
Creature of Black Lagoon	10.00+
Crocodile	5.00+
Daniel Boone	5.00+
Doctor	5.00+
Donald Duck Diecut	10.00+
Donkey Kong Jr.	5.00+
Dopey	5.00+
Dumbo	5.00+
Easter Bunny Diecut	10.00+
Engineer	5.00+
Fireman	5.00+
Fisherman	5.00+
Foghorn Leghorn	5.00+
Football Player	5.00+
Giraffe	5.00+
Golden Glow	5.00+
Gorilla	5.00+
Green Hornet	5.00+
Groom	5.00+
Henry Hawk	5.00+
Indian Brave	5.00+
Indian Chief	5.00+
Indian Squaw	5.00+

Jiminy Cricket	5.00+
Lion	5.00+
Maharajah	5.00+
Make-a-Face	20.00+
Mary Poppins	5.00+
Merlin Mouse	5.00+
Mickey Mouse Diecut	10.00+
Monkey Sailor	5.00+
Monster	5.00+
Olive Oyl	5.00+
Olympics	10.00+
Orange	5.00+
Panther	5.00+
Personalized	10.00+
Pilgrim	5.00+
Pilot	5.00+
Pineapple	5.00+
Pinocchio	5.00+
Pirate	5.00+
Popeye	5.00+
Psychedelic Eye/FLower	10.00+
Robot	10.00+
Sheik	5.00+
Space Gun	20.00+
Spaceman	5.00+
Tinkerbelle	5.00+
Uncle Sam	5.00+
Vampire	5.00+
Wile E. Coyote	5.00+
Witch (1-piece)	5.00+
Zorro	5.00+
Zombi	5.00+

CANTON

Canton was an expressly western export made in and around Canton, China, from about 1795 through the 1920's. The pattern closely resembles the Willow Ware pattern of today with its white and blue scene of teahouse, bridge, boats, and birds, all within a rain and cloud border. I am interested in unusual forms such as candlesticks, bowls, flagons, teapots, reticulated baskets, etc., or large collections. Please, no plates, platters, or teacups unless they are part of a large collection. Condition (cracks, chips, repairs, etc.)

should be carefully described and is the key to the value of a particular item. Please send a photo with complete description. I will travel anywhere in the East to make an offer on a sizable collection.

Hoby Van Deusen
28 The Green
Watertown, CT 06795
(203) 945-3456

We Pay

Cut Corner Bowls .... **600.00+**
Candlesticks, pair .... **1,000.00+**
Teapots .... **300.00+**
Garden Seats .... **4,000.00+**
Square Canisters .... **1,000.00+**
Cider Flagons .... **600.00+**

CARNIVAL COLLECTIBLES

I am buying carnival **chalkware** items by the single piece or an entire collection. I also want single decorated tumblers; I do not want sets. Send a description of the item including its condition and your price.

Thomas W. Davis
147 Longleaf Dr.
Blackshear, GA 31516

We Pay

Carnival Chalkware, small items **3.00-10.00**
Carnival Chalkware, large items **10.00-30.00**
Decorated Tumblers, each **1.00-3.00**

CARNIVAL GLASS

Even with over a thousand patterns and around sixty shapes to choose from, one thing — color — is surely what carnival glass is all about. The basic color of this glass is what gives collectors a wide choice for their particular specialization; the rainbow colors of the iridescent surface are what make a piece of carnival glass so very fascinating. Base glass colors are blue, green, red, amethyst/purple, and black; and sprayed-on colors are marigold, smoke, and white. Limited amounts were made in 'off-colors' and pastels including ice blue, ice green, teal, vaseline, aqua, and various shades of each color. A few of these were also opalized. We are interested in obtaining off-colors and opalized pieces and will pay top prices for them.

Wesley & Betty Strain
832 Carson Rd.
Ferguson, MO 63135
(314) 524-5608

We Pay

Bowls	100.00-1,000.00
Plates	150.00-2,500.00
Water Pitchers	300.00-3,500.00
Punch Bowls	400.00-5,000.00
Vases, Compotes, Rose Bowls, Others	**Write**

We purchase only old carnival glass in excellent condition with good, deep color and iridescence. We are very interested in ice blues and greens, red, and opalescents. Please send pictures (very very helpful if you don't know the pattern) along with a note describing size, etc. If you are unable to put a price on your item, please advise; but, if you can price your own merchandise, it would be very helpful. We suggest you also include an SASE for our early reply. As is our policy, once a price has been agreed to, we will send you one-half of our agreed price. You then ship the item; upon our inspection, we immediately remit the balance to you, providing items are as represented.

The Antique Place
1720A S Glenstone
Springfield, MO 65804
(417) 887-3800

J.I. CASE MEMORABILIA

In 1842, Jerome Increase Case (1819–1891) founded the J.I. Case Company in Rochester, Wisconsin. By 1852 he was demonstrating his threshing machines throughout the midwest. In 1865 the 'Old Abe' Eagle trademark was adopted. Old Abe had been a mascot for Company C in the 8th Wisconsin 'Eagle' Regiment and went through thirty-eight battles and skirmishes. In 1886 the J.I. Case Company was the largest manufacturer of steam engines in the world, and Old Abe was perched upon the globe by 1894.

J.I. Case memorabilia and Old Abe collectibles range in size from a 1" red plastic eagle pin (I will pay $2.00 for this) to a 5-foot cast iron dealer statue (which will bring you $500.00). Other items sought are listed below. Write with a complete description.

M. Hobbs
15 W 414 Fillmore St.
Elmhurst, IL 60126
(708) 279-7842

We Pay

Old Abe Books	**up to 25.00**
J.I. Case Clocks	**up to 200.00**
J.I. Case Paperweights	**up to 50.00**
Old Abe Post Standards	**up to 100.00**

CASH REGISTERS

Cash registers are becoming increasingly popular as collectibles, particularly within the past five years — especially the earlier wood and brass cabinet models. From the late 1800's until the outbreak of World War I, cash register companies, primarily in the United States, made hundreds of different fancy machines in an effort to please business owners all over the world and to more accurately and securely manage and control 'cash flow.' The beginning and primary company, National Cash Register Company of Dayton, Ohio, continues to this date to strive to meet the changing needs of businesses throughout the world.

We buy most nice wood or ornate brass cash registers that are in good condition, that can easily be restored, and are not missing major functional and/or cosmetic parts. We also buy other machines; however, prices paid for those machines tend to be lower. The following price list is reflective of prices we have paid or are now paying for such noted 'National' cash registers — unrestored, in good working order, and with no major parts missing. We urge you to contact us for prices paid on any of the hundreds of models not listed.

William (Bill) C. Danielson
Days Gone By of Tuscaloosa
18 Smith Acres
Northport, AL 35476
Parts & Restorations Ordering: 1-800-445-7811
(205) 556-1188 or (205) 339-2402

We Pay

National #1, brass 750.00
National #4, wood 1,250.00
National #5, brass 750.00
National #6, extended base 750.00
National #8, brass w/clock 650.00
National #12, brass 750.00
National #33, brass 450.00
National #92, bronze floor model 750.00
National #130, brass 550.00
National #211, brass 650.00
National #215, brass 550.00
National #216, brass 550.00
National #226, brass 450.00
National #223, brass 750.00
National #250, barber shop 600.00
National #310, brass 350.00
National #311, brass 550.00
National #312, brass 500.00
National #313, brass 450.00
National #324, brass 350.00
National #332, brass 250.00
National #442, brass 300.00
National #442, Electric 400.00
National #50, brass 550.00
National #47½, inlaid wood 1,200.00
National #747, metal 20.00
National #711, metal 50.00
Premier #1, ornate 200.00
World 400.00
American, oak, dated 1887 .... 350.00
Mc Caskey, oak, patent 1906 .... 100.00
Michigan, wood base 100.00
Simplex, oak 400.00
Ideal 100.00

CAST IRON

I collect cast iron muffin pans and baking pans. Portions of my collection of about 235 different patterns and variations have been featured in antique publications. Iron muffin pans are interesting because of the wide variety of geometric designs and figural patterns such as hearts, fruits, vegetables, etc. Many iron molds are misidentified as soap molds and sugar molds. However, if the item is made of cast iron, I am interested.

I also collect cast iron broilers and grid irons. These are cooking utensils with grids or openings which were used to broil or fry meat. In addition to collecting, I also buy, sell, and trade old cast iron cookware such as skillets, waffle irons, griddles, etc. I have been doing this for years throughout the U.S. and Canada. If it is old and cast iron (not wrought iron), I am interested.

David G. Smith
P.O. Box B
Perrysburg, NY 14129
(716) 532-5154

Muffin Pan	We Pay
Griswold #2800 Wheat Stick	350.00
Griswold #50 Hearts Star	350.00

Griswold #19 Golf Ball **150.00**
Griswold #13 Turk's Head... **300.00**
Griswold #5 .... **150.00**
Griswold #4, 4-section Vienna Roll.. **150.00**
Heart Patterns... **150.00+**
Wapak Gem Pans **75.00**
GF Filley #9, #13, or higher... **350.00**
GF Filley #1, #2, #4, or #7 .... **150.00**
W.C. Davis, 13-section **150.00**
Wagner, styles M or N.. **100.00**
Any Unusual Pan Wanted... **Call or Write**

I am looking for whatever is out of the ordinary in overall form/shape or internal style/pattern (e.g., in the internal design of waffle makers or cookie molds) of cast iron cookware. I am primarily interested in plain black metal items that you can cook in or eat/drink out of (versus trivets, mechanicals, stove parts, etc.). Always wanted is unusual or strange cast iron cookware made by Griswold, G.F. Filley, Barstow, Keen Kutter/Simmons, Buck & Wright, W.C. Davis, etc. Wanted are such items as cookie/biscuit and figural/cake molds, waffle/wafer irons, broilers, press/roll-over Springerle molds, children's/salesman's samples, plates and platters, coffee roasters, corn dog and ice cream cone makers, flop griddles, acorn pans, any ephemera (trade catalogs/cards, ads, etc.), and any item of unusual size, shape or internal pattern.

Specifically of interest are #1, #2, #7, #9, and #14 G.F. Filley molds; #7 Griswold biscuit molds; #1, #2, #4, #24, #26, and #28 bread loaf pans; #27, #28, #270, #280, #282, #283, #2700, and #2800 whole wheat grains and corn cob stick pans; #50 and #100 heart and star molds; #4 French, #21 and #22 Belgian waffler; and any company's waffle maker with an initial/logo on the inside.

With the exception of undersize (#0, #1, #2) or oversize (#11, #13, #14, #20) Griswold skillets and (#11 through #13) Dutch ovens, I mostly have enough regular pots, pans, and griddles. The listing below is not an exclusive list of wants, as I really don't know what is available. For items in good condition, I will pay the prices below plus UPS charges.

Joel Schiff
321 E 12 St.
New York City, NY 10003
(212) 777-1296

We Pay

Waffle/Wafer Irons, unusual shape or internal pattern............................ **50.00+**

Springerle/'Roll-Over' Mold Plates .... 35.00+
Ice Cream Cone Makers (cone or enclosed sandwich vs. rolled wafer)... 65.00+
Distinctive Timbale/Rosette/Patty Irons (especially club or spade).......... 5.00+
Animal/Fruit Cake Pans (bent fish, rabbit, Santa Claus) .... 60.00-100.00+
Different Pudding/Cake/Bake/Bundt Pans (swirl, crisscross)................. 40.00+
Rotary Corn Dog, Omelet, or Sandwich Grill Pans/Collars..................... 40.00+
Strange Cookie/Roll/Biscuit Mold Patterns................................... 20.00-50.00+
Coffee Roasters (ball, cylinder, 'sauce pot').. 65.00+
Different Teakettles ('tipping,' oval, square, 'cupcake' bottom) .... 20.00-60.00+
Mugs, Chocolate Pots/Possets .... 35.00+
Porrigers .... 35.00+
Plates/Platters (round, oval, etc.) .... 45.00+
Strange Broilers/Bacon Renderers (e.g., Erie)... 35.00+
Pressure Cookers/'Digesters'.. 40.00+
Unusual 'Fold-Over' Griddles (2-spot 'flop' griddles, Erie, Griswold).... 35.00+
Different 'Egg & Baconers' & 'Warm-Over' Pans (Griswold, Wagner)...... 30.00+

I am buying figural cast iron. I prefer items that are in original condition with original paint. I will buy one piece or an entire collection. Please include a phone number with your correspondence. A photo is appreciated as well and makes communication much easier. I will also buy any unusual cast iron pieces not listed below. I am a dealer and collector with twenty-two years' experience.

Graig Dinner
P.O. Box 455
Valley Stream, NY 11582

We Pay

Architectural 10.00-1,000.00
Building Stars... 15.00+
Signs & Advertising 25.00-3,000.00
Children's Toy Sad Irons... 10.00+
Curtain Tie-Backs.. 10.00+
Door Knockers... 35.00-500.00
Doorstops 40.00-2,500.00
Figural Bottle Openers... 5.00-800.00+
Figural Pencil Holders.. 10.00+
Shooting Gallery Targets 10.00-3,000.00
String Holders .... 15.00+
Match Holders.. 15.00+

I am buying old cast iron items such as those listed below. Also, please contact me if you have any unusual items. I pay any reasonable amount according to condition. A partial listing of items I seek is given below. I will answer all letters.

Muffin Pans	Dumbbells
Tart Pans	Children's Stoves
Breadstick Pans	Book Racks
Waffle Irons	Pan Racks
Doughnut Bakers	Steps
String Holders	Any Kind of Mold
Doorstops	

Mrs. Harvey Markley
611 W Beardsley Ave.
Elkhart, IN 46514

CATALOGS

My primary interest is in **trade catalogs printed before 1900**. In selected areas such as **saloon equipment, slot machines, coin-operated arcade machines, and ceiling fans, we are interested up to the 1950's**. We also buy wholesale and mail order catalogs for a number of consumer products such as toy banks, games, and gambling equipment. You may also have other trade catalogs not listed here in which we might be interested. If you think you do, please contact us, and we will let you know if we purchase them.

Having been a collector since the early 1960's, I have authored several books on saloon memorabilia and coin-operated machines: *Pinball 1*, *Slots 1*, and the latest *B.A. Stevens Billiard and Bar Goods*. These are available for $29.95 each plus $2.00 postage per book from The Coin Slot (4401 Zephyr St.; Wheat Ridge, CO 80033-3299; 303-420-2222). Please ask for a complete listing of books on slot machines, trade stimulators, arcade machines, etc.

Richard M. Bueschel
414 N Prospect Manor Ave.
Mt. Prospect, IL 60056
(708) 253-0791

Catalog	We Pay
Electrical Equipment, before 1900	**10.00**

Electrical Equipment, 1900–1920 .... **7.50**
Ceiling Fans, before 1900 .... **15.00**
Ceiling Fans, 1900–1950.. **10.00**
Saloon Equipment, before 1900, per page **1.50**
Saloon Equipment, 1900–1919, per page.. **1.00**
Slot Machines, before 1900, per page **1.50**
Slot Machines, 1900 and later, per page **1.00**
Penny Arcade Machines, per page **1.00**
Amusement Park Rides, per page.. **75¢**
Mills Novelty Co., before 1905 .... **100.00**
Mills Novelty Co., 1906–1951 .... **25.00**
Industry Novelty Co. **35.00**
B.A. Stevens (Toledo) **25.00**
R. Rothschilds Sons, before 1905 .... **75.00**
Peck & Snyder Sporting Goods.. **35.00**
D.N. Schall & Co... **75.00**
Watling Mfg. Co., before 1905 .... **75.00**
Watling Mfg. Co., 1906–1951 .... **25.00**
Kernan Mfg. Co. **35.00**
Gambling Equipment, before 1900, per page.. **1.50**
Gambling Equipment, 1900–1917, per page **1.00**
N. Shure & Co.. **15.00**
Richard K. Fox, before 1920 .... **25.00**
Bott Bros. Co. (Columbus, Ohio) **75.00**
Albert Pick & Co., before 1912... **100.00**
Albert Pick & Co., 1912–1935 .... **10.00**
Soda Fountain, per page **1.00**
Tin Ceilings **10.00**
Store Counters & Fixtures, before 1917.. **10.00**
Ogden & Co., before 1905 .... **50.00**
H.C. Evans & Co. **10.00**
Exhibit Supply Co.. **10.00**
Samuel Nafew & Co. **25.00**

I am purchasing **Christmas catalogs, toy catalogs, novelty catalogs, and fireworks catalogs through the 1960's.** I will buy one catalog or hundreds!

Jerry Bland
P.O. Box 6205
Kinston, NC 28502
(919) 522-5377

We Pay

John Smith Novelty Co. .... **5.00+**

N. Shure Novelty Co. .... **6.00+**
Christmas Catalogs.. **10.00+**
Toy Catalogs .... **5.00+**
Fireworks Catalogs.. **6.00+**

I'm buying old **Anri catalogs (wood carving)**. If possible, I would like the price lists included. I have the Club Anri catalogs. Catalogs in the best condition possible are wanted.

Doris A. Beaudoin
P.O. Box 90081
Los Angeles, CA 90009

We Pay

Early Catalogs **25.00**
1940's through 1970's Catalogs .... **20.00+**
1980's Catalogs **15.00**

I am looking for several copies of each of the following **catalogs between 1950 and 1990**. The particular years do not matter too much, but the condition must be fine or better. I will pay the amounts indicated for catalogs I need at the time I hear from you. I am also looking for an unmarked, untorn United States road map from 1950 to 1956 in fine condition. I will pay $50.00 for the first acceptable map. Also sought is a copy of a dictionary about 8½" x 11" in size which has a glossy page indicating the names of each part of a suit of armor. The page is in color and is full sized. I will pay $150.00 for such a dictionary.

Fred Drenckhahn
49 Garden St.
Boston, MA 02144
(617) 367-0869

We Pay

Johnson Smith & Co. .... **25.00+**
Edmund Scientific Co. .... **25.00+**

I have been researching the glass companies of western Pennsylvania and those of the Beaver Valley area in particular. Currently, I am trying to compile a complete and accurate history of the Phoenix Glass Company of Monaca, Pennsylvania, where my grandfather was employed as a glass blower for many years. My book on this subject will cover the period from 1880 to 1980.

I'm interested in buying **original glass company catalogs and advertising brochures**, especially those of the Phoenix Glass Company of Monaca, the Consolidated Lamp & Glass Company of Coraopolis, the Co-Operative Flint Glass Company of Beaver Falls, the Fry Glass Company of Rochester, the Dithridge Glass Company of New Brighton, the Rochester Tumbler Company of Rochester, the American Glass Specialty Company of Monaca, the Whitla Glass Company of Beaver Falls, the Beaver Falls Glass Company of Beaver Falls, and the Pittsburgh Lamp, Brass, & Glass Company of Pittsburgh. I would also consider **catalogs of any company which produced lighting glass** such as electric lamps, oil lamps, and glass shades.

I also buy related items such as magazine ads showing glassware (particularly that made by the companies listed above), company letterheads and documents, workers' badges, and post cards of glass companies of Monaca, Pennsylvania. Please price and fully describe each item. Even if you do not have items to sell, I would appreciate hearing from people who are willing to share information which may help me in my Phoenix glass research. I answer all letters and will reimburse you for postage and photos.

The Kelly Collection
Kathy Kelly
1621 Princess Ave.
Pittsburgh, PA 15216
(412) 561-3379

CEREAL PREMIUMS AND BOXES

Collector wants to buy 1960's and 1970's cereal premiums. Any in-box prizes or 'send-a-ways' from cereals such as Quisp, Quake, Cap-N-Crunch, Wheat Honeys, Crispy Critters, Trix, Twinkles, etc. are sought. I am especially looking for unassembled and unopened items in original mailing boxes. Also bought are cereal boxes before 1985 — especially discontinued cereals such as OJs, Moonstones, Pink Panther Flakes, Freekies, Kellogg's Stars, Twinkles, etc.

Roland Coover, Jr.
1537 E Strasburg Rd.
W Chester, PA 19380

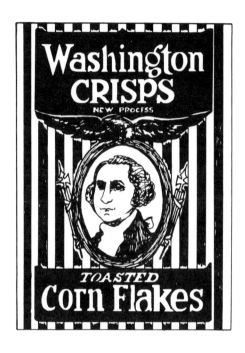

We Pay

Quisp & Quake Send-A-Ways	**25.00+**
Quisp & Quake In-Box Premiums	**8.00+**
Cereal Premium Rings	**5.00+**
TV Cartoon-Related Premiums	**5.00+**
Plastic Figures	**3.00+**
Kellogg's Snap-Together Camel & Circus Trains	**10.00+**
Cereal Boxes	**25.00+**
Store Displays & Advertising Posters	**25.00+**
Quisp Bank	**100.00+**

I am buying current (on your shelf or in your trash right now) cereal boxes. I only need clean, unmangled, whole examples — please no smelly, gooey messes! All brands are needed, including generic and store brands. I am also looking for current or recently discarded store displays, posters, banners, shelf signs, shelf cards, box tops, premiums, out-dated coupons with box pictures, etc.

To prepare boxes for shipping, remove and discard the inner liner, then gently open the box bottom to ship flat. I will pay at least 10¢ a box and will return the cost of your postage. For all other items, please contact me and enclose a SASE.

Catt Yeats
The Old Lund Store
HC 72 Box 2255
Lund, ID 83217

We Pay

Cereal Boxes	10¢+
Coupons	2¢+
Premiums	50¢+
Box Toys	25¢+
Unopened Box Toys	40¢+
Shelf Cards or Signs	50¢+
Displays, Posters, or Banners	5.00+

CHINA

I would like to buy sets, partial sets, or serving pieces from any of the following china companies:

Adams	George Jones
Adderly	Kaiser
Arabia of Finland	KPM
Arcadian	Kutani
Aynsley	Lamberton
Morgan Belleek	Lenox
Booths	Meakin
Georges Briard	Meissen
Buffalo	Minton
Castleton	Noritake
Ceralene Raynald	Oxford

Coalport
Crown Staffordshire
Denby
Epiag
Flintridge
Franciscan
Frankoma
Richard Ginori
Goebel
Gorham
Gridley
Haviland
H. & C
Herend
Homer Laughlin
Imperial Bohemian
Iroquois
Johnson Bros.

Picard
Quimper
Red Wing
Ridgeway
Rosenthal
Royal Albert
Royal Bayreuth
Royal Copenhagen
Royal Doulton
Royal Worcester
Schumann
Spode
Syracuse.
Taylor, Smith, & Taylor
Thun
Villeroy & Boch
Wedgwood
Woods & Sons

There are hundreds of other companies as well. Also wanted are any oriental items. Items must be in mint condition.

Bill Simmons
315 SW 77th Ave.
N Lauderdale, FL 33068

We Pay

Adams, Lowestoft, Covered Vegetable Bowl **25.00**
Adderly, Chelsea, Covered Vegetable Bowl... **40.00**
Belleek, Limpet, Platter, large **30.00**
Buffalo, Blue Willow, Gravy Boat **25.00**
Homer Laughlin, Fiesta, Vase, red, 12" **100.00**
Lenox, Belvidere 5314, Teapot... **50.00**
Rosenthal, Platinum Grill, Platter, large **30.00**
Royal Copenhagen, Florida Dancia, Cup & Saucer.................................... **100.00**
Royal Copenhagen, Florida Dancia, Platter, large **300.00**
Royal Copenhagen, Florida Dancia, Gravy Boat....................................... **250.00**
Royal Copenhagen, Florida Dancia, Teapot.. **275.00**
Syracuse, Celeste, Covered Vegetable Bowl **50.00**
Wedgwood, Columbia Ruby, Dinner Plate **40.00**
Wedgwood, Columbia Ruby, Vegetable Bowl, round **100.00**

I am buying porcelain made in Trenton, New Jersey, by such companies as Lenox, Willets Belleek, Ott & Brewer, Ceramic Art Co., etc. Prices range from $30.00 for common items up to $350.00 for rare pieces. I will also consider some of the lower priced pieces made by Boehm and Cybis. I am buying all dogs made by Boehm.

Richard Conti
6 Beverly Pl.
Trenton, NJ 08619
(609) 584-1080

We are currently buying china (single pieces or sets with no chips, cracks, or wear marks). These can be parts and pieces to place settings, serving pieces or complementary pieces (nut cups, candies, etc.). We are buying pieces by the following companies:

Royal Doulton
Royal Albert
Royal Copenhagen
Bing & Grondahl
Lenox (some patterns)
Noritake (some patterns)
Rosenthal (some patterns)

Prices depend on the piece. Please call for a quote. Thank you.

Bill & Beverly Rhodes
N 4820 Whitehouse
Spokane, WA 99205
(509) 328-8399

CHILDREN'S DISHES

I buy children's dishes, complete tea sets and dinner sets, and also individual pieces. Some pieces may be signed:

R.S. Prussia
R.S. Poland
R.S. Germany
R.S. Tillowitz
R.S. Silesia

R.S. Suhl
Prov. Saxe
E.S. Germany
Erdman Schlegelmilch
Rheinhold Schlegelmilch

Pieces with other marks (see Gaston, *R.S. Prussia*, Collector Books) and also unmarked items are wanted. Many known molds in children's items are not marked; therefore, a photo is required (I will return all photos). Reference Publications by Doris Anderson Lechler:

1. *Children's Glass Dishes, China, Furniture*, Vol. 1 & 2, Collector Books
2. *French and German Dishes* to be published in 1991, Antique Publications

E.S. Reynolds
P.O. Box 8231
Green Valley Lake, CA 92341

We Pay

Marked Complete Sets	to 300.00+
Other Complete Sets	200.00+
Individual Teapot	50.00+
Individual Cup & Saucer	25.00+
Individual Sugar	25.00+
Individual Creamer	25.00+

CHRISTMAS COLLECTIBLES

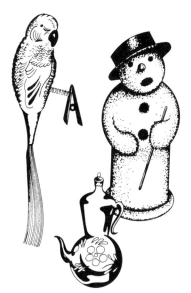

Christmas Collectibles

I am buying **Christmas tree lights**. They can be figural lights or other types of electrical lights that have been used on Christmas trees and as holiday decorations.

Cindy Chipps
4027 Brooks Hill Rd.
Brooks, KY 40109
(502) 955-9238

Figural Lights (need not work)	**We Pay**
Airplane or Train	200.00
Animals	10.00-100.00
People	10.00-200.00
Flowers or Fruit	5.00-25.00
Birds	5.00-35.00
Santas or Snowmen	5.00-300.00
Other Figures	5.00-300.00

Other Lights	**We Pay**
Bubble Lights	2.00-25.00
Matchless Wonder Stars	10.00-50.00
Other Types of Christmas Bulbs	1.00-25.00

I am looking for **glass and/or spun glass Christmas ornaments from their earliest beginnings to the 1950's**. I prefer faces with glass eyes, figures, animals, and unusual birds. Wax angels in very good condition are also wanted. Condition and uniqueness determine price.

William R. Strater
3720 Cannon Ave.
Las Vegas, NV 89121

	We Pay
Faces	25.00+
Animals	40.00+
Spun Glass Ornaments	20.00+
Wax Angels	45.00+

CIGARETTE LIGHTERS

In 1492 when Columbus landed in the West Indies and discovered America, members of his crew found the natives of that land had been using what was later to be known as tobacco for chewing, smoking, snuffing, and ceremonial purposes. People of the Mayan civilization believed the god of fire dwelt in the embers of smoldering tobacco and that by blowing the gods' smoke over them all types of diseases and wounds could be cured. Accordingly, smoking had been a privilege of the priest only, but later the people of primitive tribes adopted the custom. Still later the use of tobacco spread throughout the world. Today, some nine billion pounds of tobacco are produced annually to be used for cigarettes, cigars, etc. This is what prompted cigarette lighter manufacturers to start production about 1890. By 1940 hundreds of companies produced lighters made in all types of shapes, styles, and designs.

I am buying lighters; I prefer older ones, but I will consider all. Some types I am interested in are Ronson Touch-Tips or Ronson Strikers, Dunhill, Cartier, Tiffany, WWI and WWII, minatures, lift-arms, and novelty lighters. I also buy electric cigar lighters, as well as those that are battery-operated, and gas store counter cigar lighters. Listed below are examples of prices paid. The price can double or more than triple depending on condition and model.

Greg Zygai
4191 Hershey Rd.
Erie, PA 16506
(814) 864-7380

We Pay

Ronson Striker, Scotty Dog	**25.00+**
Ronson Striker, any other dog	**20.00+**
Ronson Striker, Pelican	**25.00+**
Ronson Touch-Tip w/Clock	**100.00+**
Ronson Touch-Tip, Art Deco	**25.00+**
Ronson Bartender	**200.00+**
Dunhill, plated, leather banded	**15.00+**
Dunhill, Tinder Pistol	**30.00**
Occupied Japan, Pull Lamp	**15.00+**
Occupied Japan, Camera	**15.00+**
Occupied Japan, Piano	**15.00+**
Parker, Nude, battery-operated	**15.00+**
Musical Knight	**15.00**

CIVILIAN CONSERVATION CORPS

I am interested in items from the Civilian Conservation Corps, established April 5, 1933, by President Franklin Roosevelt. Nicknamed the 'Tree Army' or C.C.C., the agency provided useful work and vocational training for unemployed young men between the ages of 18 and 25. At that time, there were a quarter of a million men out of work. The first 'camp' was established at Luray, VA. There would be at its height over fifteen hundred camps spread across the country. Because of Congress' unwillingness to appropriate the funds necessary to continue the program, the C.C.C. closed its doors in 1942. During the brief existence of the Civilian Conservation Corps, many items were produced with the C.C.C. initials or emblem. I am interested in all material used by the C.C.C., especially sleeve patches for the various camps (usually these have the company number and C.C.C. on them), tokens or paper scrip used at camp commissaries, flags or pennants with the company or unit number on them, etc.

The prices below are minimums. If you have something unusual or something in mint condition, I will pay more. However, I need to see a photo or the actual item.

Thomas W. Pooler
22152 McCourtney Rd.
Grass Valley, CA 95959-7661

We Pay

Unit/Company Sleeve Patches	35.00+
Company Flags or Guidons	75.00+
Dinnerware w/Symbol, each	25.00
Pins, Paper Script, Insignia, each	10.00+
Company or C.C.C. Souvenir Pennants	20.00
'Sweetheart' Pillowcases	15.00+
'Honor' Medal w/Ribbon	100.00+
Belt Buckles, Rings, Tie Clips, each	25.00

CLOCKS

I buy **antique clocks, especially clocks made before 1890** — single pieces or entire collections. Traveling a distance to view a collection is not a problem. Send photos or call 1-800-277-5275. Below are prices for mint original clocks.

Mark Peer
P.O. Box 15351
Sarasota, FL 34277-1351
1-800-277-5275

We Pay

Welch, Spring & Co.	**up to 800.00**
S.B. Terry	**up to 1,000.00**
Eli Terry	**up to 1,500.00**
English Weight-Driven Wall Clocks	**2,000.00**
American Weight-Driven Wall Clocks	**2,500.00**
German Weight-Driven Wall Clocks	**1,500.00**
English Grandfather Clocks	**3,000.00**
American Grandfather Clocks	**5,000.00**
Brewster	**500.00**
China Clocks	**450.00**
Fancy Repeating Carriage Clocks	**1,000.00**
Florence Kroeber	**600.00**
Ansonia	**500.00**
Seth Thomas	**600.00**
Waterbury	**1,200.00**
French Statue Clocks	**900.00**

Clocks

American Fusee Clocks **900.00**
English Fusee Clocks **2,500.00**

I am interested in purchasing small, novelty, animated clocks for my collection. These clocks are called **pendulettes** as they have a small pendulum which makes the clock run. The clocks were made by such companies as Lux, Keebler, Westclox, and Columbia Time. The first ones were made in the 1930's of pressed wood, metal, and porcelain. After WWII, they were made of plastic. Most clocks have some form of animation. There were many variations of these clocks. I am interested in all the pendulettes but am especially looking for the following that I lack for my collection. I will pay anywhere from $15.00 to $500.00, depending on condition and rarity.

Boy Scout, pressed wood
Bulldog, pressed wood
Calico Horse, plastic
Christmas Wreath, pressed wood
Clown, pressed wood
Country Scene, metal
Dog House, pressed wood
Dutch Boy & Girl, pressed wood
Dutch Mill, porcelain
Fort Dearborn, pressed wood

Rabbit, plastic
Little Boy Blue, pressed wood
ABC, pressed wood
Mary Had a Little Lamb, pressed wood
Scotty Dog, pressed wood
Ship's Wheel, plastic
Schmoo, plastic
Sunflower, plastic
Woody Woodpecker, plastic

Carole Kaifer
P.O. Box 232
Bethania, NC 27010
(919) 924-9672

I collect **cast iron blinking-eye clocks**. I buy incomplete and non-working examples. I also like **double dial calendar clocks, clockwork toys, and banks**. Please see some examples below and let me hear from you.

Dr. 'Z'
1350 Kirts #160
Troy, MI 48084
(313) 642-8129

We Pay

Sambo **1,000.00-2,500.00**
Topsey **1,250.00-2,750.00**

Santa **2,000.00-4,000.00**
Dog, Lion, or Owl **1,500.00-2,500.00**
Weeden Manufacturing Co. Clockwork Bank **500.00-1,250.00**
Clockwork Toy **500.00-1,250.00**
Double-Dial Calendar Clock **750.00-5,000.00**

Wanted to buy are clocks made by **Seth Thomas, New Haven, Ansonia, Ithaca, Waterbury, Howard, Gilbert, Sessions, Ingraham, E.N. Welch, etc.** Prices depend on condition and originality. I can also use **parts such as cases, dials, pendulums, weights, etc.**

David Hong
2625-146th Ave. SE
Bellevue, WA 98007

I am interested in purchasing **animated pictures with clockworks** (or sand operated). I will pay $250.00 and up for animated clocks and $200.00 and up for comic watches in mint condition with their boxes. Other interests are **ships in bottles, ship prints, and Black collectibles**.

Walter David
833 Troy St.
Elmont, NY 11003

CLOTHING

Wanted: **vintage clothing and accessories before 1940 for women, men, and children**. I am collecting anything an individual would have worn, adorned themselves with, or carried from head to foot. All colors are desirable. I prefer good to excellent condition. I can repair or salvage the unusual (lace, trims, buttons, etc.). All sizes are needed. Inquiries enclosing a SASE will be answered. I will phone or travel when possible to see collections. All prices are negotiable.

Betty Yates
P.O. Box 759
Greenville, TN 37744

We Pay

Women's Evening & Daytime Dresses & Suits	**8.00-100.00**
Children's Clothing	**10.00-40.00**
Men's Clothing	**8.00-80.00**
Hats & Hatpins	**1.00-15.00**
Shoes (high-button especially wanted)	**3.00-20.00**
Lace, Trims, Buttons, Etc.	**1.00-10.00**
Handbags, Daytime & Evening	**5.00-25.00**
Jewelry	**3.00+**

I am a very serious buyer of **vintage clothing from about 1800 to the 1950's**. I prefer good quality, nice things with great style. Of course, this is subjective. Exact prices depend upon condition, material, quality of workmanship, size, and style. I'll be happy to look at any older clothing you have. Any inquiries enclosing a SASE will be answered. I do not buy faded, ripped, stained, or fur items. I also buy textiles, interesting accessories, and jewelry (see my listing in this book under jewelry).

Pahaka September
19 Fox Hill
U. Saddle River, NJ 07458
(201) 327-1464

We Pay

Daytime Outfits, 1800's–1919 .... **5.00-75.00**
Daytime Outfits, 1920's (flapper) **5.00-50.00**
Daytime Outfits, 1930's (bias cut, lounging pjs, etc.) **5.00-35.00**
Daytime Outfits, 1940's (rayon print dresses, gabardine suits) **5.00-45.00**
Daytime Outfits, 1950's (circle skirts, large-size cashmere
    sweaters, etc.) **5.00-25.00**
White Cotton Victorian & Edwardian Outfits (stains OK)............. **20.00-125.00**
Wedding Dresses, 1800's–1930's **20.00-125.00**
Older Lace Bridal Veils & Headpieces **10.00-50.00**
Children's Fancy Dresses or Outfits.. **5.00-45.00**
Embroidered Robes, Shawls (oriental, paisley, Spanish, etc.)....... **10.00-150.00**
Fancy Evening Wear, 1800's–1919 .... **15.00-100.00**
Fancy Evening Wear, 1920's (beaded, fancy) **25.00-150.00**
Fancy Evening Wear, 1930's–1950's.. **5.00-75.00**
Men's Suits, 1920's–1930's (button fly, no vents).......................... **10.00-50.00**
Men's Clothing, 1800's–1950's (fancy robes, Hawaiian shirts, ties,
    etc.) **2.00-50.00**
Purses, 1930's or older (beaded, mesh, or unusual compacts) **7.00-55.00**
Purses (Bakelite boxes, crazy looking, alligator, etc.)....................... **5.00-55.00**
Fancy Dresser Accessories & Perfume Bottles (mint condition)........ **2.00-50.00**
Hats, 1800's–1919 (fancy, wide-brim, feathers, fruit, etc.)............. **10.00-75.00**
Hats, 1920's (cloche, helmet-type & wide-brim)................................ **8.00-65.00**
Hats, 1930's–1940's (must be mint & unusual)................................. **4.00-25.00**
Shoes, Lace-Up or High-Button (men's or women's) **10.00-50 00**
Shoes, 1920's–1940's (larger sizes preferred) **5.00-25.00**
Shoes, 1950's (must be mint & unusual)... **2.00-20.00**
Shoes, 1960's stylish 'Frankenstein' platforms **2.00-10.00**
Fashion Magazines & Patterns, 1800's–1940's **1.00-5.00**
Designer Label Clothing & Accessories (Poiret, Worth, Bone Soners, Pacquin,
    Fortuny, Adrian, Schiaparelli, Balenciaga, Chanel, Lilly Dache, Betsy
    Johnson, etc.)... **20.00-1,000.00**
Unused Fabric Material (1940's rayon prints, outer space or cowboy prints,
    cut velvets, brocade curtains, other older material, etc.)..................... **Write**

Clothing

I am interested in purchasing motorcycle attire from the late 1800's to the early 1900's. Below is a partial list of items I would be interested in buying. Please write or call for prices I will pay. If writing, please include a complete description of the item along with a photo (if possible) and a SASE for a reply.

Kidney Belts   Uniforms
Boots   Riding Caps
Breeches   Leggings
Scarf Hats   Gloves
Jackets

Bruce Kiper
Ancient Age Motor Co.
21301 Coakley Lane
Land O'Lakes, FL 34639
(813) 949-9660

COCA-COLA

I will buy any Coca-Cola advertising made before 1970. Because Coca-Cola put their name on almost anything including chewing gum and silverware, it is not possible to list all my wants. Please send an accurate description and a photo if possible. I am a collector who buys trays, calendars, small signs, cartoons, toys, blotters, salesman's samples, and most any item with the Coca-Cola script logo in near-mint to mint condition.

Terry Buchheit
Rte. 7, Box 62
Perryville, MO 63775

Calendars   We Pay

1914, 1916, 1917, or 1922, each 200.00
1923, 1926, 1927, or 1929, each 150.00
1936 or 1937, each 100.00
1939 or 1940, each 90.00
1941 through 1949, each.. 50.00

Trays   We Pay

1910 or 1913, each 150.00
1920 .... 125.00
1921 through 1925, each.. 100.00
1926 .... 110.00
1927 through 1929, each 100.00
1931 .... 175.00
1932 .... 100.00
1933 through 1937, each.. 75.00
1938 through 1948, each.. 50.00

Other Items   We Pay

Child's Toy Stove, ca 1930's.. 200.00
Cut-Out Cardboard Santa Claus Sign .... 25.00+
Light-Up Sign .... 75.00+
Toy Trucks or Cars, each .... 25.00+
Syrup Bottle w/Metal Cap, ca 1900–1920.. 100.00
Cartoons .... 5.00+
Playing Cards w/Box, ca 1909–1963, complete............................ 10.00-100.00
Blotters .... 5.00+
Free Drink Coupons... 5.00+
Match Holder Ash Tray (matches hang down from top of bottle), ca 1940's. 100.00
50th Anniversary Cigarette Box, frosted glass, 1936 .... 90.00
Match Striker, porcelain 75.00

Any Cigarette Lighter w/Coke Logo .... **5.00+**
Box of Straws w/Coca-Cola on Straws, ca 1940-1950 .... **20.00**
Pocket Mirror (send photo for quote), 1906-1922.................................. **100.00+**
Vendor Coin Changer (gives nickels when dime or quarter is inserted) ... **75.00**
Salesman's Sample of Counter Dispenser w/Carrying Case, 1960's **200.00**
One-Gallon Syrup Can, ca 1930-1950 .... **25.00**
Syrup Keg w/Label, wooden .... **50.00+**
Seltzer Bottle w/Coke Logo .... **25.00+**
Display Bottles .... **100.00+**
Miniature Cartons or Cases of Glass Bottles of Coke.............................. **10.00+**
Coca-Cola Flyer, 3-wheel scooter, 1930-1931 .... **500.00**
Clocks, pre-1960 .... **25.00+**
Radio, bottle shape, 1933, 30" **200.00**
Cooler Radio, 1950.. **100.00**
Radio, vending machine shape, 1963-1972 .... **25.00**
Thermometers .... **25.00+**
Menu Boards, wood, metal or chalkboard, each .... **25.00+**

In conjunction with our apothecary and drugstore museum exhibits, we are interested in buying any pre-1970 Coca-Cola items. We especially prefer pre-1940 items pertaining to or advertising Coca-Cola. We are only interested in items in mint or near-mint condition. Signs, trays, gum jars, and dispensers are of special interest to us. We also buy other soft drink advertising items, such as Moxie, Hires, Dr. Pepper, Pepsi, etc. Our prices shown are often starting prices; your item(s) could easily be worth more to us. We prefer pictures and asking prices be sent before shipping any item.

Days Gone By
18 Smith Acres
Northport, AL 35476
(800) 445-7811
(205) 556-1188 or (205) 339-2402

We Pay

Bottles.. **5.00-150.00**
Cardboard Signs... **20.00-250.00**
Chewing Gum Jar **100.00-500.00**
Clocks **50.00-1,200.00**
Cooler Radios **20.00-500.00**
Coolers... **20.00-100.00**
Dispenser, syrup **25.00-1,250.00**
Display Bottle.. **25.00-100.00**

Menu Board... 20.00-100.00
Playing Cards 20.00-75.00
Salesman's Sample Cooler 100.00-1,000.00
Seltzer & Syrup Bottles... 50.00-150.00
Serving Trays 15.00-1,500.00
Signs, metal... 20.00-200.00
Signs, porcelain 20.00-500.00
Signs, light-up.. 50.00-500.00
Thermometers 25.00-125.00
Tip Trays.. 15.00-500.00
Toy Trucks 20.00-200.00
Watch Fobs.. 20.00-120.00

The Coca-Cola Company has spent more money advertising a single product than any other company in the world. This is evidenced by the numerous types of items which bear the Coca-Cola trademark. The earliest advertising dates back to the 1880's, even before Coca-Cola was sold in bottles. The bottling of Coca-Cola began in the 1890's, but fountain sales were far greater until the 1920's.

I buy quality Coca-Cola items and will pay fair prices for items that interest me. I also collect other soft drink brand items (Pepsi, Dr. Pepper, 7-Up, R.C., Nehi, Orange Crush, Moxie, Suncrest, Nu Grape, Grapette, Nesbitts, etc.) as well as other types of advertising (gum, ice cream, automotive, and country store items). Condition is very important to me, so please describe any flaws the item has when you call or write. If possible, a photo is very helpful in determining the identity, age, and value of the item.

Marion Lathan
Rt. 1, Box 430
Chester, SC 29706
(803) 377-8225

We Pay

Calendars, 1890's 1,000.00-6,000.00
Calendars, 1900–1910... 700.00-2,000.00
Calendars, 1911–1919... 500.00-1,500.00
Calendars, 1920–1925... 200.00-600.00
Calendars, 1926–1937... 100.00-400.00
Calendars, 1938–1940... 75.00-200.00
Calendars, 1941–1950... 50.00-100.00
Calendars, 1951–1969... 10.00-50.00
Serving Trays, 1890's.. 500.00-3,500.00

Serving Trays, 1900–1909 .... **700.00-2,500.00**
Serving Trays, 1910–1928 .... **300.00-700.00**
Serving Trays, 1929–1936 .... **200.00-400.00**
Serving Trays, 1937–1942 .... **75.00-200.00**
Serving Trays, 1948–1958 .... **25.00-75.00**
Chewing Gum Jars **150.00-350.00**
Metal Signs, 12" round **25.00-55.00**
Metal Signs, 16" round **50.00-100.00**
Metal Signs, 18" round **50.00-100.00**
Metal Signs, 24" round **50.00-175.00**
Metal Signs, 36" round **50.00-175.00**
Cardboard Signs, 1900–1920 .... **300.00-3,000.00**
Cardboard Signs, 1921–1930 .... **150.00-600.00**
Cardboard Signs, 1931–1940 .... **75.00-300.00**
Cardboard Signs, 1949–1950 .... **50.00-150.00**
Cardboard Signs, 1951–1969 .... **10.00-100.00**
Menu Boards, 1930's **100.00-300.00**
Menu Boards, 1940's **50.00-200.00**
Menu Boards, 1950's **10.00-100.00**
Light-Up Signs, 1950's **100.00-800.00**
Light-Up Signs, 1960's **50.00-200.00**
Thermometers, through 1915 .... **100.00-250.00**
Thermometers, 1920's–1930's **50.00-200.00**
Thermometers, 1940's–1960's **10.00-150.00**
Clocks, 1880's–1900 .... **300.00-3,000.00**
Clocks, 1900–1940 .... **75.00-1,500.00**
Clocks, 1940–1950 .... **50.00-300.00**
Clocks, 1950–1969 .... **20.00-275.00**
Cooler Radios, 1950's **50.00-500.00**
Toy Trucks w/Bottles, 1930's **50.00-500.00**
Salesman Sample Coolers, 1920's **500.00-5,000.00**
Salesman Sample Coolers, 1930's **100.00-1,000.00**
Bottles, stopper tops **50.00-500.00**
Bottles, paper labels **20.00-100.00**
Bottles, straight sides **5.00-20.00**
Display Bottles, usually 20" tall & up **50.00-700.00**
Syrup & Seltzer Bottles **25.00-300.00**
Wood Syrup Kegs **25.00-100.00**
Wood 6-Packs **10.00-25.00**
Display Racks, 1930's **50.00-200.00**
Display Racks, 1940's–1950's **30.00-150.00**
Watch Fobs, w/celluloid facing **100.00-800.00**
Bookmarks, early 1900's **50.00-500.00**
Post Cards, early 1900's **10.00-500.00**
Coupons, early 1900's **5.00-300.00**
Blotters, early 1900's **20.00-300.00**
Playing Cards, early 1900's **20.00-400.00**
Sheet Music, early 1900's **10.00-300.00**

Records, 1950's **10.00-20.00**
Fans, early 1900's **20.00-100.00**
Photos (originals only), 1900–1930's **10.00-30.00**
Letterhead & Invoices, early 1900's **5.00-35.00**
Cigar Bands **10.00-40.00**
Advertising Manuals, 1930–1950's... **10.00-150.00**
Decals, 1930's–1950's... **5.00-100.00**
Magazine Ads, 1900–1906, color **10.00-150.00**
Magazine Ads, 1900–1906, black & white **2.00-15.00**
Many Other Items Not Mentioned... **Call or Write**

COIN-OPERATED MACHINES

If it is operated by a coin and it was **made prior to the 1960's**, then you
ought to send me a photo so I can send you some cash for your machine. If

you have one or a hundred, I'm the one to write. Please send a photo, a description of your machine's working condition and appearance, and a SASE. I'll answer you and send you a list of books on coin-operated machines that you can purchase to learn more about your machine.

For working games, I'll pay as listed below. For machines that pay out automatically, I'll pay three times these amounts. For jukeboxes, I'll pay five times the amounts listed. For gumball and vending machines, I'll pay 50% of these prices.

Ken Durham
909 26 St. NW
Washington, DC 20037

We Pay

1950–1960 Machines	**50.00**
1940–1950 Machines	**100.00**
1930–1940 Machines	**150.00**
1920–1930 Machines	**175.00**
1910–1920 Machines	**200.00**
1900–1910 Machines	**250.00**
1890–1900 Machines	**300.00**

A.M.R. Publishing Company seeks to buy a variety of items such as **jukeboxes, player pianos and piano rolls, nickelodeons and their rolls, phonographs, radios, and any literature related to these items**. Please see also our listings under 'Player Pianos' and 'Phonographs' in this book.

Our catalog, *A.M.R. Publishing Company Jukebox*, lists over 400 different jukebox and service manuals, radio and phonograph instruction manuals, player piano and organ service manuals, etc. It is available from us for $2.00. However, you need not buy our catalog for us to be interested in your item. We will purchase individual items or large collections. Prices vary per item.

A.M.R. Publishing Company
P.O. Box 3007
3816-168th Place NE
Arlington, WA 98223
(206) 659-6434 or FAX (206) 659-5994

We Pay

Jukeboxes from 1900 to 1960	**300.00-6,000.00**
Original Jukebox Brochures	**2.00-50.00**

I am buying old **jukeboxes of the 1950's and gumball machines of the 1950's to the 1920's or older**. I am also looking for **parts and manuals** for machines. Listed below are examples of prices I will pay.

George M. Kesely
8140 Jefferson Ave.
Munster, IN 46321

We Pay

Jukeboxes	**Write**
Jukebox Manuals	**5.00+**
Advance Gumball	**20.00+**
Columbus Gumball	**25.00+**
Regal	**20.00+**
Victor	**20.00+**
Smiling Sams	**50.00+**

Wanted: **coin-operated penny arcade** items. Penny arcades were started in 1890. A large range of machines appreared — fortuneteller, card-drop, shooting, strength, football, etc. Also bought are **slot machines**. A slot machine is any machine with a coin slot that involves gambling or speculation on gambling. These came into being in the 1890's.

Thomas McDonald
2 Ski Dr.
Neshanic Station, NJ 08853-9314
(908) 369-3100

Arcade	**We Pay**
Clam Shell Mutoscope	**1,000.00-2,000.00**
Fortuneteller	**500.00-5,000.00**
Cupid's Post Office	**500.00-1,500.00**
Chester Pollard Games	**1,000.00-2,000.00**
Challenger Duck Shoot	**100.00-200.00**
Novelty Merchantman	**800.00-1,500.00**
Counter Top Games	**100.00-1,000.00**

Slot Machine	**We Pay**
Mills, Caille, Floor Wheels	**4,000.00+**
Jennings, Today Vendor	**400.00-1,000.00**
Jennings, Golf Ball	**500.00-900.00**

Coin-Operated Machines

Mills Baseball Vendor... **1,000.00+**
Pace Machines... **500.00+**
Watling Rol-A-Top... **2,000.00+**
Common Machines, working.. **650.00+**
Parts & Manuals .... **Write**
Rare Machines .... **Write**

I am interested in buying **all types of coin-operated machines** including slot machines, trade stimulators, vending machines, and skill games. My special interest is pinball machines from the early 1930's. Very early games sat on counter tops, and you simply shot marbles into holes and counted your score. These evolved to include legs and intricate mechanical mechanisms to make the games more interesting. Some had batteries to operate devices to give the balls more action or to pay out coins to skillful players. I pay at least $100.00 for games that are complete and in good working condition. Listed below are some of the prices I will pay for only a few of the more desirable games. Let me know what you have. I also buy games that are rough or incomplete and related advertising and paper items.

I buy certain later pinballs, parts, and related items from all later machines. These include back glasses, play boards, advertising material, instruction books, photographs, etc.

Hal O'Rourke
Box 47
Lanexa, VA 23089
(804) 966-2278

We Pay

Bingo.. **150.00**
Baffle Ball **200.00**
Ballyhoo **200.00**
Blue Seal... **250.00**
Five Star Final... **200.00**
Jigsaw (World's Fair).. **600.00**
Register **300.00**
Official Baseball **400.00**
World's Series **500.00**
Games That Pay Out Coins .... **200.00+**
Later Pinball Back Glasses... **25.00-100.00**
Play Boards **10.00-50.00**
Instruction Books **1.00-5.00**

Other Coin Machines   **We Pay**

Mills Slot Machines 500.00-1,500.00
Jennings Slot Machines .... 1,000.00+
Watling Slot Machines .... 1,000.00-4,000.00+
Trade Stimulators 100.00-500.00
Skill Games 100.00-500.00

I am looking to buy **pinball machines manufactured from 1950 to 1970 as well as back glasses and miscellaneous parts**. Whether they are operational or not, call me — I'm interested! I am willing to purchase a single piece or an entire collection. Please find listed below some of the collectibles sought.

Rob Berk
2671 Youngstown Rd. SE
Warren, OH 44484
(216) 369-1192 or (800) 323-3547

                                                                We Pay

1950–1959 Pinball Machines .... 150.00+
1960–1970 Pinball Machines .... 100.00+
1950–1970 Pinball Back Glasses .... 20.00+
1950–1970 Miscellaneous Pinball Parts .... 1.00+

I am interested in buying **coin-operated pinball machines from the 1930's through the 1950's** that are not already in my collection. I can have most machines picked up by a private nationwide hauler; I pay shipping. The cosmetic condition of the game is most important. Sometimes photos are requested to help in determining the condition. I need to know the name of the game along with the manufacturer, its condition, and any detailed information you may have. These all help in determining value. Also wanted are any parts, literature, or photos relating to pinball games.

Richard Conger
Silver Ball Ranch
1947 Coffee Lane
Sebastopol, CA 95472

Niagara by Gottlieb, 1951	**600.00**
Liberty by Gottlieb, circa 1943	**400.00**
Nine Sisters by Williams, 1953	**500.00**
Contact by Exhibit, 1939	**400.00**
Wall Street by Jennings, 1936	**600.00**

I am paying top prices for any early or unusual vending **gumball machine**. I am especially seeking any animated machines by Pulver (tall or short cases), Manneken, AMCO (Scoopy), and Blinky. Also bought are cases, mechanisms, backs, and figures. Wooden or porcelain machines that are L-shaped are wanted. Strong prices are paid for any animated gum, fancy globe or tab gum machines. Please also include a description of any parts you may have.

Elliot J. Baratz
49 Lewis Rd.
Swampscott, MA 01907

We Pay

Pulver Red Case	**475.00+**
Pulver Red Cop & Hobo	**550.00+**
Colored Case Cop & Hobo	**625.00+**
Colored Case	**550.00+**
Tall Cases	**1,000.00+**
Manneken Baker Boy	**1,000.00+**
Scoopys	**900.00+**
Blinkys	**2,500.00+**

I am buying **coin-operated machines from the 1800's to the 1950's**, whether a single piece or a collection. I have collected for many years. I buy in any condition and will also buy parts.

Lynn Slordal
5046 Arrowhead Rd.
Duluth, MN 55811

We Pay

Slot Machines.. **700.00+**
Jukeboxes .... **500.00+**
Coke Machines.. **500.00+**
Popcorn Machines .... **200.00+**
Trade Stimulator... **100.00+**
Viewing Machines .... **800.00+**
Claw Machines.. **800.00+**
Gum Machines w/Metal Feet .... **100.00+**

COINS

I am buying **coins, diamonds, jewelry, sterling, gold, silver, and platinum bullion**. I also will pay the highest prices for **scrap gold, silver, and platinum**. Please contact me before selling. Samples of my buying prices are listed below. A coin's date, mint mark, and condition will affect its value.

Coronado Coins
P.O. Box 181440
942 Orange Ave.
Coronado, CA 92178-1440
(619) 437-1435 (9am–5pm, Monday–Friday)

Coins

Coins
We Pay

Half Cents	up to 4,000.00
Large Cents	up to 10,000.00
Two Cents	up to 1,000.00
Three Cents	up to 5,000.00
Five Cents	up to 5,000.00
Half Dimes	up to 20,000.00
Dimes	up to 8,000.00
Twenty Cents	up to 5,000.00
Quarters	up to 10,000.00
Half Dollars	up to 100,000.00
Dollars	up to 100,000.00
Gold Coins	up to 40,000.00

Diamonds
We Pay

.25 Carat	up to 275.00
.50 Carat	up to 1,200.00
1 Carat	up to 4,000.00
2 Carat	up to 15,000.00
3 Carat	up to 20,000.00

New or Used Gold, Silver, & Platinum
We Pay

Class Rings	up to 200.00
Anything Marked 10K, 14K, 18K, .750, or Plat	Call or Write
Dental Gold, Watch Cases, Service Pins, Chains, Stick Pins, Glasses	Call or Write

Sterling Silver
We Pay

Antique Tableware	up to 10,000.00
Flatware, complete sets	up to 4,000.00
Serving Trays	up to 1,500.00
Tea Sets	up to 5,000.00
Silver Bars, Franklin Mint Items, Private Mint Items, or Anything Marked Sterling or Ster	Call or Write

Jewelry
We Pay

Brooches	up to 10,000.00
Cigarette Cases	up to 3,000.00
Bracelets	up to 15,000.00
Faberge, Cartier, Tiffany, Napier, Van Cleef, & Arpels	Call or Write

We buy **all coins, U.S., foreign, or gold; and paper currency of the Civil War, etc**. We have been in business since 1953; thirty-five of our years in business have been in the same location. We are also very interested in **anything pertaining to Paducah, Kentucky**: books, magazines, post cards, jugs, dishes, etc. Send your items by registered mail for our appraisal. We also buy **stamp collections, old post cards, fountain pens, jewelry, gold, silver, and costume jewelry**.

Hoskins Coins, Stamps, & Jewelry
120 S Third St.
P.O. Box 368
Paducah, KY 42002
(502) 442-4531

U.S. Coins We Pay

U.S. Coins	We Pay
Half Cents	15.00+
Large Cents	5.00+
Half Dimes	3.00+
Indian Cents	40¢+
Seated Dimes	2.50+
Twenty-Cent Pieces	30.00+
Bust Quarters	25.00+
Bust Half Dollars	15.00+
Seated Dollars	60.00+
Trade Dollars	30.00+

I purchase old **elongated coins from World's Fair Expositions or other major events dating from 1893 to 1965**. Prices paid depend upon the quantity produced, scarcity, rarity, condition, denomination, etc. Please write describing condition and include your price.

'Doug' Fairbanks, Sr.
5937 Beadle Dr.
Jamesville, NJ 13078-9534

Numismatic Assets Co., **buys all U.S. coins in any amount or condition** — singles, rolls, sets, accumulations, or entire collections. As coin retailers we can pay you up to full *Red Book* or *Coin World Trends* for many coins. We consistently pay market highs — you have the satisfaction of knowing that you are receiving the highest prices you will encounter for all your coins. Handsome premiums are paid for scarce and Gem coins.

We have twenty-two years of professionalism in numismatics. Perfect business references are available upon request. We are members of the American Numismatic Association. Please ship your coins with confidence by insured or registered mail for immediate, same-day, confidential cash offers. Your coins are fully insured while in our vaults. We will travel to your home, bank, or office to buy your coins if circumstances dictate. Write or call collect for details.

Now it is up to you. Package your coins securely and take them to the post office. Keep in mind that 90% of all coin transactions are made through the mail and that it is quite safe. Your postal clerk will help you with packaging and insured-registered mail procedures to make the transaction convenient and risk-free. 'Superb service and excellent buying prices' is a hard philosophy to live up to, but we have no complaints — and neither do our customers. Write for our free twenty-four page *Guide for Selling Your Coins*. We are paying top-market prices for anything gold or silver!

Numismatic Assets Co., Inc.
P.O. Box 47003
Indianapolis, IN 46227
(317) 887-3224

COLLAPSIBLE DRINKING CUPS

We are buying collapsible drinking cups (also called telescoping cups or folding cups). We are interested in cups made before the 1940's. Listed below are some of categories sought. Let us know what you have. We would also like to correspond with collapsible cup collectors.

M. &. T. Schoeffler
1624 Terrace St.
Arlington, TX 76012

We Pay

Aluminum	**1.00+**
Other Metals	**2.00+**
Cups w/Lids	**3.00+**
Cups w/Handles	**5.00+**
Cups in Leather Cases	**10.00+**

COLLECTOR PLATES

I am currently collecting portrait plates of women. I prefer older plates with pictures from the Victorian era, but I will consider buying others as well. The color of the plates does not matter as long as they are in good condition. I am willing to pay good prices depending on the rarity, age, and condition of plates. A photo of your plate is prefered but not necessary. The average price range I am currently paying is from $10.00 to $40.00. However, exceptions may be made.

Cindy Theilacker
6860 Bluebonnett Dr.
Cocoa, FL 32927
(407) 631-6582 (after 6 pm)

COMIC BOOKS

I have clients with immediate needs for specific comic books. I will pay the amounts shown for the first copy I receive of each of the following books in very fine or better condition.

Andrew Egendorf
P.O. Box 646
Weston, MA 02193
(617) 647-1025

We Pay

Walt Disney Comics & Stories, #138	35.00
Walt Disney Comics & Stories, #153	35.00
Walt Disney Comics & Stories, #163	35.00
Marge's Little Lulu, #44	45.00
Marge's Little Lulu, #67	40.00
Marge's Little Lulu, #76	40.00
Marge's Little Lulu, #97	35.00

Any Condition   **We Pay**

Chilly Willy, 4-color #1122, complete	25.00

Chilly Willy, 4-color #1281, complete **25.00**

I am interested in Famous Funnies comic books from the 1930's. These books were my first experience with mail-order purchases and I have fond memories of awaiting their delivery. I gave up on my subscription somewhere after #30 and subsequently gave my collection away. I would now like to obtain at least one of the copies of the first series. If these early copies are not available, I would then be interested in later issues as long as they had the same format and subjects (Buck Rogers, Hairbreadth Harry, etc.).

Good condition would be appreciated but not necessary. Somehow through the years, I managed to save bubble gum cards from the same era — Wild West, Indian cards, G-Man, etc. So whether you would like to arrange for a trade or be paid for your comic books, please contact me.

Bob Arriola
4130 Opal Cliff Dr.
Santa Cruz, CA 95062
(408) 475-3950

COOKBOOKS

Cookbooks are one of the few historical records that housewives had a part in producing. The evolution from early recipes to the modern directions for preparing a similar dish make for interesting reading and give us an idea of some of the primitive conditions with which early cooks had to deal. I collect all sizes and types of cookbooks: foreign, hardcover, softcover, booklets (particularly those of brand name products as Junket, Brer Rabbit Molasses, etc.). The older the item, the better. Single items or collections are wanted. No ripped or stained booklets are wanted. I also collect all sorts of **needlework, decorative tole-painted items, Quimper pottery, and Belleek china.** Please write with a description of any item from these categories, your price, and phone number.

Lori Hughes
253 Magda Way
Pacheco, CA 94553

COOKIE CUTTERS AND COOKIE-RELATED ITEMS

I am buying all items which will shape cookies and various cookie-related paper items of all types. Some new items are wanted as well as old examples. Listed below are some of the things I am interested in finding.

Phyllis S. Wetherill
5426 27th St. NW
Washington, D.C. 20015

Cookie-Shaping Tools   We Pay

Carved Wooden Molds	up to 1,000.00
Ceramic Molds or Stamps	2.00+
Metal Molds	10.00+
Wafer Irons	20.00+
Old Hand-Made Tin Cookie Cutters	20.00+
Old Manufactured Cookie Cutters	2.00+
Signed Metal Cutters	2.00+
Early Hallmark Cutters	5.00+
Early Plastic Cutters	5.00+
Cutters in Original Boxes	10.00+

Cookie-Related Paper Items   We Pay

Cookie Cookbooks to 1930	10.00+
Cookie Cookbooks after 1930	5.00+

Gingerbread Boy Storybooks to 1950.. **10.00+**
Hansel & Gretel Storybooks to 1950.. **10.00+**
Newer Cookie Storybooks .... **5.00+**
Turn of the Century or Foreign Post Cards w/Cookies............................. **2.00+**
Greeting Cards w/Cookies .... **1.00+**
Miscellaneous Cookie Items (posters, booklets, etc.) .... **2.00+**

I want to buy **hand-made, hand-soldered cookie cutters and metal cookie cutters that were factory-made advertisements**. All inquiries enclosing a SASE are answered. I pay $2.00 to $30.00.

Betty Yates
P.O. Box 759
Greenville, TN 37744

COOKIE JARS

My wife and I are avid collectors of cookie jars. We are most interested in colorful varieties and do not restrict ourselves to any special manufacturer. We would welcome old as well as new jars for our collection. Older marked pottery jars are **Shawnee, McCoy, Brush, and Hull**. Some new pottery marks include **Treasure Craft, Omnibus, and Vandor**. Newer jars are sometimes marked with sticker labels which eventually peel off. However, a jar does not need to have any marking to interest us. We are especially interested in figural comic characters, Red Riding Hoods, and colorful jars. We would prefer the jars be in good condition. Inside rim chips are acceptable and small chips, flakes, or paint loss will be considered. All correspondence will be answered promptly. The following list is of jars currently not in our collection. It is impossible to list all the jars we would like to have, and we have many more on our want list. Please write, describing your jar and its condition.

Clifford Saxby
P.O. Box 130
German Valley, IL 61039
(815) 362-2941

Abington   We Pay

Fat Boy	45.00
Baby	30.00
Rocking Horse	50.00
Pumpkin	30.00
Mother Goose	50.00

American Bisque   We Pay

Blackboard Characters	45.00
Cheerleaders	40.00
Spaceship	35.00
Buck Lamb	35.00
Clown on Stage	35.00
Tortoise	40.00
Davy Crockett	45.00
Jack-in-Box	35.00
Majorette	35.00
Popeye	60.00
Rabbit in Hat	25.00
Sweet Pea	55.00
Donkey w/Milk Wagon	20.00
Granny	20.00
Yarn Doll	20.00
Pelican	30.00

Leprechaun.. 50.00
Kangaroo.. 40.00
Mother Goose 35.00
Davy Crockett Head 160.00

National Silver   We Pay

Mammy.. 70.00
Chef... 70.00

Pearl China   We Pay

Mammy.. 90.00
Chef... 90.00

Robinson Ransbottom   We Pay

Peter Pumpkin Eater 45.00
Cow Jumped Over Moon 40.00
Clay Jars.. 45.00
Old King Cole.. 50.00
Oscar.. 30.00
Snappy... 45.00

Sierra Vista   We Pay

Girl w/Cookies 45.00
Dennis the Menace.. 45.00
Stagecoach... 55.00
Davy Crockett 50.00

Walt Disney Productions   We Pay

Mickey Mouse on Drum 50.00
Donald Duck on Pumpkin 50.00
Mickey Mouse Clock... 45.00
Mickey Mouse on Cake... 55.00
Big Al... 35.00
Mickey-Minnie Turnabout 35.00
Dumbo Turnabout... 35.00
Snow White... 50.00
Disney Bus.. 45.00
Tweedle Dee.. 25.00

Cookie Jars

Ee-Yore 40.00
Boy w/Balloons 55.00
Circus Horse 55.00
Clown Head 50.00
Elephant w/Monkey 70.00
Humpty Dumpty 50.00
Little Angel 55.00
Little Red Riding Hood 55.00
Peter Pan 65.00
Puppy Police 50.00
Stylized Siamese 40.00
Stylized Owl 40.00
Treasure Chest 25.00
Clock 25.00
Raggedy Ann 30.00
Elephant w/Bonnet 55.00
Fish 30.00
Clown 40.00
Sitting Hippo 45.00
Squirrel w/Top Hat 40.00
Panda 35.00
Teddy Bear 35.00

Hanna Barbera   We Pay

Yogi Bear 55.00
Wilma Flintstone 60.00
Dino w/Golf Bag 60.00

Hull   We Pay

Little Red Riding Hood w/Brown Shoes 40.00
Little Red Riding Hood w/Red Shoes 50.00
Little Red Riding Hood w/Poinsettias 50.00

McCoy   We Pay

W.C. Fields 55.00
Friendship 7 Spaceship 50.00
World Globe 50.00
Snoopy in Doghouse 45.00
Tepee 65.00
Indian Head 75.00
Kittens in Basket 95.00
Yosemite Sam 50.00

Elephant	50.00
Betsy Baker	45.00
Christmas Tree	85.00
Dalmatians	85.00
Hamm's Bear	55.00
Jack-O'-Lantern	80.00
Mac Dog	25.00
Mr. & Mrs. Owl	35.00

Unknowns   We Pay

Woody Woodpecker	40.00
Pixie Head	15.00
Howdy Doody	55.00
Century 21 House	40.00
Pinnochio	50.00
R2D2	40.00
CP30	40.00
Tug Boat	35.00
Cookie Cop	30.00
Campbell Kid	45.00
Tattle-Tale Woman	65.00
Olive Oyl	65.00
Barefoot Boy	50.00
Angel Face	35.00

I am buying American-made figural (animals, people, buildings, and other objects) cookie jars manufactured by the following companies: Brush, Regal China, Hull, McCoy, Shawnee, Metlox, American Bisque, and others. Special interests include Black Americana, Disney, cartoon characters, other personalities (real or fictitious), and any jars with gold trim, decals, and/or hand decorating. I am also interested in any other cookie jar that could be considered rare or unusual. I prefer jars in excellent to mint condition (no cracks, chips or repairs) but will consider some examples with minor damage and will pay less accordingly. (See my listing under Shawnee Pottery in this book for additional cookie jar listings.) If you have a cookie jar you wish to sell which you can't identify, please send me a photo with SASE.

Stephanie Horvath
745 14th Ave. S
St. Cloud, MN 56301

We Pay

Abingdon Hippo	75.00

Abingdon Little Miss Muffet **95.00**
Abingdon Mother Goose.. **150.00**
Abingdon Witch.. **150.00**
American Bisque Baby Huey... **200.00**
American Bisque Caspar the Friendly Ghost................................... **300.00**
American Bisque Flintstones (Fred, Wilma, Dino, Rubble House).......... **150.00**
American Bisque Popeye.. **150.00**
American Bisque Olive Oyl... **200.00**
American Bisque Sweet Pea **250.00**
Brayton Black Mammy **200.00**
Brush Circus Horse **150.00**
Brush Purple Cow **200.00**
Brush Covered Wagon **100.00**
Brush Humpty Dumpty **50.00**
Brush Little Red Riding Hood **125.00**
Brush Panda **65.00**
Brush Peter Pan.. **125.00**
Brush Raggedy Ann **75.00**
California Originals Superman or Wonder Woman **65.00**
California Originals Mickey Mouse on Drum................................... **65.00**
Hull Little Red Riding Hood... **65.00**
McCoy Astronauts.. **125.00**
McCoy Coalby Cat... **75.00**
McCoy Christmas Tree... **150.00**
McCoy Circus Horse **65.00**
McCoy Black Mammy w/Cauliflowers **250.00**
McCoy Black Mammy, 'Dem Cookies Sho Am Good' on skirt **200.00**
McCoy Hillbilly Bear **300.00**
McCoy Stagecoach **250.00**
McCoy Two Kittens in a Basket **200.00**
McCoy Jack-O'-Lantern... **150.00**
Pearl China Black Mammy **200.00**
Pearl China Black Chef **150.00**
Pearl China Watermelon Mammy **250.00**
Pearl China Panda... **200.00**
Pottery Guild Elsie the Cow **70.00**
Red Wing King of Tarts... **85.00**
Red Wing Jack Frost Sitting on a Pumpkin...................................... **125.00**
Regal China Peek-a-Boo Bunny **200.00**
Regal China Baby Pig Wearing a Diaper **65.00**
Regal China Goldilocks... **75.00**
Weller Black Mammy **350.00**

I am interested in buying **figural cookie jars.** These are cookie jars made
in the shapes of people, animals, cars, trains, spaceships, cartoon characters,

and almost any other shape you can imagine. I am especially interested in cartoon character and spaceship cookie jars, but I will buy any that are unusual, pretty, cute, or in any other way appealing to me. Many of these jars do not have any names on the bottom to tell who made them, but some do. Some of the companies I look for are Brush, Hull, McCoy, Abingdon, Brayton, and Poppytrail. I will consider buying cookie jars that have small chips if they are ones I like, but I will not buy any that are cracked. I will also pay more for those that are decorated with gold trim or with the original paper stickers still on them. Below are some of the prices I will pay for cookie jars that I want.

Marilyn Hammond
P.O. Box 965
Los Molinos, CA 96055

We Pay

Peek-a-Boo Bunny in Sleepers	100.00+
Count Dracula, Muppets	100.00+
Black Chef or Mammy	80.00+
Elephant Holding Ice Cream Cone in Trunk	50.00+
Pig Dressed in Tux w/Top Hat & Cane	60.00+
Humpty Dumpty	40.00+
Cow w/Cat on Her Back	40.00+
Baby Pig w/Gold Safety Pin in His Diaper	50.00+
Little Red Riding Hood	50.00+
Davy Crockett	50.00+
Jack-O'-Lantern	30.00+
Jack-O'-Lantern, McCoy	100.00+
Any marked Brush, Metlox or Poppytrail on bottom, each	30.00+
Any decorated w/gold	50.00+
Indian, Wigwam, Cowboy, Old Granny, Turkey, Etc.	40.00+

I would like to buy **all McCoy** cookie jars which are in good condition — no chips or nicks. I am willing to pay high book prices on items that are in perfect condition. I will also pay shipping charges or will pick up where possible.

Bobbi Drexler
Rte. 7, P.O. Box 345
Brigadoon Subdivision
Benton, KY 42025
(502) 362-4986

I am interested in **McCoy** cookie jars in good condition with no chips or cracks. I will pay $10.00 and up depending on the individual piece. Also of interest are other old cookie jars. Please send photo (which I will return) or detailed description. All inquiries enclosing SASE will be answered.

D.F. Yates
229 Forkner Dr.
Decatur, GA 30030

CREDIT CARDS

I am putting together a historical credit card collection. I am buying old charge coins from department stores, metal charge plates, and paper or plastic credit cards. I will buy by the box or single items. Offers will be made for all credit pieces, not just on better specimens. Please send your credit pieces or photocopies of them for offers. Listed below are examples of prices paid for credit cards in excellent condition.

John Robbins
P.O. Box 3138
W Sedona, AZ 86340
(602) 634-1164

We Pay

	We Pay
Charge Coins	5.00
Metal Charge Plates	3.00
Paper Credit Cards	5.00-20.00
Plastic Credit Cards, pre-1970	5.00-25.00

I collect credit cards, charge plates, and charge coins. Most are made of metal, paper, or plastic. I am interested in U.S. Visa, Mastercard, American Express, store, airline, gas, restaurant, or any other piece that was issued to be used for credit. These same items are wanted from any other country.

Lin Overholt
P.O. Box 8481
Madeira Beach, FL 33738
(813) 393-5397

We Pay

Credit Cards... **2.00**
Abused Cards .... **less than 2.00**
ATM Cards .... **25¢**
Sample or Test Cards .... **10¢**
Blanks .... **5¢**

COTTAGES

I am seeking cottages from the Dept. 56 Snow Village and the Wade Villages collections.

Patsy Fryberger
(216) 724-8572

Snow Village   **We Pay**

Mansion, dark green roof.. **200.00+**
Stone Church, small version .... **200.00+**
General Store, except white.. **200.00+**
Skating Rink .... **300.00+**
Victorian House, peach... **250.00+**
Mobile Home.. **400.00+**
Single Giant Tree, 11" **200.00**
Adobe House .... **375.00+**
Cathedral Church, original w/dome... **400.00+**
Gabled House, rust & gray .... **200.00+**
Gingerbread House (coin bank)... **200.00+**
Countryside Church, Meadowland .... **225.00+**
Aspen Trees .... **100.00+**
Sheep, set of 12 .... **75.00+**
Others.. **50.00-200.00+**

Wade Village   **We Pay**

Miscellaneous Pieces... **10.00+**

COUNTRY STORE

Country store items, some of which are listed here, are wanted. Please send photos. I will pay top prices for quality items.

Coffee Mills
Coffee Dispensers
Bolt Cabinets
Spool Cabinets
Dye Cabinets
Ribbon Cabinets
Other Display Cabinets

Bean Counters
Racks
Tins
Signs, metal or paper
Advertising
Catalogs

Del Williard
2707 Arcadia Ave.
Erie, PA 16506
(814) 838-3344

CUSTARD GLASS

Custard glass was first developed in England in the early 1880's. The first American custard glass was made in 1898 by Harry Northwood. It was made in patterned tableware pieces as well as in souvenir items and novelties. We buy custard glass in good condition, no reproductions please. The following list reflects the prices we will pay; we will also buy pieces not listed.

Delores Saar
45-5th Ave. NW
Hutchinson, MN 44350
(612) 587-2002

Everglades   **We Pay**

Pitcher 325.00
Jelly... 100.00
Spooner 60.00
Butter... 150.00
Sugar.. 80.00
Creamer 75.00
Master Berry 100.00
Sauce 25.00
Cruet 500.00

CZECHOSLOVAKIAN COLLECTIBLES

At the close of World War I, Czechoslovakia was declared an independent republic and immediately developed a large export industry. The factories produced a wide variety of glassware as well as pottery and porcelains until 1939, when the country was occupied by Germany. The following list reflects prices we will pay for items marked 'Made in Czechoslovakia.' We will consider buying other items not listed.

Delores Saar
45-5th Ave. NW
Hutchinson, MN 55350
(612) 587-2002

We Pay

Art Glass Vases... 15.00
Cut Glass Perfume Bottles 40.00

Czechoslovakian Collectibles

Christmas Ornaments 5.00
Rhinestone Bag... 25.00
Portrait Vase, 5¾" 15.00
Elephant, 4½" 17.50
Teapot w/Girl Finial 645.00
Creamer, Lady, 6¼" 10.00
Creamer, Cow, 6¼" 20.00
Wall Pocket, Bird/Pineapple, 7" 12.50
Salt, 8"... 30.00
Art Deco Figure, 9¾" 30.00
Kerosene Lamp, painted milk glass, 12¾" 45.00

DECANTERS

We are interested in buying the following listed liquor decanters and will buy one piece or a collection. Specify condition and whether or not they are in their original boxes. Please no chipped, damaged, or missing parts.

Tom & Vicky Grams
2767 Lorenzo Ave.
Costa Mesa, CA 92626
(714) 545-1425

We Pay

Grenadier, 1974, Coit, San Francisco, Fireman Statue........................... 250.00+
Grenadier, Others Wanted.. Write
Beam, Duesenberg, any color 75.00
Beam, Fire Chief, 1928.. 50.00
Beam, Fire Truck, Ford, 1930, Model A 60.00
Beam, Fire Truck, Mack, 1917... 50.00
Beam, Police Car, Ford, 1929 .... 45.00
Beam, Police Paddy Wagon, Ford, 1930 .... 65.00
Beam, Convention Corvettes .... Write
Ezra Brooks, Race Cars, 1970 & 1971 (3)..................................... 15.00
Ezra Brooks, Others Wanted .... Write
Baseball, Beam, Brooks, Lionstone, Others Wanted .... Write
Budweiser, Clydesdale, 1978 .... 75.00

DEPRESSION GLASS

I am buying depression glass in all colors and patterns. I will also buy **elegant glassware** of the depression era such as Heisey, Cambridge, Fostoria, Duncan and Miller, Tiffin, Fenton, Imperial, Paden City, etc. I also want **kitchen glassware** such as reamers, canisters, refrigerator dishes, mixing bowls, cruets, butter dishes, cruets, cheese dishes, shakers, spice sets, measuring cups, rolling pins, etc. All items must be in perfect condition — free from nicks, chips, cracks, mold roughness or scratches. I will pay 30% to 60% of the prices in Hazel Weatherman's or Gene Florence's price guides.

William D. Ogden
3050 Colorado Ave.
Grand Junction, CO 81504
(303) 434-7452

I am buying **cobalt depression glassware in Moderntone, Ships, Aurora by Hazel Atlas, and Hazel Atlas Crisscross**. Also wanted are other cobalt items such as canisters, curtain tiebacks, drawer pulls, towel rods, coasters, water bottles, knives, forks, spoons, etc.

Mr. & Mrs. Carl W. Raymond
P.O. Box 2203
Newnan, GA 30284

We Pay

Moderntone Cobalt Dinner Plate... **10.00**
Moderntone Cobalt Salt & Pepper Set... **27.50**
Aurora Cobalt Bowl **7.00**
Hazel Atlas Cobalt Canister Set (5)... **225.00**
Cobalt Curtain Tieback **15.00**
Cobalt Drawer Pull.. **8.00**
Cobalt Spoon or Fork **15.00**
Cobalt Coaster **4.00**
Cobalt Crisscross Refrigerator, 8" x 8" **60.00**
Cobalt Ships Tumbler.. **7.00**

I want only undamaged items in **English Hobnail** and **Lincoln Inn** patterns of depression glass. Salt and pepper shakers in genuine ruby red glass (patterned or plain, but not flashed) are wanted. I pay postage and insurance charges.

Homer Neel
4213 Westridge Dr.
N Little Rock, AR 72116

English Hobnail   **We Pay**

Plate, square, 8" **8.00**
Dinner Plate, green, pink or turquoise, 10"... **17.50**

Lincoln Inn   **We Pay**

Bonbon, handled or square, red **10.00**
Cereal Bowl, red, 6"... **9.00**
Fruit Bowl, red, 5".. **8.00**
Olive Bowl w/Handles, red **10.00**
Finger Bowl, red... **12.00**
Bowl, footed, red, 9¼" or 10½" **23.50**
Cup, red... **7.50**
Plate, red, 9¼" or 12".. **11.00**
Saucer, red... **3.00**

Salt & Pepper Shakers   **We Pay**

Genuine Ruby Red Glass (pattern or plain), single...................................... **30.00**
Genuine Ruby Red Glass (pattern or plain), pair .... **up to 65.00**

Depression era glassware has been a fascination for me since I was twelve years old, and I began my first collection. I am interested in purchasing mint pieces to further collections for myself and my mother as well as items for resale. All patterns will be considered if reasonably priced. The following list of patterns will be considered at 50% of current book values.

American Sweetheart (pink & monax)   Mayfair or Open Rose (pink in blue)
Cameo (green)   Patrician (all colors)
Dogwood (pink)   Princess (all colors)
Hocking Sandwich (clear)   Royal Lace (all colors)
Iris (iridescent & clear)   Sharon (pink & amber)
Lace Edge (pink)

Pamela Wiggins
10701 Sabo #202
Houston, TX 77089
(713) 944-7520

We buy and sell all patterns and colors of depression glass. We are also interested in depression-era glass **kitchenware and elegant glassware.** If you have any items you wish to sell, send us a list along with a SASE. We will then make you an offer. Or send us your list along with the amount you would like to receive for the items. All items must be in mint condition — i.e., no chips, cracks, scratches, etc.

Auntie Em's Attic
486 103rd St.
Niagara Falls, NY 14304-3628
(716) 283-3626

I want to buy Fire-King jadite dinnerware in patterns **Alice and Jane Ray.** I also am looking for McKee jadite dinnerware in the **Laurel** pattern.

Susan Hirshman
540 Main St.
Woodland, CA 95695

Jane Ray

        We Pay

Plate, dinner	**3.00**
Plate, salad	**3.00**
Bowl, soup	**5.00**
Bowl, cereal	**3.00**
Bowl, fruit	**2.00**
Cup & Saucer	**2.50**
Platter	**7.00**

Alice

        We Pay

Plate, dinner	**8.00**

Laurel

        We Pay

Plate, dinner	**8.00**
Plate, salad	**6.00**
Bowl, cereal	**6.00**
Bowl, fruit	**4.00**
Cup & Saucer	**5.00**
Platter	**20.00**

We will pay the prices listed below for **Manhattan** in crystal or colors. Please give sizes and a general description of each piece. We only want items without cracks, chips, or sickness. Minor scratches are alright. We will buy any number of pieces. We also buy other depression-era glassware such as **Katy Blue**, **Jubilee**, **Cherry Blossom**, **Iris**, **Orchid** by Heisey, and **Rosepoint** by Cambridge. We buy most patterns of depression glass. Prices vary according to the desirability of patterns and whether or not we need pieces for our own collections. The following is only a partial list of Manhattan pieces.

Dennis & Sandi Boone
No Horse Antiques
Rte. 1, P.O. Box 86
Reynolds, IL 61279

Manhattan   **We Pay**

Ash Tray w/Advertising, round 10.00
Bowl, 9½" fruit, open handles, ftd.. 12.50
Bowl, 5⅜" cream soup, handled 8.00
Candy Dish w/Cover 18.99
Comport.. 10.50
Cup 7.50
Plate, 8½" salad 5.50
Tumbler, 10-oz, ftd 7.50
Vase 7.50

I buy depression glass in all patterns and all colors except clear and amber. I am especially seeking **pink Cherry Blossom, cobalt Moderntone, and pink Princess** . All glass must be mint condition and original — no reproductions please! I will pay 50% of book price plus shipping.

Charmaine Galindo
2805 SW 116th St.
Seattle, WA 98146

I am buying any pink depression glass, especially these patterns: **Florentine #1**, **Sharon**, and **Royal Lace** (also wanted in cobalt blue). Etched pink glassware in all patterns and pink kitchenware are sought as well.

Diane Genicola
25 E Adams Ave.
Pleasantville, NJ 08232
(609) 646-6140

DEPRESSION GLASS KNIVES

I am buying glass knives of the depression years (1920 through 1940). These knives are made entirely of glass and were available in several colors: crystal, light blue, light and forest green, pink, amber, and opal (milk glass). I am also the editor of *The Cutting Edge*, quarterly newsletter of the Glass Knife Collectors Club.

Adrienne S. Escoe
Glass Knife Collectors Club
P.O. Box 342
Los Alamitos, CA 90720
(213) 430-6479 (evenings)

We Pay

Crystal Candlewick	**200.00+**
Crystal Plain Handle	**100.00+**
Crystal Westmoreland Sanitary, ribbed	**100.00+**
Opal (milk glass) Stonex	**100.00+**
Amber Aer-Flo (Grid)	**125.00+**
Forest Green Aer-Flo (Grid)	**125.00+**
Westmoreland Midget Thumbguard	**100.00+**
Pink Short Plain Handle	**100.00+**
Other Glass Knives	**4.00-70.00**

Glass fruit and cake knives are wanted, especially colored ones — opal (milk glass), amber, emerald green, and those with ribbed handles or clear blades and colored handles. All responses will be answered. Please price and describe.

Michele Rosewitz
P.O. Box 3843
San Bernardino, CA 92413

DIONNE QUINTUPLETS

I am looking for anything pertaining to the Dionne Quints, Dr. Dafoe, Nurse Yvonne Leroux, or any of their other nurses, family, mid-wives, Madame Legros and Lebel, Quintland items, etc. Some are marked Corbeil or Callander, Ontario, Canada. I am especially looking for items made of paper, china, metal, cloth, and plaster, including little china and celluloid dolls. Listed below are examples of items wanted with prices paid.

Mrs. Donald Hulit
226 Cape Rd.
Standish, ME 04084
(207) 642-3091

We Pay

Tea Sets w/Picture of a Quint, metal .... 8.00+
Plate or Bowl, china... 50.00+
Mug, china... 25.00+
Real Photo .... 15.00+
Pillowcases, satin or cotton.. 35.00+
Handkerchief, cotton, crepe or embroidered.. 20.00+
Coloring Book .... 25.00+
Play Mother Goose Booklet w/Quints.. 12.00+
Jewelry (necklace, bracelet, pins, etc.).. 30.00+
Sheet Music, except Quintuplet Lullaby .... 20.00+
Souvenirs of Quintland .... 15.00+
Colored Blotter... 15.00+
Christmas Cards w/Quints or Dr. Dafoe... 15.00+
Sunny Days Fan .... 15.00+
Miscellaneous Paper Items, except for magazine ads .... 5.00+

DISNEY COLLECTIBLES

I am looking for just about anything from the 1930's and early 1940's. The following prices are usually the minimum I will pay for items in excellent condition. All items are from the 1930's unless noted otherwise.

Bob Havey
P.O. Box 183
W Sullivan, ME 04689
(207) 422-3083

We Pay

Mickey Mouse Radio 600.00
Snow White Radio 500.00
Mickey Lamp (sitting in chair).. 600.00+
Donald Lamp (standing by post) .... 600.00+

Disney Collectibles

Pop-Up Books .... **125.00+**
Movie Poster .... **500.00+**
First Mickey Mouse Book, 1930 .... **300.00+**
Mickey Mouse Waddle Book with Waddles .... **1,000.00+**
Merchandise Catalogs .... **200.00+**
Christmas Promotion Books .... **200.00+**
Minnie's Yoo Hoo (store music) .... **400.00+**
Fantasia Figurines by Vernon Kilns, 1940's **100.00-700.00**
Laguna Pottery Pieces, 1940's .... **100.00+**
Bavarian China Pieces or Sets .... **75.00+**
Wind-Up or Celluloid Toys **200.00-Thousands**
Reverse Paintings .... **100.00+**
Uncut Paper Dolls & Cut-Out Books .... **100.00+**
Many, many, more items wanted .... **Call or Write**

I am buying Disney children's china dishes, planters, cookie jars, salt and pepper shakers, etc. Especially wanted are items listed below.

Calvin L. Hackeman
8865 Olde Mill Run
Manassas, VA 22110
(703) 368-6982

We Pay

Cookie Jars, early non-turnabout featuring Disney characters..... **45.00-100.00+**
Dumbo Planter .... **25.00+**
Frog Character Planter .... **35.00+**
Unusual Salt & Pepper Shakers.. **10.00-25.00+**
Children's China, Mickey/Minnie, Three Little Pigs, or Snow White & Dwarfs;
sets or individual pieces .... **Call or Write**

DOCUMENTS

America West Archives is buying all types of old paper, especially paper from the western half of the United States dating from the 1840's through the 1920's. This includes old documents, letters, checks, stocks and bonds, maps, photographs, and many other types of old paper. We prefer documents to be in good condition and not damaged. We will buy a piece or a complete grouping, depending upon their age, condition, area they are from, and the subject matter they contain. We are full-time dealers and are buying for resale. Because of the wide range of prices these types of documents can sell for based upon the above factors, we have not given specific examples of what we can pay — some documents are worth no more than a dollar while others may be worth $100.00 or more. Contact us giving a description of your item.

American West Archives
P.O. Box 100
Cedar City, UT 84721
(801) 586-9497

DOG COLLECTIBLES

Any dog and fox items are wanted — especially Russian wolfhound and Borzoi dogs. Other breeds we are interested in include English Bulldogs,

Afghans, Pugs, Great Danes, Samoyeds, Bull Terriers, Collies, German shepherds, Pomeranians, and Pekingese. Figurines in any material (porcelain, china, small bronzes, cast iron, metal, composition, etc.), plates, mugs, tins, books, prints, cigarette cards, post cards, and thimbles are just some of the items wanted. I will buy, sell, and trade to find wanted breeds.

Cynthia Greenfield
12309 Featherwood Dr. #34
Silver Spring, MD 20904
(301) 622-5473

We Pay

Figurines	**50.00+**
Paper Items	**3.00+**
Books	**5.00+**
Plates	**15.00+**

Wanted to buy: porcelain pure-bred dog figurines manufactured by Boehm, Mortens Studio, Royal Doulton, or others. The price offered ranges from $10.00 to $600.00 depending on the individual piece and its condition.

Jeffrey Jacobson
6424 Jefferson Ave.
Hammond, IN 46324

DOLLS

Barbie has become dolldom's most popular representative. Introduced in 1959, she did not excite dealers but charmed her little girl owners and soon gathered an adult collector following. An 11½" dimensional 'paper doll,' Barbie's sucess was assured by the many and varied clothing outfits that were sold with her.

Barbie catapulted the Mattel Toy Company into the world's number-one position as producer of women's wear. Her tiny garments reflected the western world's fashion evolution through hem lengths, accessories, sewing methods, and textile development. Mattel offered little girl Barbie owners greater play opportunities and attracted new adult fans each year as Barbie and her expanding family reflected new cultural and racial attitudes through changes in hairstyle, make-up, friends, and relatives.

Prices fluctuate widely on collectible Barbie and her possessions. They are based on age, desirability, and condition. Deduct 50% from the listed price if the item has been removed from its box or package; deduct another 25% if the item shows use or wear. We are also interested in **G.I. Joe and other personality celebrity dolls, paper dolls, and Breyer horses**.

Gretchen & Wildrose
Playdolls
5816 Steeplewood Dr.
N Richland Hills, TX 76180
(817) 581-4477

We Pay

#1 Barbie	**3,000.00**
#2 Barbie	**3,000.00**
#3 Barbie	**500.00**
#4 Barbie	**350.00**

Barbie w/Bendable Limbs... **500.00**
Bubble Cut Barbie **90.00**
#1 Ken... **125.00**
#2 Ken... **75.00**
#1 Alan **65.00**
First Ken w/Bendable Limbs **250.00**
#1 Midge... **75.00**
Midge w/Bendable Limbs.. **200.00**
Other Barbie & Family Dolls **10.00-500.00**
3 Rare 900-Series Outfits **500.00**
Other 900-Series Outfits... **10.00-200.00**
1600 Series Outfits.. **10.00-250.00**
Pan American, Other Rare 1600's, Pucci, & Other Special **500.00-1,000.00**
Structures & Accessories **5.00-350.00**

I am buying **Barbie and her friends**. I will buy one piece or a whole collection. I also buy **Mattel-tagged outfits and any related items** such as houses, cars, books, games, etc. I will buy mint-in-box or used items.

Denise Davidson
834 W Grand River
Williamston, MI 48895
(517) 337-2501

We Pay

1959–1961 Ponytail Barbies **75.00-1,500.00**
1962–1965 Barbies.. **40.00-200.00**
1966 Barbies & Friends.. **25.00-75.00**
Complete Outfits... **15.00-150.00**
Accessories, Shoes, Jewelry **5.00-30.00**
Houses, Cars, Etc... **20.00+**

I am interested in **hard plastic and composition** dolls with the same type of bodies or cloth bodies. Some **rubber, early vinyl, and small bisque** dolls are wanted as well. **Damaged dolls with usable parts** are OK too. A special want is a 24" Effanbee Sweetie Pie doll with a mohair wig in any condition. Please send a detailed description of your doll's condition, size, any identification marks, and your price. Listed below is a sample of items and prices.

J. Mc Donald
20763 Hartland St. #2
Canoga Park, CA 91306

We Pay

Japan Bisque, small, jointed .... 5.00+
German Bisque, small, jointed .... 15.00+
Vogue Ginnys & Nancy Ann Muffies .... 15.00+
Terri Lee 60.00
Shirley Temple, 1957, 12" .... 35.00+
Shirley Temple, 1972, 15" .... 25.00+
Marked Composition .... 20.00+
Marked Hard Plastic .... 20.00+
Sun Rubber 5.00
Tagged Doll Clothes 3.00
Doll Parts... Write

Who knows what mysteries lie in your attic? I am looking for 12" **G.I. Joe, Captain Action, and Johnny West dolls and their equipment**, as well as other military, science fiction, and western theme action figures. Most of these figures were made in the 1960's and 1970's and may still be lurking in your attic or basement. These dolls featured detailed uniforms, equipment, and vehicles that were often accurate scale reproductions of real gear. **Major Matt Mason, Star Wars, Mego dolls, and monster toys** are wanted as well as **comic character toys** that are too numerous to mention here. Many other items were scaled for these action figures. I am also interested in any loose clothing, equipment, and vehicles.

Prices vary widely on most toys. Of course, condition, age and scarcity will all affect price. I have paid $10.00 to $40.00 per figure, averaging $20.00 each for dolls in good condition and more for rare pieces. I have had good results by making offers. Please write with a description of what you have; or, better yet, send photos. Include a phone number and the best time to call, and I will call with an offer promptly. All letters will be answered.

Paul Ivy
2300 McCullough St.
Austin, TX 78703

I buy **antique or collectible dolls from 1900 through 1960**. The condition of the doll is very important as this determines price. Photos are a big help in selling the doll faster. I do not buy vinyl dolls, new dolls, rag dolls, or badly crazed or crackled composition dolls. As I do not repair dolls, I need dolls only in good condition. Character dolls most wanted are those with expression to their faces. Approval boxes are welcomed and postage will be paid.

Cindy Lewis
2150 Lomita Blvd.
Lomita, CA 90717
(213) 539-4575

We Pay

Ginnys, hard plastic	20.00-30.00
Alexander, hard plastic	25.00-75.00
Tonis	20.00-40.00
Composition Dolls	20.00-60.00
Nanettes	30.00-45.00
Bisques	50.00-150.00
Clothes	1.00-10.00
Doll Furniture	1.00-20.00

I am interested in **dolls of the 1950's to present day**. Specific dolls I seek are Chatty Cathy, Giggles, Julie (36" and taller), Saucy, and Marilyn Monroe dolls. I am also looking for **books on doll collecting by Pat Smith**. Specific books by Pat Smith are listed below. I will pay fair prices.

Modern Collector's Dolls, Vol. 2.
Modern Collector's Dolls, Vol. 3
Antique to Modern, Vol. 1
Antique to Modern, Vol. 2
Antique to Modern, Vol. 3

Louise Ramsay
Rte. 2, Box 99A
Pekin, IN 47165

My interests in doll collecting are varied — from Barbie to Shirley Temple to Jan Hagara to Dionne Quints. I'm interested in dolls, their clothing, and their accessories. Still wanted is a doll-sized camelback trunk, a wicker doll buggy, and other interesting doll items. I would like to find Patricia R.

Smith's book *Modern Collector Dolls*, Second Series. Price depends on condition of the item.

Sandi Waddell
2791 C.R. 302
Durango, CO 81301
(303) 247-1568

I am both a dealer and collector. I own Child's Play Doll & Toy Museum & Shoppe located in Wisconsin Dells, Wisconsin. I am always looking for rare and unusual items for the museum plus dolls and toys for resale. I prefer items from the mid-1800's through the 1950's. I pay very fair prices, depending on age and condition. I am especially looking for a **Freundlich Corp. Navy Wave doll** of composition made in 1942. Also wanted is the **Freundlich soldier doll.** These have molded caps. I want these to complete a museum display and will pay $100.00 to $175.00 each. I buy other military dolls. Also wanted is an **aluminum head doll marked Giebeler-Falk Doll Corp. with a 6-point star and a G.** I will always buy **hand-painted dolls from the 1940's and 1950's priced for resale.** I really like **composition and character dolls circa 1920 through 1950.** I usually pay too much for these.

Child's Play Doll & Toy Museum & Shoppe
P.O. Box 506
Wisconsin Dells, WI 53965
(608) 254-4200

DOOR PUSH PLATES

I collect porcelain door push plates that were used on entrance doors to grocery stores, drugstores, and in any store in general that sold manufacturers' products. They were mostly attached to screen doors where you normally reached out to push the door in or out. The push plate was colorful and advertised the company's product; it often carried the wording 'push' or 'pull' as well. The plate was usually mounted on the inside, with the instructions to push rather than to pull. Size of the plates varied, but the average was 4" x 7". These were made of enameled steel (more commonly called porcelain). Some examples that exist are: Red Rose Tea, Tetley Tea, Salada Tea, Chesterfield Cigarettes, Dr. Caldwell's Pepsin Syrup, and Vick's.

I buy according to condition. Please send photocopy or photo with a description for a price quote. I will pay $50.00 to $100.00 for nice additions to my collection. I pay postage.

Betty Foley
227 Union Ave.
Pittsburgh, PA 15202
(412) 761-0685

DR. PEPPER COLLECTIBLES

Dr. Pepper was introduced in 1885 at Waco, Texas, by the Artesian Mfg. & Bottling Co. They produced many advertising products that were given to their customers. They distributed nearly as many different items as Coca-Cola, Pepsi-Cola, Moxie, etc. If you have an unusual item, please send a description (a photo, if it is difficult to describe). Be sure to mention condition, and I will try to give you a fair offer for it. Pre-1950 items are preferred, but I would consider any good piece. Please include SASE.

Robert Thiele
620 Tinker
Pawhuska, OK 74056

EGG SEPARATORS

I collect tin egg separators with advertising around the edge. I will pay from $5.00 to $7.50 each, depending upon rarity and condition.

Jim Goldsmith
8102 SE Thirteenth
Portland, OR 97202
(503) 233-7334

EGG TIMERS

Figural egg timers were produced primarily during the 1930's and 1940's and were made mainly in Japan or Germany; some are marked accordingly. Figures can range from maidens to animals to clowns to bellboys — the variety is almost limitless. Many figurals no longer have the timer piece (sand tube), but they are still easily recognizable by either a hole going through a portion of the back of the figure or a hole going through a stub of a hand or arm (this is where the egg-timer tube would have been connected, enabling it to turn). The sand tube was made of thin glass and easily broken. Figurals are mostly in the 3" to 5" range in height. All are made of ceramic (china or bisque) and can be one solid allover color or painted in detail. Minor crazing in the figure is acceptable, but timers may have no major chips or breaks. The sand tube can be present or missing — either is acceptable.

Jeannie Greenfield
R.D. #2, Box 2105
Caldwell Rd.
Stoneboro, PA 16153

We Pay

German w/Timer... **20.00+**
German w/out Timer .... **10.00+**
Japan, Made in Japan, or Occupied Japan w/Timer .... **10.00+**
Japan, Made in Japan, or Occupied Japan w/out Timer........................... **5.00+**
Black w/Timer .... **45.00+**
Black w/out Timer .... **35.00+**
No Markings w/Timer... **5.00+**
No Markings w/out Timer .... **3.00+**

I am a collector buying porcelain or china figurines which have hourglass egg timers attached. The figurines must be undamaged. Those without timers, but which have the hole through which the timer can be attached, are okay as I have extra egg timers. All replies will be answered. I have paid from $3.00 to $45.00. Thank you!

Margaret S. Welty
P.O. Box 14
Milton Center, OH 43541

EGGBEATERS, MIXERS, AND CHURNS

I am a serious collector/dealer of old and unusual cast iron eggbeaters, glass-bottomed mixers, mayonnaise mixers, churns, stoneware beater jars, and the like. I prefer items be pre-1925, in excellent condition and working order, with no broken or missing parts. I do buy mixer bottoms or tops, though, so don't throw them away. I am also interested in catalogs (general hardware and housewares) prior to 1930, pamphlets and product literature relating to mixers, etc.

As a dealer I need to buy reasonably so I can resell. As a collector I will pay a premium for something I need for my collection or for mixers with original labels (no missing parts, like the funnels that are so often missing from mayo mixers), original containers, and literature.

Always of interest are the following for resale: old cast iron kitchen collectibles, pot scrubbers, advertising pot scrapers, glass and metal shaker sets and canisters, old scales, advertising match safes, old tin (wood or paper) food containers, Monarch or Ben Hur containers, or what have you?

Describe fully as to all markings, dimensions, condition, and price desired. I have listed below the minimum price I will pay for items I want or need in excellent condition and working order. A returnable photo is very helpful. I will respond to all offerings and reimburse postage.

R.J.C. — Mixer Mania
5535 Forbes Ave.
San Diego, CA 92120

We Pay

Cast Iron Eggbeaters	**15.00+**
Advertising Beater Jars & Beaters	**20.00+**

Aurelius Bros. Side by Side Triple Beater .... **60.00+**
Glass Measuring Cup w/Skirted Beater .... **18.00+**
E-Z Mixer, dated 1903 .... **200.00+**
Ladd #1 or #2 Glass-Bottomed Mixers .... **80.00+**
Keystone #20 by North Bros. .... **100.00+**
S&S Hutchinson or S&S #2 .... **90.00+**
Universal Mayo Mixer/Cream Whipper (various sizes) .... **125.00+**
Silvers & Co. Mixer (various styles) .... **65.00+**
Borden's Archimedean or Similar .... **15.00+**
Catalogs, Pamphlets, Etc. .... **1.00+**

FAIRBANK

I collect most any item marked 'Fairbank.' A photograph or photocopy would be helpful in describing an item. I pay 15% finders fee if the information leads to a purchase. Please, no magazine ads for Fairy Soap or Gold Dust. Also no expensive tin signs are wanted. Reproductions will not be considered; originality must be guaranteed. Listed are items I am interested in buying — it is in no way complete. Items must be in good or better condition.

Soap: Fairy, Santa Claus, Sunny Monday, Pumo, Clarette, Mascot, White Star, Golden West, Gold Dust, Dandy, & Silver Dust. (Especially wanted are mint bars.)

Cottolene Cooking Oil: Tins & dated items, especially Gold Label.

Fairbank Scales: Small counter-top size, any related item, or any dated advertisements.

Fairbank Lard Co.: Any dated item.

Fairbank Meat Co.: Any dated item.

Fairy Calendars: Must be in excellent-to-mint condition.

There were a lot of items offered either as gifts, premiums, or by mail order. A few that I know of are: Gold Dust jewelry, watch fobs, children's fairy tale books or kitchen toys, gift plates, and a Fairy Soap doll made in 1912. I will pay book price, if there is one, or a 'value to me' negotiated price. Contact Jim or Ellen at the address or phone number given below.

Fairbank House of Antiques & Upholstery
113 E 5th
Kennewick, WA 99336
(509) 586-6839

FANS

I am buying electric desk fans with brass blades and/or brass guards that were made from about 1890 to 1930. Some brand names are Emerson, Diehl, General Electric, Jandus, Menominee, Western Electric, Westinghouse, etc. I am interested in obtaining unusual examples or fans with decorated bases. We pay from $25.00 to $250.00 depending on condition and rarity.

Dempse B. McMullen
P.O. Box 402
Natchez, MS 39120
(601) 446-9037

We are a wholesale and retail antiques store that specializes in antique mechanical fans of almost any type — electric, battery-operated, fuel-driven, water-powered, etc. We also collect mechanical fan paraphernalia such as old electrical company catalogs by General Electric, Westinghouse, Emerson, Robbins & Myers, etc., and any type of fan advertising such as signs, window displays, ceramics, etc. from fan manufacturing companies. We buy, sell, repair, and make parts for obsolete fans, especially ceiling fans; and we handle a wide assortment of switches, blades, etc. We buy unusual fans of all kinds. Send your price and a photo with first letter.

The Fan Man, Inc.
4614 Travis
Dallas, TX 75205
(214) 559-4440

FAST FOOD COLLECTIBLES

We are called 'POE-pourri' and we collect fast food premiums (toys), store displays, older uniforms, glasses, books, and anything else to do with fast food. We primarily trade with other collectors; however, we do buy items that we need in our collection and to trade. Fast food stores include: McDonald's, Burger King, Wendy's, White Castle, Hardee's, Arctic Circle, Bo Jangles, Captain D's, Carls Jr., Dairy Queen, Domino's, Frisch's Big Boy, El Pollo Loco,

Fast Food Collectibles

Jack-In-The-Box, Little Caesar's, Long John Silver's, Pizza Hut, Pizza Time, Showbiz Pizza, Taco Bell, Arby's, Denny's, and Whataburger. The following are prices we normally pay.

POE-pourri
220 Dominica Circle E
Niceville, FL 32578-4068
(904) 897-4163

We Pay

Fast Food Premiums & Toys, mint in package or mint & no package	**50¢+**
McDonald's Uniforms, Hats, Belts, etc.	**1.00+**
McDonald's Enameled Pins..	**50¢+**
Fast Food Pin-Back Badges & Buttons	**25¢+**
Hummel (Goebel) Co-Boy Display Plaque (in German)	**25.00+**

Books

We Pay

Big Mac: The Authorized Story of MacDonald's, by Max Boas & Steve Chain, NY-Mentor, 1976 .... **5.00+**
McDonald's: Behind the Arches, by John F. Love, Bantam, 1986 .... **8.00+**
Grinding It Out: The Making of McDonald's, by Ray Kroc & Robert Anderson, Henry Regnery Co., 1977 .... **7.00+**

Orange Roofs, Golden Arches: The Architecture of an American Chain Restaurant by Phillip Langdon, NY, Alfred A. Knopf, 1986 .... **10.00+**
White Towers, by Paul Hirshorn & Steve Izenour, MIT Press, 1979.......... **1.00+**
Ronald Revisited, The World of Ronald McDonald, Bowling Green U Popular Press, Bowling Green, OH 43405 .... **5.00+**

I am a private collector of **Big Boy** memorabilia. I am looking for all unusual and unique items produced prior to 1980. Listed below are some of the items I am seeking.

Glenn J. Grush
8400 Sunset Blvd.
Los Angeles, CA 90069
(213) 656-4758

We Pay

Ceramic Banks	**35.00+**
Bobbin' Head Nodder	**75.00+**
Big Boy Lamp	**125.00+**
Advertising Items	**10.00+**
Statue, ceramic, 14"	**175.00+**
Salt & Pepper Set, ceramic	**75.00+**
Ash Tray	**10.00+**
Original Artworks	**35.00+**
Tableware w/Big Boy Logo	**10.00+**

FIESTA

Fiesta dinnerware was first introduced in 1936 by Homer Laughlin and gained immediate popularity. After extensive research and planning, a simple yet colorful line was presented. Though some of the original five colors were dropped and others added over the years, Fiesta remains a distinctive line of dinnerware and accessories collected by many.

I am interested in all Fiesta in good (no chips or cracks) to mint condition and will pay approximately 50% of retail book prices and more for some accessories. Below is a partial list of items and prices. Prices range according to color of item. Higher prices are paid for rare colors or pieces.

Country Livin'
P.O. Box 953
425 S Main
Canyonville, OR 97417
(503) 839-4717

We Pay

Bowl, cream soup 10.00-35.00
Bowl, fruit, 4¾" 7.00-22.50
Plate, 6".. 1.50-3.00
Plate, 9".. 2.00-7.00
Saucer... 1.00-2.25
Teacup... 6.00-10.00
Carafe... 50.00-75.00
Coffeepot 50.00-75.00
Creamer 4.00-12.00

I am buying all pieces of Fiesta dinnerware made by the Homer Laughlin China Company of Wheeling, West Virginia: cups and saucers, plates, bowls, tumblers, water pitchers, etc. All colors are wanted.

Diane Genicola
25 E Adams Ave.
Pleasantville, NJ 08232
(609) 646-6140

FIGURINES

Collector is in the market to buy all types of dancing, dressed, or nude **figural ladies**. Figurines may be found in porcelain, glass, ceramic, brass, or precious metals. Listed below are different designs in which a figure may be found.

German ceramic frog centerpiece
English candle holders
Woman modeled w/wolfhounds (A. Santini)
Nude supports bowl centerpiece
Ceramic figure modeled after Dorothy Lamour
Bookends
Vanity mirrors
Clocks
Vases
Cocktail stem glasses
Weller or Rookwood figural planters

Lenora's Fine Antiques
5802 Morningside Dr.
Richmond, VA 23226
(804) 282-3904

I am interested in fine quality, mint condition **animal, children, and nude** figurines in bisque, china, pottery, porcelain, or metal. Signed items such as Rosenthal, Heubach, Coalport, Wedgwood, Noritake, Labino, Lalique, Lenox, etc. are preferred. Pieces may be painted porcelain or molded pottery, but they must be mint. No Hummels are wanted. Please send photo and price.

K. Hartman
7459 Shawnee Rd.
N Tonawanda, NY 14120

Wanted to buy: **porcelain pure-bred dog** figurines manufactured by Boehm, Mortens Studio, Royal Doulton, or others. The price offered ranges from $10.00 to $600.00, depending on the individual piece and condition.

Jeffrey Jacobson
6424 Jefferson Ave.
Hammond, IN 46324

FIREWORKS MEMORABILIA

I am hoping to hear from anyone that has any old firecracker labels, packs, or bricks from 1890 to 1960. I am willing to purchase a single item or an entire collection. Please find listed below some of the collectibles I am seeking.

Rob Berk
2671 Youngstown Rd. SE
Warren, OH 44484
(216) 369-1192 or (800) 323-3547

We Pay

1890–1929 Firecracker Labels	**20.00+**
1930–1949 Firecracker Labels	**10.00+**
1950–1970 Firecracker Labels	**5.00+**
1890–1929 Firecracker Packs	**50.00+**
1930–1949 Firecracker Packs	**30.00+**
1950–1970 Firecracker Packs	**10.00+**
1890–1929 Firecracker Bricks	**100.00+**
1930–1949 Firecracker Bricks	**80.00+**
1950–1960 Firecracker Bricks	**60.00+**

Fireworks catalogs and related artifacts are wanted! I need fireworks catalogs, firecracker packs and labels, cardboard boxes and boxed items, sparkler and cap boxes, salesmen's display boards and samples, and anything related to old-time U.S. fireworks manufacturers.

I am especially interested in locating items and information on the following manufacturers and distributors:

Victory Fireworks Co., Elkton, MD
Triumph Fussee & Fireworks Co., Elkton, MD
Pain's Firework Co., NYC
Keystone Fireworks Co., Dunbar, PA
Rochester Fireworks Co., NY
Baltimore Fireworks Co., Baltimore, MD
National Fireworks Co., Boston, MA
Havre De Grace Fireworks Co., MD
Unexcelled Fireworks Co.
Lloyds Fireworks Co., NYC
M. Backes Sons, Wallingford, CT
Banner Fireworks Co., OH
Essex Specialty Co., Berkeley Heights, NJ
Hitt's Fireworks Co., WA

Please write or phone me for an immediate cash offer!

Barry Zecker
P.O. Box 1022
Mountainside, NJ 07092
(908) 232-6100 (8 am to 8 pm)

FISHBOWLS AND STANDS

I buy fishbowls and holders. The holders are very decorative — possibly with mermaids, dolphins, men in fishing boats, sailing ships, or maybe even an elephant with a palm tree as motifs. They can be a combination of cast iron, brass, or pot metal with a bronze finish. The bowls have a large range of shapes and colors. The color could be clear, vaseline, green, amber, even a deep root beer shade, or cobalt blue. Since there is an enormous range of motifs, color, and finish, the listings below serve only as a starting point.

Alyce R. Fillion
834 Beech St.
Lake Odessa, MI 48849
(616) 367-4566

We Pay

Cast Iron Standard w/Bowl	**300.00+**
Cast Iron Standard Alone	**150.00+**
Table Model w/Bowl	**175.00+**
Table Model Alone	**100.00+**

FISHING COLLECTIBLES

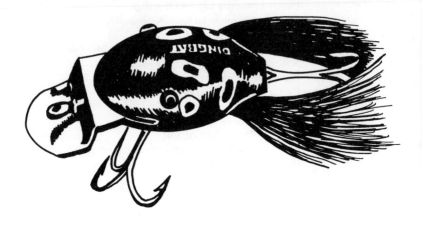

Little did James Heddon know when he carved the first wooden lure many years ago that he would not only change the way fishing would be done from then on but would also unknowingly start one of the most interesting categories of collectibles today.

Collecting old fishing tackle has really caught on in the last few years and still hasn't reached its peak. Old wooden lures are still the most popular items, but many other fishing-related items are also of interest to collectors. I am interested in buying old fishing lures and related items as well as some hunting items. The prices listed here are for examples in excellent condition, although more rare items are still sought after, even in lesser condition. I am known for paying top dollar for things I am looking for. Please call anytime. I want other items also besides those listed below.

Randy Hilst
1221 Florence, Apt. 4
Pekin, IL 61554
(309) 346-2710

Lure	We Pay
Winchester	75.00-150.00
Heddon Underwater Minnow	20.00-35.00
Detroit Glass Minnow Tube	75.00-150.00
South Bend Truck Oreno	100.00-200.00
South Bend Plug Oreno	25.00-35.00
Shakespeare Revolution	50.00-75.00
Shakespeare Paddler	15.00-20.00
Garland Cork Head Minnow	30.00-45.00
Kent Frog	75.00-150.00

Creek Chub Pikie	**2.00-5.00**
Creek Chub Wee Dee	**75.00-100.00**
Creek Chub Beetle	**25.00-35.00**
Chippewa Lure	**40.00-50.00**
Charmer Minnow	**50.00-75.00**
Flying Helgramite	**750.00-1,500.00**
Al Foss Oriental Wiggler	**3.00-7.00**

Related Items	**We Pay**
Reel, Winchester	**30.00-50.00**
Reel, Meek	**40.00-50.00**
Camp Glass Minnow Trap	**20.00-30.00**
Lure Boxes	**1.00-10.00**
Lure Catalogs	**10.00-30.00**
Fishing & Hunting License Buttons	**3.00-10.00**
Duck Calls	**5.00-25.00**

I am buying all types of vintage old and used fishing tackle. I'm collecting fishing lures, reels, fish decoys, glass minnow traps, and other miscellaneous tackle. Listed below are some of the things that I am seeking. I also want anything old or unusual. If you have anything else not listed, please send me a list along with detailed descriptions, prices, and photos.

The Fisherman
Gary L. Weber
468 E. Metz Rd.
Columbiana, OH 44408

	We Pay
Lures, wooden	**5.00-1,000.00**
Lures, metal	**1.00-1,000.00**
Reels, bait casting	**10.00-1,000.00**
Reels, spinning	**10.00-100.00**
Reels, fly	**10.00-1,000.00**
Fish Spearing Decoys (frogs, fish, turtles, etc.)	**5.00-1,000.00**
Fishing Spears	**5.00-50.00**
Fishing Lure Boxes	**2.00-100.00**
Fishing Tackle Catalogs	**5.00-500.00**
Folk Art Fishing Lures, handmade	**5.00-1,000.00**
Glass Minnow Traps	**25.00+**

Fishing Collectibles _____

Tackle Boxes, metal & wood **10.00-100.00**

I am buying old hunting and fishing items. Items made before 1950 are most preferred. Listed below are some of the things I am seeking.

Dar Hoag
3614 Arapahoe Trail
Beaverton, MI 48612

We Pay

Michigan Hunting/Fishing Licenses, 1928–1932 (button form) ....**25.00+**
Michigan Non-Resident Hunting/Fishing Licenses, 1928–1932 (button
    form) .... **50.00+**
Michigan Hunting/Fishing Licenses, 1895–1939 .... **4.00+**
Marble Arms Products.. **Write**
All Types of Fishing Tackle .... **Write**
Knives .... **Write**
Shotgun Shell Boxes, cardboard .... **Write**
Advertising .... **Write**
Other Items Relating to Hunting or Fishing .... **Write**

Collecting hunting and fishing license badges is one of today's fastest-grownning hobbies. Especially popular among sportsmen and gun collectors, they span the period from about 1913 until 1942 when the World War II war effort caused the a switch from metal and celluloid-covered badges to paper licenses. The only state to continue their use was Pennsylvania.

These badges were required to be worn on outer clothing for identification purposes. Some states such as Michigan and Wisconsin issued badges for only a few years. California, Minnesota, and New Mexico issued them for one year only. Apparently they were not too popular in these areas. Badges were issued in other states for many years.

Generally, each year was a different color, and many depicted animals or fish. Several combinations were issued as well — deer, hunting, fishing, trapping, small and large game, non-resident, and aliens. All badges are highly desirable and valuable in today's collectibles market.

Prices shown below are for hunting and fishing badges in nice condition. Deer, trout, plain trapping, non-resident, and mint condition badges are worth more.

Terry Martin
545 Crest Circle
Webster, NY 14580

State	We Pay
NY or NJ	**10.00+**
CT, WI, or WV	**20.00+**
AR, MD, TN, VA, or MN	**30.00+**
GA, NC, SC, MS, MI, or Canada	**40.00+**
DE, NM, or OH	**50.00+**
FL	**200.00+**
PA	**Not Wanted**

Wanted: hunting, fishing, trapping, and guide licenses and pin-back buttons. The buying prices listed are for buttons in good to excellent condition. Buttons with stains, cracks, or other damage might be purchased, depending on the extent of damage. Those from certain southern states (such as South Carolina, Florida, Georgia, and Mississippi) and Ohio will bring the highest prices. Buttons with birds, fish, or animals also bring better prices.

James C. Case
R.R. 1, Box 68
Lindley, NY 14858
(607) 524-6606

Paper Licenses	We Pay
Common Licenses, any state, pre–1910	**20.00-50.00**
Common Licenses, any state, 1910–1920	**10.00-30.00**
Common Licenses, any state, 1920–1935	**2.00-15.00**
NY Non-Resident Hunting, 1905	**500.00+**
PA Fishing License, 1922	**150.00-250.00**
PA Hunting Back Tags, pre–1924	**40.00-200.00**

Celluloid Buttons	We Pay
Common Date Resident, any state, pre-1945	**3.00-30.00**
Common Date Non-Resident, any state, pre-1945	**5.00-50.00**
Rarer Resident Button, any state, pre-1945	**25.00-100.00**
Rarer Non-Resident Button, any state, pre-1945	**50.00-250.00**

Resident Button from Ohio, Hawaii, Florida **40.00-150.00**
Non-Resident Button from Ohio, Hawaii, Florida **100.00-300.00**
NY Alien Button, pre-1942 .... **150.00-500.00**
NY Non-Resident, pre-1942 .... **30.00-200.00**
NY Resident Trapping Button, 1940 or 1941 .... **150.00-300.00**
NY Non-Resident Trapping Button, 1940 or 1941 .... **200.00-400.00**
NY Resident Duplicate Button, 1941 .... **100.00-300.00**
NY Non-Resident Duplicate Button, 1941 .... **200.00-400.00**
PA Non-Resident Fishing, 1923-1939, ... **25.00-150.00**
MI Resident Hunting or Deer **25.00-100.00**
MI Non-Resident Hunting or Deer **100.00-300.00**

FLASHLIGHTS

I am buying pre-1935 flashlights, such as Eveready, Winchester, Bond, Franco, Delta, Burgess, French Flasher, etc. The older the better. I mostly want the novelty type and small fiber tube type 'C' and 'D' cell. Also wanted are display items, old batteries, bulbs, and literature. All types and makes will be considered. All items must be complete and in good condition. Send photocopy of the item with a complete description and price.

John Rex
P.O. Box 6384
Lynnwood, WA 98036

We Pay

Early Eveready, Fiber Tube, Ring Switch .... **20.00+**
Eveready, Daylo Pistol Type .... **10.00+**
Chase Bomb (skater's) Flashlight .... **10.00+**
Eveready Lapel (scarf) Pin Light .... **20.00+**
Bright Star Pocket Watch Flashlight .... **30.00+**
Chase/Bond Lanterns, Owl or Lighthouse .... **10.00+**
Vest Pocket Lights, Plated, Fiber Case .... **10.00+**
Burgess Vest Pocket 'Snaplite' .... **15.00+**

FLORENCE CERAMICS

I buy anything made by Florence Ceramics to picture in a book that I am writing. I pay anywhere from $15.00 for small, simply molded, 'plain Jane' items and up to $500.00 for fancy, elaborately hand-detailed and applied-decorated figurines. Mint condition items are preferred, but damaged items will be considered. The list below reflects only a few items that are needed. If you have Florence to sell, send a fully-detailed description of the item (including condition, size, colors, marking on bottom, pose, etc.). Photos are very helpful! For a prompt reply include price desired and SASE. I am also interested in hearing from other Florence Ceramics collectors, as I am planning a Florence newsletter. Sample prices below are for items in mint condition. Generally the more hand-applied detailing, the higher the price.

Audree Gada
4431 Chapman Rd.
Modesto, CA 95356

	We Pay
Original Catalogs or Literature	Name Your Price
Male Figurines	20.00-50.00
Figural Grouping	25.00-50.00
Matched Sets (2 or more figurines)	75.00-350.00
Lady Figurine, basic	40.00-75.00
Lady Figurine, fancy w/applied detail	75.00-350.00
Figurines w/Brocade Fabric	150.00-300.00
Figurines after Famous People (Scarlett, Rhett, etc.)	65.00-350.00
Animals, Birds, or Jewelry	25.00-75.00
Figurine Flower Holders	15.00-50.00
Clocks, Lamps, Wall Plaques, or Busts	50.00-175.00
Miscellaneous Knick-Knack Items	15.00-50.00
Figurine Powder Boxes	50.00-100.00
Religious Items	30.00-150.00

FLOW BLUE

We buy Warwick vases marked I.O.G.A. as well as other Warwick Flow Blue items. We prefer items in excellent condition. Vases with portraits rather than florals are of particular interest, but we are always interested in any unusual pieces. Listed below are examples of prices we will pay. Photos of items would be appreciated. All letters will be answered promptly.

Jeff & Sandy Mauck
142 N 19th St.
Wheeling, WV 26003
(304) 277-2356

We Pay

Brown Bouquet Vases w/Portraits... 125.00
Tobio Pitchers w/Portraits 110.00
Plates 25.00
Cracker Jar 75.00
Urn... 150.00

FOSTORIA

We will pay the prices listed below for blue **June** by Fostoria. Please give sizes and a general description of each piece. Only items without cracks, chips, or sickness are wanted. Minor scratches are alright. We will buy any number of pieces. We also are buying pink **June** and other patterns such as **Versailles and Chintz by Fostoria, Caprice and Rosepoint by Cambridge, Orchid and Rose by Heisey, as well as other depression-era glassware.** We buy most patterns of depression glass. Prices vary according to desirability of patterns and whether or not we need pieces in our collections. The following is only a partial list of pieces in blue June.

Sandi & Dennis Boone
No Horse Antiques
Rte. 1, P.O. Box 86
Reynolds, IL 61279

We Pay

Ash Tray	27.50
Bowl, 10½" oval	50.00
Bowl, 7" soup	25.00
Bowl, 6" cereal	20.00
Bowl, 5½" handled cream soup	20.00
Candy Dish w/Cover, ½ lb.	90.00
Goblet, ¾-oz. cordial	47.50
Ice Bucket w/Metal Handle	65.00
Pitcher, 48-oz.	225.00
Plate, 10¼" dinner	45.00
Platter, 12"	55.00
Sauce Boat w/Underplate	125.00

FOUNTAIN PENS

Fountain pens produced between 1880 and 1945 are very collectible, as well as some produced later (such as Parker's Spanish Treasure pen). The most valuable pens represent major brands like Parker, Sheaffer, Waterman, Wahl-Eversharp, Conklin, and Swan. Pens commanding the best prices are those that are either very large, very fancy, or very rare.

I prefer very fancy and rare pens but will consider purchasing any high-quality pen that is in excellent condition and free from defects such as cracks, damage, or missing parts.

The following list reflects the current prices I pay for fountain pens. Some of these pens have identifying numbers stamped on the end of the holders. Prices are for pens in excellent condition. I have published a book on collectible fountain pens. Write for further information on the book or if you have fountain pens to sell. Please send a photocopy of pens you wish to sell.

Glen Bowen
2240 N Park Dr.
Kingwood, TX 77339

We Pay

Parker #41 or #31 Sterling or Gold-Filled Filigree	**400.00**
Parker #47 Pearl Sided w/Floral Design Gold-Filled Cap	**500.00**
Parker #15 Pearl Sided w/Gold-Filled Filigree Cap	**400.00**
Parker #45 Pearl Sided w/Gold-Filled Filigree Cap	**400.00**
Parker #37 or #38 Gold-Filled or Sterling Snakes	**2,000.00**
Parker #59 or #60 Gold-Filled or Sterling Indian Aztec Design	**2,000.00**
Parker #58 Gold-Filled Partial Indian Aztec Design	**500.00**
Parker #35 or #36 Gold-Filled or Sterling Floral Pattern	**500.00**
Parker #52 or #53 Gold-Filled or Sterling Swastika Design	**500.00**
Parker #39 or #54 Gold-Filled or Sterling Floral Pattern	**400.00**
Parker #40 Gold-Filled or Solid Gold Floral Design	**400.00**
Parker, #43 or #44 Gold-Filled or Sterling Floral Design	**400.00**
Parker #14 or #16 Gold-Filled or Sterling Filigree Design	**200.00**
Parker #33 or #34 Gold-Filled or Sterling Overlay	**200.00**
Parker #62 Gold-Filled Floral Engraved Pattern	**500.00**
Waterman #452, #454, #0552, or #0554 Gold-Filled or Sterling	**150.00**
Waterman #456, #458, #0556, or #0558 Gold-Filled or Sterling	**400.00**
Waterman #552, #554, #555, or #556 Gold Overlay	**250.00-1,000.00**
Waterman Ripple Pattern #7, #56, or #58	**100.00-500.00**
Waterman Ripple Pattern #52, #54, or #55	**50.00-200.00**
Waterman 100-Year Brown, Black, or Burgundy	**50.00-200.00**
Waterman 100-Year Blue, Yellow, Red, or Green Transparent	**200.00**
Waterman #20 Black, Red, or Red & Black Pattern	**500.00-1,000.00**
Waterman Patrician, Multicolored	**100.00-250.00**
Wahl-Eversharp Gold-Filled or Sterling #2, #3, #4, #5, or #6	**100.00**
Wahl-Eversharp Oversize in Various Colors, Roller Ball Clips	**100.00-200.00**
Wahl-Eversharp Oversize Doric (fluted sides) in Various Colors	**100.00-200.00**
A.A. Waterman Gold-Filled or Sterling Overlay	**100.00-500.00**
Aiken-Lambert Gold-Filled or Sterling Overlay	**50.00-200.00**
Conklin Crescent Filled, Gold-Filled or Sterling	**50.00-300.00**
John Holland Gold-Filled or Sterling Filigree	**50.00-300.00**
Paul Wirt Gold-Filled or Sterling Overlay or Filigree	**50.00-300.00**
Parker Duofold Sr., Blue or Yellow	**100.00-200.00**
Parker Duofold Sr., Red, Green, Black & Pearl, or Black	**25.00-100.00**

I am buying all high-quality fountain pens manufactured from 1884 to 1950. I'm especially interested in the 'large' men's pens made by Parker, Waterman, Le Boeuf, Conklin, Wahl-Eversharp, Swan, Mont Blanc, Chilton, and other fine manufacturers. I am paying especially high prices for fancy pens with silver or gold overlays, filigrees, or mother-of-pearl. I will buy one pen or a collection.

Howard Share
4349 La Vale Court
Clemmons, NC 27012
(919) 766-6579

We Pay

Parker Duofold Sr., Yellow	200.00
Parker Duofold Sr., Blue	175.00
Parker w/Mother-of-Pearl	1,000.00+
Parker w/Overlay of Gold or Silver	500.00+
Parker Snake Pen	10,000.00+
Parker Aztec Indian Pen	5,000.00+
Waterman Patrician, any	300.00+
Waterman #58, any color	200.00+
Waterman #458	1,000.00+
Wahl-Eversharp, lg size	100.00+
Le Boeuf, lg size	200.00+

Purchasing fountain pens is my passion! I especially desire to buy Parker, Waterman, Wahl-Eversharp, Swans, Mont Blanc, and Swan pens and pencils. My specialities are very large or very fancy pen types. Please write or call if you have pens to sell.

Phil Glatz
164 N Garfield Ave.
Mundelein, IL 60060
(708) 949-4280

We Pay

Parker #37 or #38 Sterling or Gold-Filled Snakes	900.00
Parker #59 or #60 Sterling or Gold-Filled Indian Aztec Design	900.00
Parker #58 Gold-Filled Partial Indian Aztec Design	150.00
Parker Giant	300.00

Fountain Pens

Parker Duofold Sr., Yellow or Blue	**50.00-100.00**
Waterman #20 Black, Red, or Red & Black	**200.00**
Waterman #552, #554, #555, or #556 Gold Overlay	**100.00-500.00**
Waterman Patrician, Multicolored	**100.00-200.00**
John Holland, Gold-Filled or Sterling	**50.00-200.00**
All Giant Pens	**50.00-500.00**

We purchase old fountain pens and also some mechanical pencils that are in good condition. We particularly like fancy ones. We pay a lot for those that have gold or silver overlay or mother-of-pearl. Photos are appreciated, especially on fancier ones. Also bought are some better pens for parts. Brands such as Parker, Sheaffer, Conklin, Waterman, Le Boeuf, and Eversharp, are preferred. Those of lesser quality are Esterbrook, Eclipse, Franklin, Boston, Salz, Betzler, Bicks, Abon, Wearever, etc. We also buy fancy dip pens and good condition old mechanical pencils. Higher prices will be paid for more fancy pens.

Once we have agreed on a purchase price, we will send one-half of the amount to you. Upon receiving and inspecting your items, we will send the balance providing items are as represented. Please send photos with your correspondence.

The Antique Place
1720A S Glenstone
Springfield, MO 65804
(417) 887-3800 (10 am to 6 pm)

FRANKART

I am buying Frankart nude figural lamps, bookends, ash trays, and more. These items were made in the 1920's and 1930's; they are cast metal and most pieces are marked 'Frankart Inc.' with patent number, 'patent applied for' or copyright and/or year. Original finish normally is paint in green, black, or gun-metal gray. Listed below are some descriptions and what I am paying for pieces in good to mint condition.

David Wroblewski
P.O. Box 51223
Indianapolis, IN 46251-0223
(317) 925-2469

We Pay

Lamp, nude stands in front of frosted glass panel, 10½"..........................**225.00**
Lamp/Clock, 2 kneeling nudes hold a circular disc, 10½".......................**925.00**
Lamp, nude standing on geometric base looks down into 3" glass globe . **400.00**
Lamp, nude figure w/fan, made entirely of glass, on metal base, 11½"... **975.00**
Lamp, kneeling nude looks into 10" glass disc, also came as mirror....... **625.00**
Lamp, 2 nudes standing on sides of carved rectangular glass plate **650.00**
Lamp, nude holding 10" glass disc.. **800.00**
Lamp, 2 nudes holding horizontal glass cylinder **700.00**
Lamp, 2 nudes support 7" glass plate around 3" glass cylinder, 13" **1,000.00**
Floor Ash Tray, nude arises out of tobacco plant, glass tray **500.00**
Floor Ash Tray, nude stands on horseshoe base, 23"............................... **375.00**
Ash Tray, nude holds ceramic dish to side, 10"....................................... **135.00**
Ash Tray, nude holds dish to side, glass cigarette box on base.............. **285.00**
Bookends, nude on back with legs up, 10", pair....................................... **265.00**
Bookends, nude sits on ribbed pedestal, arms extended to back, 8½", pair.. **285.00**

GAMBLING

I buy early gambling items that are used for cheating or devices that were used to make a legitimate item into a cheating device. It is difficult to identify some of these or figure out how they work. So don't hesitate to write me; send a description and a photo, if possible. All inquiries answered.

R.E. White
6924 Teller Ct.
Arvada, CO 80003

We Pay

Card Trimmers... **up to 1,000.00**
Card Corner Rounders.. **up to 800.00**
Card Holdouts, simple .... **up to 200.00**
Card Holdouts, complicated .... **up to 1,000.00**
Dice Drops .... **up to 300.00**
Complete Decks of pre-1900 Cards.. **up to 75.00**
Gambling Motif Pocket Watches.. **up to 200.00**
Faro Case Keepers .... **up to 300.00**
Faro Layouts .... **up to 200.00**
Cheating Dice Cups .... **up to 300.00**

I buy old clay composition, ivory, or any other type of **poker chips, gambling supply catalogs and old gambling-related books, U.S. playing cards, gambling equipment, and unique chip holders.** As for chips, they must not be plain but have a design which would appeal to the general public. Also those with private initials or names are not wanted. Please send me a sample or a photocopy of each design. For approximately 100 chips of the following three types in good or better condition, I pay at least $20.00 plus postage and insurance.

Inlaid clay composition chips: These usually have a white laminated paper or plastic inlay recessed into the chip, flush with the chip's surface.

Engraved clay composition chips: These are slate or ceramic-like. The design is created by fine lines pressed into the chip surface, and then 'engraved' lines are usually filled with paint.

Catalin chips: These are marbleized red, green, and yellow chips.

Robert Eisenstadt
140 Cadman Plaza W
Brooklyn, NY 11201
(718) 625-3553

GAME ROOM DECORATIONS

I am buying items to decorate game rooms and dens. These items can be bar, sports, western, or brewery signs and decorations. Anything that will enhance the appearance of a game room. I prefer items made prior to 1950 but will consider all items. Below is a partial listing of the items I am seeking.

Alan D. Conway
1696 W Morton Ave.
Porterville, CA 93257

We Pay

Beer Signs	**3.00+**
Beer Lights	**5.00+**
Sports Advertising Signs	**3.00+**
Beer Clocks	**10.00+**
Baseball or Football Decorations	**2.00+**
Pool or Billiard Decorations	**2.00+**
Slot Machine, non-working, good appearance	**50.00+**
Old Sports Scenes	**3.00+**
Beer Steins	**3.00+**
Coin-Operated Game Dispensers, small	**15.00+**
Western Sign or Decorations	**3.00+**

GAS PUMP GLOBES

Gas pump globes were first introduced in the early 1910's; they were used to advertise the brand of gas being sold at the gas stations. Some globes simply had brand names on both sides. The most desirable globes had pictures on them such as Indians, lions, old cars, flowers, birds, etc. There are four basic types of gas pump globes. The earliest globes were one-piece milk glass with advertising on both sides. Then there were metal-rimmed globes with glass lens inserts held in place with metal snap rings. Next were the glass bodies with two glass advertising lenses held on by two or three tiny bolts on each lens. Last were the plastic globe bodies with two glass lenses, and these were the most common. I will pay the following prices for original gas pump globes in nice condition (not cracked or faded).

Walt's Antiques
2513 Nelson Rd.
Traverse City, MI 49684
(616) 223-7386

We Pay

One-Piece Glass Globes .... **200.00+**
Metal-Rimmed Bodies w/2 Glass Lenses.. **185.00+**
Glass Bodies w/2 Glass Lenses.. **125.00+**
Plastic Bodies w/2 Glass Lenses.. **65.00+**

GLASSWARE MADE BEFORE 1950

I am interested in collecting glass manufactured before 1950. I prefer glass having a pattern or some design. I especially like amberina, cranberry, vaseline, Fenton, Loetz, depression glass, Coin Dot, Daisy and Button — just to name a few. Approval boxes are welcomed, but please pack them well. Listed below are a few of the things I am seeking and the price I will pay.

Cindy Lewis
2150 Lomita Blvd.
Lomita, CA 90717
(213) 539-4575

We Pay

Glass Chickens	**10.00-50.00**
Glass Hats	**5.00-20.00**
Vaseline Vases	**10.00-75.00**
Amberina	**10.00-100.00**
Daisy & Button, amberina	**5.00-50.00**
Cranberry	**10.00-50.00**
Pink Depression	**5.00-50.00**
Dolphins	**10.00-75.00**
Cross Candlesticks, per pair	**20.00-50.00**
Fenton Bowls & Vases	**5.00-40.00**
Loetz	**35.00-100.00**

GLOW LIGHTS

I am buying glow lights. They are clear light bulbs with figures inside them. I am also looking for any advertisements for them and other related materials.

Cindy Chipps
4027 Brooks Hill Rd.
Brooks, KY 40109
(502) 955-9238

We Pay

Parisphere & Trylon, 1939 World's Fair	**400.00**
Signs of the Zodiac	**30.00+**

Glow Lights

Dogs	25.00+
Donald Duck	200.00+
Flowers	15.00+
American Flag	50.00+
Mickey Mouse	400.00
Santa & Little Girl	30.00+
Ram & Fence	20.00
Airplane or Sailboat	25.00
Popeye	75.00+
Catholic Shrines	40.00+
Howard Johnson	50.00
Star of David w/Wreath	40.00+
Star of David w/Menorah	40.00+
'Jesus Saves'	40.00+
'God Loves You' or 'God Loves Me'	40.00+
Smiling Face	40.00+
Bucking Bronco	50.00
Bulbs w/Letters or Numbers in Them	40.00
Other Styles	10.00-400.00

GOEBEL

172

I am buying Goebel cat figurines and Goebel cat-related items. I want pieces no longer in production and that were produced for European distribution only. I will pay $20.00 or more for items.

Linda Nothnagel
Rt. 3, Box 30
Shelbina, MO 63468
(314) 588-4958

GOLF MEMORABILIA

Golf ball markers have been made from many substances including gold, silver, plastic, and hard rubber. Used to mark the golf ball's location on the green, they come in many shapes and sizes — usually round but sometimes in arrow shapes.

I seek all kinds of markers from the rare gold ones to today's easy-to-find plastic types. Value depends on the piece, who may have used it, age, and the metal content. A gold marker identifiable as having been used by Walter Hagen or Bobby Jones sure beats one of plastic used by Norm Boughton, so please write a complete description of what you have and the price you desire for it. Other golf memorabilia is also wanted. Please describe and price what you have. Listed below are sample prices for golf ball markers.

Norm Boughton
1356 Buffalo Rd.
Rochester, NY 14624

Golf Memorabilia

Identifiable to: **We Pay**

Hogan, Jones, Palmer, Nicholas, Etc. **5.00-100.00**
Major Championships **3.00-25.00**
Companies... **10¢-$50.00**

We buy thousands of **golf balls** a year in all sizes, shapes, designs, materials such as leather, pimples or dimples, range, floaters, mesh, lattice, brambles, sizes 27½ and 28, plus many odd shapes and markings. We buy them in all grades: new, mint, excellent, very good, some good, fair, middling fair, poor, and even those with cuts in some cases.

Values of balls for collectors depend on age, manufacturer, and markings (club name or insignia, company name or logo, name of golf or other event, date, etc.). Balls relating to historical events such as the 'First Landing on the Moon,' balls with printed names of famous (or infamous) persons or important occasions, and autographed or personally-signed balls are wanted. Balls autographed by U.S. Presidents, their secretaries, or their dogs are especially valued. Do you have any that were signed by Gary Hart?

We buy all balls that have been issued for commemorative events, World's Fairs, tournaments, races, as well as those of foreign origin. Balls with slogans 'Tee for Two,' greetings 'Merry Christmas,' and similar ones are very desirable. But, please, no expletives or unprintable four letter ones. However, 'Happy Hooker' is alright.

If it looks unusual, it could be valuable. There are innumerable makers of balls — big ones and small ones. Some of the biggies are Spaldings, Wilson, Acushnet, and Dunlop. Some of the teenies and oldies are: Holmac, Wanamaker, Worthington, and Kempshall. There are hundreds of brand names like Kroflite, Top-Flite, Titleist, as well as thousands of variations in markings. We like them all.

We pay top dollar for any unusual or different make, design, marking, imprint, or other variation. We buy one ball or collections of hundreds. Send us a complete detailed description of what you have. Good clear pictures are essential in some cases. We will give you a preliminary estimate within two weeks if we are interested. At that time you can elect to send them to us for inspection and final estimate. We will then send you a check or return the lot to you. No reproductions please. Be sure to enclose your name, complete address, and telephone number. Some of the prices we pay are listed below.

Hotchkiss House, Ltd.
Golf Balls Unlimited
P.O. Box 11
Sanibel Island, FL 33957

We Pay

Leather/Feather Balls, made before 1898 .... **up to 3,000.00**
Gutty (Gutta Percha) Balls, smooth or hammered........................ **up to 1,000.00**
Rubber Core Balls, before 1915, mint .... **up to 300.00**
Rubber Core Balls, before 1915, used .... **up to 150.00**
Rubber Core Balls, before 1930, mint .... **up to 100.00**
Rubber Core Balls, before 1930, very good...................................... **up to 50.00**
Rubber Core Balls, before 1930, good.. **up to 20.00**
Most Balls, made before 1930, mint .... **up to 25.00**
Most Balls, made before 1930, good.. **up to 10.00**
Most Balls, made before 1930, fair .... **up to 5.00**

Most Balls, after 1950   **We Pay**

Personally Signed by Celebrities .... **up to 100.00**
Commerative Dated/Named Events, Games, Etc............................... **up to 50.00**
Logos of Country Clubs, Organizations, or Individuals in Cartons, per
   dozen.. **up to 35.00**
Logos of Some Companies or Societies in Cartons, mint, per dozen...**up to 25.00**
Logos of Above 2 Listings, mint, each.. **up to 5.00**
Unusual Makes, Brand names, Designs, or Variations, each............. **up to 5.00**

I am interested in buying **porcelain, pottery, silver, and art relating to golf dating from around 1900 through 1930**. I will pay up to $1,000.00 for an unusual item.

Sari Blecker
25 Crocker St.
Rockville Centre, NY 11570

GRANITEWARE

I am currently buying unusual graniteware, any old swirls, duchessware, end of day, and children's items. I am also interested in related items such as trade cards, advertising, and salesman's samples. Prices paid are directly related to color, condition, and rarity. Original labels are a plus.

John Markworth
121 Clark St.
Richmond, MO 64085

Coffee Biggin	**200.00**
Coffee Mug	**50.00**
Cocoa Dipper	**100.00**
Spoon	**25.00**
Muffin Pan	**125.00**
Mixing Bowl	**75.00**
Mendets	**20.00**
Magazine Advertisements	**20.00**
Water Buckets, large	**75.00**
Skillets	**75.00**
Covered Buckets	**125.00**
Child's Cup & Saucer	**80.00**

I am buying all items in swirl graniteware and the more unusual gray graniteware. Color and condition are very important when determining price.

Listed below are some of the pieces I need in mint condition, along with prices I will pay.

Daryl D. Alpers
P.O. Box 2621
Cedar Rapids, IA 52406
(319) 365-3857

We Pay

Butter Churn, green swirl	1,000.00
Butter Churn, blue swirl	1,000.00
Muffin Pan, green swirl	400.00
Muffin Pan, blue swirl	200.00
Match Safe, gray	200.00
Biscuit Cutter, gray	250.00
Cream Can, swirl	100.00
Cream or Sugar, swirl, ea	200.00

LOUIS ICART

As the author of the book, *Louis Icart: The Complete Etchings*, I am interested in purchasing etchings, oil paintings, and illustrated books by Louis Icart. During the 1920's and 1930's, Icart etchings became the rage, not only in his native France but in America as well. There are still many etchings hiding in the attics and basements of American households. The etchings were printed from a copper plate and then colored by hand. They are always pencil signed in the lower right. Many have a raised seal at the lower left which looks like a windmill. There may be copyright information printed at the edge of the image. Of course, condition is very important. Tears, creases, stains, or spots will lower the value considerably. Icart did about 500 different etchings, and there is a wide range of values depending on rarity and popularity of a particular etching. His oil paintings are less common; they are always signed in oil paint and most look quite impressionistic. Books which he illustrated are much more common in France than in America and usually have more erotic themes than his regular 'bedroom' etchings. Other artists which were also popular during this time were Hardy, Ablett, Milliere, and Felix.

William R. Holland
1708 E. Lancaster Ave.
Suite 133
Paoli, PA 19301
(215) 648-0369 or (215) 647-7099
FAX (215) 647-4448

Common or Small Icart Etching	500.00+
Icart Illustrated Book	600.00+
Single Icart Bookplate	20.00+
'More Popular' Icart Etching	1,200.00+
'Very Popular' Icart Etching	2,000.00+
Icart Oil Painting (except war or smalls)	7,500.00+
Hardy, Ablett, Milliere, & Felix	100.00+

ICE CREAM SCOOPS

I need assistance in locating unusual ice cream scoops (dippers) to purchase as surprise gifts (birthday, Christmas, etc.) for my husband. Depending on condition and rarity, I am willing to pay $300.00 through $500.00 and up. Some unusual scoops sought were manufactured by Mosteller Manufacturing; Schupfer & Eaton Co.; Pi-Alamoder, Inc.; Modern Specialty Co.; and Bohlig Manufacturing Co.

Lillian M. Cole
14 Harmony School Rd.
Flemington, NJ 08822
(908) 782-3198

INDIAN ARTIFACTS

This is a broad term for arts and crafts produced by North American Indians. I specialize in the Pueblo Indians of the Southwest. I do not purchase stone items such as arrowheads, axes, etc. Today there is a resurgence of interest in American Indian way of life, history, culture, and artifacts. It is important to respect the cultures — past and present — avoiding items related to secret ceremonies (e.g., Hopi masks and religious articles and feathered items of all tribes). Therefore, in offering your items for sale, please take this into consideration. Perhaps a museum is best suited for these items. You may want to consult Lar Hothem's Book *North American Indian Artifacts*. Prices are for items in good condition.

John W. Barry
Indian Rock Arts
P.O. Box 583
Davis, CA 95617
(916) 758-2561

We Pay

California Baskets	**25.00-1,000.00**
Southwest Baskets	**75.00-300.00**
Pueblo Pottery, general	**25.00-500.00**
Pueblo Pottery, by Maria Martinez	**200.00-1,500.00**
Pueblo Paintings	**50.00-300.00**
Hopi Kachinas (pre-1950)	**125.00-400.00**
Photographs of Pueblo Indians	**3.00-200.00**
Books on Pueblo Indians	**5.00-50.00**

Bows & Arrows (pre-1900) **100.00-500.00**

I will pay the highest prices for **fine authentic antique American Indian and cowboy** material. I am interested in purchasing fine original pieces or entire collections.

Rex Arrowsmith
P.O. Box 2700
Santa Fe, NM 87504
(505) 982-0225

We Pay

Southwestern Pottery .... **10.00 to 10,000+**
Southwestern & Western Baskets............................... **10.00 to 10,000+**
Beadwork .... **10.00 to 10,000.00+**
Bows, Arrows, Pipes, Clubs .... **10.00 to 10,000.00+**
Spurs, Chaps, Saddles .... **10.00 to 10,000.00+**
Photographs, Paintings... **10.00 to 10,000.00+**
Holsters, Saddle Bags .... **10.00 to 3,000.00+**
Western Documents & Signs .... **10.00 to 5,000.00+**
Navajo Rugs .... **10.00 to 10,000.00+**

JARS

I want to buy jars embossed with the word '**JUMBO**' and an elephant head. These jars were made by the Frank Tea & Spice Co., Cincinnati, Ohio. They contained peanut butter, pepper sauce, and mustard. Another version is an elephant figural in clear or green glass. Lids screw onto the bottom of this figural. Other wants are Frank's Dove brand jars in various shapes: cat, dog, monkey, owl, parrot, and rabbit. I will also buy just the original jar lids for the above jars in any quantity. Prices depend on condition and quantity. Please write or call before shipping.

John Decker
660 Crockett
Elmhurst, IL 60126
(708) 832-1449

We Pay

Jumbo Jars, larger than 2 pounds	**10.00+**
Jumbo Jars, 1 pound or less	**5.00+**
Jumbo Figural Elephant	**15.00+**
Dove Brand Figurals	**10.00+**

JEWELRY

I'm a quality dealer of antique and collectible fashion jewelry, and I am always interested in finding new buying sources. If you have anything interesting that you'd like to sell, I'd certainly like to hear from you. Please be sure that your items are in top condition; but if you have special things with small problems, they too may be acceptable if you will describe any damage accurately and price the piece accordingly. A photograph or photocopy of any merchandise for sale is most appreciated. You can be sure of a quick response if I'm interested.

As I deal in all sorts of jewelry except gold and gemstones, there are many categories of jewelry that I always need. The prices below are only a guide, and there is always an exception to the rule — but they will serve as a good starting point for us. I will buy one piece or entire box lots.

Brenda's Bric-a-Brac
1441 N Market St. Exit
E Palestine, OH 44413
(216) 426-2636

We Pay

Bakelite Bangles, narrow w/carving	5.00-12.00
Bakelite Bangles, wide w/carving	15.00-45.00
Bakelite Bangles, wide w/carving, hinged	25.00-75.00
Bakelite Bangles, polka-dot or reverse-carved	100.00+
Pins, Bakelite figurals	25.00+
Pins, rhinestone, large & gaudy	10.00+
Bracelets, rhinestone, large & gaudy	10.00+
Designer Jewelry	15.00-150.00+
Lockets, ornate sterling, old	15.00+
Charm Bracelets, sterling, old	30.00+
Pins, gold-filled Victorian, interesting & fancy	8.00-20.00
Cameos, shell, lava, Bakelite, celluloid, gutta percha	15.00-100.00
Bangles, gold-filled Victorian, ornate	25.00-45.00
Chatelaines, sterling	75.00-150.00
Pins, Victorian to 1940's, heavy sterling figurals	20.00-45.00
Hat Pins, ornate & gaudy w/good color	20.00+
Figural Pins, Hula girls, flamingoes, animals, large & heavy	15.00-35.00
Tremblers	15.00+
Brass Jewelry (set w/stones is best), old	10.00+
Lavalieres, old	15.00-55.00
Marcasite Jewelry, old	25.00-75.00

I am a dealer in all types of jewelry. I carry a full line of gold, silver, fine, and costume jewelry. I specialize in designer costume jewelry and 1960's jewelry such as peace signs, etc. I buy all types of jewelry — new or old. I am always looking for designer costume jewelry such as Eisenberg, Hobe, Miriam Haskell, Schiaparelli, and Har. I will consider any quantity or pieces in any condition.

Patsy Comer's Antiques & Jewelry
7445 Reseda Blvd.
Reseda, CA 91335
(818) 345-1631

We Pay

Eisenberg	**15.00+**
Miriam Haskell	**15.00+**
Weiss	**5.00+**
Hobe	**15.00+**
Jomaz	**12.00+**
Har	**12.00+**
Regency	**12.00+**
Bogoff	**10.00+**
Boucher	**12.00+**
Carnegie	**15.00+**
De Mario	**12.00+**
Robert	**15.00+**
Schiaparelli	**15.00+**
Trifari, old	**8.00+**
Coro, sterling, old	**12.00+**

I buy many types of jewelry. Below are examples with prices paid. I usually advise sellers to photocopy pieces (machines are found in post offices and libraries). I can choose or refuse items ahead of time this way. It is difficult to give specific prices, as there is so much variation. A large, unusual, mint condition piece will fall in the high end of the range. Some rare items might exceed these prices. I am not interest in jewelry that is brand new, reproduction, poor quality, or severely damaged. All letters enclosing a SASE will be answered. If you price the item, it saves time; if not, I will make an offer.

Pahaka September
19 Fox Hill
U Saddle River, NJ 07458
(201) 327-1464

We Pay

Victorian, Art Nouveau, Art Deco	**5.00-250.00**
Lacy Brass w/Colored Glass Stones, 1920's–1930's	**10.00-75.00**
Trifari or Coro Big Bug or Animal, clear Lucite body, usually gold-washed sterling	**25.00-200.00**

Designer Costume Jewelry, 1930's–1960's: Pennino, Boucher, Mazer, Jomaz, KJL, Miriam Haskell, older Trifari, Hobe, Hollycraft, Eisenberg, Ciner, Schiaparelli, etc., & unmarked pieces if outstanding **15.00-175.00**
Bakelite, heavily carved, animals, fruit, unusual **20.00-75.00**
Egyptian, imagery **5.00-75.00**
Funny or Whimsical (dancers, fruit, bugs, etc.) **3.00-50.00**
Earrings, very large or very long & hanging **2.00-20.00**
Mexican, large pieces w/excellent craftsmanship **10.00-75.00**
Designer Contemporary Jewelry by: Marci Zelmanoff, M. Laws, M. Barnaby, Pahaka, Georg Jensen, Glenda Arentzen, Sam Kramer, William Harper,
   etc. **20.00-250.00**
Woven Hair Jewelry, 1850–1900, good condition only **10.00-65.00**
Jewelry w/Carved Colored Glass Fruit or Leaves **5.00-65.00**
Compacts w/Chain Handles, older **15.00-100.00**

I am buying vintage costume jewelry and estate jewelry by the piece or box full, signed or unsigned. Certain designers are of special interest: Har, Schiaparelli, and McClelland Barclay.

The Curiosity Shop
P.O. Box 964
Cheshire, CT 06410
(203) 271-0643

We Pay

McClelland Barclay .... **50.00+**
Har Dragons & Genies .... **35.00+**
Corodvettes .... **35.00+**
Gold Rings w/Stones .... **45.00+**
Gold Brooches .... **45.00+**
Lilly Dache .... **50.00+**
Schiaparelli .... **40.00+**
Trifari, sterling .... **75.00+**
Chanel .... **40.00+**
Christian Dior (dated) .... **50.00+**
Corocraft, sterling .... **35.00+**
Mazer, sterling .... **50.00+**
Bakelite Polka-Dot Bracelets .... **100.00+**

I am interested in buying costume jewelry from the mid-1800's to the 1960's. I would also like to buy any small item a lady would carry in her purse such as compacts, perfume bottles, pill boxes, etc. I want mint condition things only.

Beth Nehez
1404 Gordon Rd.
Lyndhurst, OH 44124

We Pay

Rhinestone Pins, unsigned .... **10.00+**
Bracelets .... **10.00+**
Most Signed Pieces .... **15.00+**
Rings, sterling w/stones.. **18.00+**
Compacts... **5.00+**
Older Victorian Jewelry **20.00**

We are currently seeking **Whiting & Davis jewelry circa 1900 through the 1960's**. Please, no snake bracelets. We also want ads for Whiting & Davis jewelry.

Terri & Dennis Lamothe
P.O. Box 40421
St. Petersburg, FL 33743
(813) 343-9100

We Pay

Rings **5.00**
Necklaces.. **15.00**
Pins **10.00**
Bracelets **10.00**
Earrings.. **7.00**
Ads, black & white **2.00**
Ads, color **3.00**
Premiums for Original Tags & Boxes .... **Write**

We would like **signed pieces as well as good older pieces** such as cut crystal, Aurora Borealis or Venetian glass beads; rhinestone brooches, earrings, necklaces, bracelets, etc. We also like cameos, jet glass, pearls, etc. We also want any old or unusual jewelry.

Joyce & Max Knight
101 Victory
Ponca City, OK 74604
(405) 765-5974

We Pay

Miriam Haskell, Eisenberg, Etc. .... **10.00+**
Trifari, Hobe, Kramer, Richter, Robert, Etc. .... **5.00+**
Richelieu, Marvella, Deltah, Faberge, Etc. .... **2.00+**
Castlecliff, Vendome, Hattie Carnegie, Czechoslovakian .... **2.00+**

I want to buy **fine signed and unsigned pieces of costume jewelry** by the following designers. Best condition is appreciated. Highest prices are paid.

Hobe   Coro
Pennino   Jomaz
De Rosa   Ciner
Miriam Haskell Mazer
M. Boucher   Robert De Mario
Trifari

Karyn Shaudis
1370 Southwind Circle
Westlake Village, CA 91361
(818) 377-5298 (3 pm to 9 pm P.S.T.)

We buy jewelry of all kinds: gold or silver, old costume jewelry of any kind, diamonds, rings, necklaces, etc. We also buy old fountain pens, coins, stamp collections, post cards, and anything pertaining to Paducah, Kentucky (i.e., pottery, post cards, books, advertising). We have been in business since 1953 and have a reputation for honesty. Send your items by registered mail for our offer, or call. We are closed Sundays and Wednesdays.

Hoskins Coins, Stamps, & Jewelry
120 S Third St.
P.O. Box 368
Paducah, KY 42002
(502) 442-4531

I collect all types of old jewelry, especially rhinestone costume jewelry. If you've not been happy with the prices you've been offered by dealers, send me your asking price or their offers. I will buy one piece or several pieces, including pieces needing minor repairs. Name brand costume jewelry is nice, but I will consider any well-made piece. No phone calls, please.

Edna Zemites
3543 Lawnview
Corpus Christi, TX 78411

I buy old carved celluloid bracelets, rings, earrings, pins, and children's items. Most often these are stamped 'Japan' on the inside of bracelets or on the back of other items. These usually come in solid colors or in mixed pastel colorations. I prefer only the mixed-colored items. Older items in general have turned a dark cream color on the inside from aging. Most often the carvings consist of roses, daisies, or lily of the valley, as well as leaves. Given below is a sampling of prevailing prices. Children's bracelets and unusual items often bring much more.

Mike Newell
2113 Nottingham
Cape Girardeau, MO 63701

We Pay

Bracelets	20.00-30.00
Rings & Earrings	10.00-15.00
Pins	5.00-10.00
Children's Bracelets or Unusual Items	Call or Write

I am looking for old, odd, and unusual jewelry from the 1920's through the 1960's. Whole estates or single items in good to mint condition are wanted. No beads, pearls, or chains are desired. We are seeking early perfume bottles, flapper belt buckles (metal or Bakelite), and shoe buckles as well. We will pay top dollar commensurate with quantity, quality, and condition. Please send list with description and asking price, also photos if possible. It is impossible for us to list specific prices we are willing to pay for jewelry that is sight unseen. Please also include your phone number with your correspondence.

Tom & Vicky Grams
2767 Lorenzo Ave.
Costa Mesa, CA 92626
(714) 545-1425

After buying and selling costume jewelry for some time now, I have accumulated quite a few pieces that need to be repaired and restored to their original beauty. It is a hobby that I find enjoyable and would like to continue, but I am running short of materials. Therefore I would like to purchase reasonably priced jewelry and related items such as pill boxes, compacts, etc. that are missing stones or are broken. I can also use single earrings for repairs. Especially needed at this time are earrings by Miriam Haskell.

When I find such items, I buy them in bulk — but will consider single items as well. And of course I can also use items needing little or no repair. Please let me know what you have.

Pamela Wiggins
10701 Sabo #202
Houston, TX 77089
(713) 944-7520

We Pay

Bulk Lots .... **4.00+**
Single Items for Repair .... **50¢+**
Single Items in Good Condition .... **1.00+**

JIGSAW PUZZLES

I am buying jigsaw puzzles with outer space scenes on them that are circa through the 1950's. They can be interlocking or frame-tray puzzles. These were children's puzzles that have fictional scenes on them. Some are related to TV programs, and some are generic scenes of rockets, space ships, and space-suited people. Superman puzzles are of special interest. I am also seeking board games, records, and greeting cards of the same description and time period. Listed below are some puzzles I want to find.

Donald Sheldon
P.O. Box 3313
Trenton, NJ 08619
(609) 588-5403

We Pay

Buck Rogers, through 1940's	**45.00+**
Flash Gordon, 1940's	**35.00+**
Captain Video, 1950's	**25.00+**
Rocky Jones, 1950's	**25.00+**
Rex Mars, 1950's	**20.00+**
Rip Foster, 1950's	**20.00+**
Generic Space Scenes, 1950's	**20.00+**
Captain Universe, 1960's	**20.00+**
Jetsons, 1960's	**25.00+**
Lost in Space, 1960's	**30.00+**
Superman, through 1950's	**30.00+**

KENTUCKY DERBY AND HORSE RACING

We are buying Kentucky Derby and Churchill Downs items. We prefer Kentucky Derby glasses prior to 1974. We specialize in single pieces and unique items. Listed below is a sample of the items we buy. Please give us a call or drop us a line for a fast cash offer for your items.

Gardner's Collectibles
Jim & Betty Ann
3110 Tremont Dr.
Louisville, KY 40205-2936
(502) 454-0595

We Pay

Pre-1950 Derby Glasses	**30.00-250.00+**
Pre-1960 Derby Glasses	**20.00-175.00+**
Pre-1974 Derby Glasses	**7.00-25.00+**
1940 Plastic Beetleware Cup	**150.00+**
1940 Derby Shot Glass	**125.00+**
1942 Derby Aluminum Tumbler	**95.00+**
KY Derby Programs	**1.00-15.00+**
Churchill Downs Items	**1.00-15.00+**

Derby Ticket Stubs & Return Checks .... **1.00+**
Derby Tote Tickets .... **1.00-100.00+**
KY Derby Festival Pegasus Plastic Pins, pre-1980 .... **10.00-200.00**
KY Derby Festival Pegasus Metal Pins .... **2.00-100.00+**
Mint Julep Aprons .... **5.00-50.00+**
KY Derby & Horse-Related Swizzle Sticks .... **5¢-1.00+**
Silver & Silverplated Mint Julep Cups .... **5.00-150.00+**
KY Derby Coins & Souvenirs .... **25¢-20.00+**

Thoroughbred horse racing and Kentucky Derby memorabilia are wanted. I have been collecting since 1953 and will pay good prices for unusual and hard-to-get items. I am buying older programs, cigarette cards, post cards, glasses, books, games, photos, prints, plates, and any other items related to thoroughbred racing and the Kentucky Derby. I will consider any item but would like the seller to price it according to what they desire to receive.

Gary L. Medeiros
1319 Sayre St.
San Leandro, CA 94579
(415) 351-6193

We Pay

Pre-1960 Programs **1.00-100.00**
Glasses **5.00-150.00**
Cigarette Cards .... **50¢-20.00**
Post Cards .... **50¢-20.00**
Games **5.00-500.00**
Books **5.00-350.00**

As a private collector, I am seeking any item that relates to the Kentucky Derby. All paper items are needed including programs, books, and advertising items. I especially want pre-1965 Kentucky Derby glasses. If your item is Kentucky Derby related, we would be interested in hearing from you. Send lists with description, condition, and your price. I will respond to all letters. No collect calls please.

Greg Wade
1320 Ethel
Okemos, MI 48864-3009
(517) 349-8688

KEY CHAIN LICENSE PLATES

The specific key chain license plates I am seeking are painted brass with 'B.F. Goodrich' or 'Goodrich Tires & Batteries' embossed on the reverse side. They are approximately 1½" x ⅝", not to be confused with the smaller type in a metal case that was mailed to vehicle owners from 1942 through 1971 by the Disabled Vets for the purpose of soliciting donations. B.F. Goodrich tags were available for 10¢ apiece through promotions held in their stores from 1939 through 1942. Although 10¢ sounds insignificant today, the depression syndrome still hung on, and many people would not freely spend a dime on a key chain license plate.

I am seeking B.F. Goodrich tags from all states for my collection. Prices paid for them vary depending on paint, condition, and rarity (tags from lesser-populated states are scarce). Price guides frequently value these at $15.00 to $20.00 each. Please inquire as to prices paid for specific states and conditions.

Edward Foley
227 Union Ave.
Pittsburgh, PA 15202
(412) 761-0685

KITCHENWARE

I am interested in buying kitchen glassware of the depression years, especially the pieces listed below by **Jeannette Glass**.

Susan Hirshman
540 Main St.
Woodland, CA 95695

We Pay

Canister, Spiral by Jeannette Glass, Coffee or Sugar, Delphite **80.00**
Canister, Spiral by Jeannette Glass, Coffee or Sugar, Jadite **40.00**
Canister, Tea, Delphite **60.00**
Shakers, Sugar, Flour or Paprika, Delphite.. **20.00**
Shakers, Sugar, Flour or Paprika, Jadite **12.00**
Butter Dish, Delphite **80.00**
Butter Dish, Custard... **35.00**
Salt Box, Jadite.. **75.00**
Salt Box, Custard.. **40.00**
Batter Jug w/Lid, Jadite.. **150.00**
Spice Jars, square, Jadite.. **10.00**
Mixing Bowls, black, any size.. **15.00-25.00**
Napkin Holder, black.. **80.00**

I will pay over book value to get **Jeannette Glass Company's canisters (coffee, sugar, flour, tea), salt shakers, and paprika shakers in Delphite blue**. *Kitchen Glassware of the Depression Years*, by Gene Florence, may be useful as reference. I will also pay top dollar for any stoneware, ceramic, or glass rolling pin that I do not have in my collection. No wooden or new rolling pins are wanted. Also bought are **sewing items, colored Victorian glass, and old Christmas collectibles**.

Joan McGee
Rt. 2, Box 36
Mountain Home, AR 72653
(501) 491-5161

I seek **T.G. Green kitchenware china made in England**. Dishes have blue and white stripes that are slightly raised or polka dots that are slightly recessed. The storage pieces (canisters, pitchers, bottles, jars, etc.) often have the contents word printed in black. The mark is a shield under glaze printed in either black or green. They made everything from plates to rolling pins. Pieces must be in mint or near-mint condition. I also buy **flow blue, blue Hall china, and anything else blue and white (graniteware, crockery, fabrics,**

cobalt glass, poison bottles, etc.). Please send photos, prices, and descriptions.

Deborah Golden
Rt. 2, Box 2365A
Grayling, MI 49738

KNIVES

I am interested in buying any and all patterns of old original pocket and hunting knives. I am especially interested in Sunfish or Elephant Toe patterns before 1960. I buy only old knives — no new knives or limited edition knives. Describe pattern, handle material, condition, or ship insured with price wanted.

Robert Lappin
P.O. Box 1006
Decatur, IL 62523
(217) 428-2973

We Pay

Winchester	20.00+
Remington	15.00+
Remington Bullets	200.00+
Cattaraugus	10.00+
Keen Kutter	10.00+
Marble Knives	20.00+
Sunfish	50.00-1,500.00
Elephant Toes	50.00-1,500.00

KITSCH, FROM TURN-OF-THE-CENTURY TO ART DECO

I seek the unusual, strange, and unique pieces from American culture from the turn-of-the-century through the Art Deco period. We can re-wire lamps and smooth up furniture, but we prefer items almost ready to go. Strong quality design is a criterion. We're interested in anything copper, primitive items, or Arts and Crafts items. Adirondack, Art Deco, Kitsch, and western items are of interest. Wanted are utilitarian objects as well as handsome ones. Photos are helpful and will be returned. Measurements of items are requested. We pay UPS on three or more small items ordered. If you're coming to Santa Fe, query by mail or phone so that you may bring us things to buy. We are always interested in networking with mid-country traders and dealers and would be delighted to have your visit.

The Gallery of Antiques
Carol Berge
307 Johnson St.
Santa Fe, NM 87501
(505) 986-1774

Kitsch   **We Pay**

Shell Items (lamps, boxes, Miami Beach souvenirs), lamps need not work, but
    shells must be intact **15.00-25.00**
Tiered Lampshades or Handmade Lampshades............................. **10.00-20.00**
Tramp Art (small items, especially shelves or boxes) .... **Call**

Art Deco Items   **We Pay**

Coffeepots, West Bend 15-cup, aluminum in 2-globe shape w/Bakelite han-
    dles **8.00-10.00**
Clocks, blue mirror, any size in working condition **20.00-25.00**
Toasters, Sunbeam, in working condition **10.00-15.00**
TV Lamps, figurals as such as black jaguar, working condition only.......... **Call**
Plastic Eames Chairs, sets of 2-6, in good condition **30.00-40.00**
Bertoia or Knoll Chairs, each... **50.00**

Western   **We Pay**

Antler Table Lamps **25.00-35.00**
Western Motif Lampshades, any size, clean & intact **15.00- 35.00**
Horn Chairs & Footstools.. **75.00-80.00**

Table Lamps, copper or brass w/western influence	**20.00-45.00**
Prints, Remington or western scene, old & framed	**15.00-25.00**
Tables, made by W.P.A., small	**20.00-35.00**
Ranch Oak or Texas Oak Tables, small	**10.00-20.00**

Miscellaneous   **We Pay**

Odd or Unusual Old Table Lamps, wood or metal	**25.00**
Wicker Chairs or Tables	**50.00-80.00**
Japan Lustreware Tea Sets, for 4-6, matched & complete	**25.00-30.00**
Trunks w/Flat Tops, pre-1915, intact, large or small	**20.00-50.00**
Cedar Chests w/Flat Tops, good condition	**45.00-60.00**

LABELS

As a historian who researches, collects, and writes about western agricultural advertising practices from the 1850's to the present, I am continually seeking anything related to this area. This includes labels, agricultural books and magazines, price cards, etc. from Washington, Oregon, California, British Columbia (Canada), Florida, or elsewhere throughout the U.S. In addition, I collect items relating to San Francisco's many commercial lithographers who created most of this advertising. Some well-known brands would be Sunkist, Skookum, Blue Anchor, Pure-Gold, Del Monte, Libby's, Earl Fruit Co., and Wenoka. Some of the lithographers I'm researching are Schmidt Litho Co., H.S. Crocker, Traung, Mutual, Olsen, Louis Roesch, and others. Outside San Francisco, I seek labels and items from Ridgway (Seattle), Simpson-Doeller (Baltimore), Western (Los Angeles), and Stecher Lithograph (Rochester).

I offer exhibits, lectures, slide shows, informal appraisals, collector information, and other services. I offer a 1991 value guide, detailing over five thousand citrus, apple, and pear labels from the Pacific states. I will buy lots, collections, miscellaneous bulk, or single items. I can help you find a buyer and also offer a collector referral service. Please include SASE with your inquiry or call. I take this work very seriously, so thanks for your help. A sampling of specific items wanted are given below.

Fruit & Vegetable Crate Labels
Salmon & Seafood Can Labels
Fruit & Vegetable Can Labels
Raisin & Dried Fruit Labels, pre-1950
Skookum Dolls
Sunkist Juicers & Extractors
San Francisco City Directories, 1870–1920
Orange, Apple, & Pear Crates w/Labels
Pamplets, Posters, Books from Agricultural Fairs or Shows

Post Cards w/Western Orchards or Farm & Fruit Scenes
Litho Salesman's Samples & Stock Label Books
Posters, Lithographs, Printings, or Agricultural Magazines, 1880–1950's
Old Sheet Music by San Francisco Printers or w/CA Scenes
Blue Anchor Magazine Set, bound, 1924–1950's

I have several unrelated wants as well: **electric race cars, track, and accessories by Aurora, A.F.X., and H.O; piano rolls by Ampico, Duo-Art, or non-QRS; and George Steck upright player pianos (intact)**.

Pat Jacobsen
437 Minton Ct.
Pleasant Hill, CA 94523

LAMPS

I will pay premium prices for unusual or embossed student lamps or cast student lamps by Harvard, Aladdin, or Mammoth, as well as many other lamps, shades, or parts. Please see listings below for other sought-after items. A photograph of your item is helpful.

Lamps

Angle	Sinumbra
Astral	Solar

Banquet
Finger
Gone-with-the-Wind
Hanging
Hitchcock
Moderator
Organ

Store
Student
Syphon
Table
Wall
Wedding

Shades

Angle
Astral
Ball
Cased
Domed
Etched
Gas
Hanging

Pinwheel
Reverse-Painted
Ribbed
Solar
Spider
Student
Tiffany

Parts

Advertising
Bases
Burners
Catalogs
Chimneys
Frames

Founts
Harps
Literature
Shade Rings
Wicks

Del Williard
2707 Arcadia Ave.
Erie, PA 16506
(814) 838-3344

Emeralite lamps and Bellova lamps are bought, sold, and traded. I'm a collector at heart but buy duplicates of pieces I already have to use for trading or resale. I will also buy bases alone, if they are unusual, and parts for Emeralite lamps. Write, sending photos if possible, or call collect evenings or weekends.

Bruce Bleier
73 Riverdale Rd.
Valley Stream, NY 11581
(516) 791-4353

We are paying top prices for lamps and **night lights** in any of the following shapes or figures: monkey, rabbit, dog, owl, parrot, lovebird, flower or fruit basket, or any others made by U.S. Glass or Cambridge Glass Co. We also buy bases and globes for red, green, or yellow satin glass kerosene lamps. Please send descriptions or photos with your asking price.

Wesley & Betty Strain
832 Carson Rd.
Ferguson, MO 63135
(314) 524-5608

LARKIN

As a writer and publisher of material concerning the history and products of the Larkin (Soap) Company (ca 1875 through the 1950's), I am interested in buying all types of Larkin paper and ephemera. I particularly seek Larkin catalogs, calendars, cards, booklets, diecuts, pictures, and letters. Please note: some Larkin paper is only identified by one of their products (i.e.: Sweet Home Soap, Boraxine, White Woolen, Modjeska, Creme Oatmeal, People's Mfg. Co., etc.). I will pay the following prices depending on condition and rarity.

Walt Ayars
Echo Publishing
P.O. Box 279, 307 Third St.
Summerdale, PA 17093

We Pay

Larkin Catalogs & Books **5.00-40.00**
Larkin Calendars **15.00-50.00**
Larkin Diecuts **5.00-35.00**
Larkin Cards, Letters, & Pictures **2.00-10.00**

LAW ENFORCEMENT

I am interested in purchasing single items or collections in the field of crime and law enforcement. Particular emphasis is on badges and items from the early west and midwest through the 1930's. Items relating to gangsters of the 1930's such as Pretty Boy Floyd, Bonnie and Clyde, and the Barkers are of special interest. Please send photocopies and prices.

Antiques of Law & Order
Rt. 7, Box 53A
Mena, AR 71953
(501) 394-2863 (after 5 pm)

We Pay

Badges, solid gold 14K, 10K, etc. .... **100.00+**
Badges, sterling silver .... **25.00+**
Name Badges .... **25.00+**
Other Badges .... **10.00+**
Photos .... **5.00+**
Reward Posters .... **5.00+**
Officers' Weapons .... **50.00+**
Crime-Related Items .... **10.00+**

LICENSE PLATE ATTACHMENTS

I collect cast aluminum license plate attachments also known as crests, piggybacks and add-ons. These attachments were made of a heavy sand-cast aluminum. The purpose of these crests was largely promotional. They were sold for about fifty-nine cents in all tourist meccas. Florida must have been like heaven for the traveling salesman who wrote orders for these crests. It seems every city and beach in Florida had a crest boasting its name and slogan. Examples would be: 'Miami Beach,' 'Land of Sunshine,' or 'World's Playground.' They all seemed to have adornments flanking both sides of the name — for instance, Florida with a palm tree on one side and a sailfish on the other.

I have sufficient 'Miami,' 'Miami Beach,' and 'Florida.' I want attachments from other Florida cities, towns, beaches, as well as cities and towns from other states. I am paying $10.00 to $25.00 depending on rarity and condition. I will also consider broken ones if repairable. Please contact me for prices.

Edward Foley
227 Union Ave.
Pittsburgh, PA 15202
(412) 761-0685

LICENSE PLATES

I am interested in buying **car license plates from different states**. I prefer plates from the 1980's to the present. Plates are wanted in good condition only; I buy whole collections or single pieces and have some I will trade. Different or unusual license plates are of special interest.

Douglas A. Fink
9 Kenalcon Dr.
Phoenixville, PA 19460

_____

One of the most collectible types of **Michigan license plates** are those that were issued for motorcycles. The state of Michigan started making motorcycle plates in 1910, the same year as car plates. Those from 1910 through 1914 were made of porcelain or steel. Plates from 1915 through 1919 were of stamped steel and had an aluminum 'state seal' affixed to the upper left-hand corner. Those from the following years were stamped steel embossed with 'Mich,' the year, and the number. The word 'cycle' wasn't put on motorcycle plates until the 1970's. Motorcycle plates in general are about one-fourth the size of car plates and were even smaller in the 1940's and 1950's. The only cycle plate that was vertical instead of horizontal was the 1924 plate. I will pay the following prices for Michigan motorcycle plates in nice condition. I also pay top prices for all other types of old and unusual Michigan license plates in nice condition.

Walt's Antiques
2513 Nelson Rd.
Traverse City, MI 49684
(616) 223-7386

Porcelain Plates w/only minor rim chips   We Pay

1910	500.00
1911	400.00
1912	300.00
1913	200.00
1914	150.00

Steel Plates   We Pay

1915–1919 w/Aluminum 'State Seal' Attached	125.00-150.00
1920–1929	85.00-125.00
1930–1942	50.00-85.00
1943–1949	20.00-50.00

_____

I collect license plates from all states. The porcelain examples are my favorites, but certain early tin plates are desirable. Some early plates from

Hawaii, Alaska, and various southern states will warrant very respectable prices. Old motorcyle plates made prior to 1960, Presidential Inaugural plates dated 1969 or earlier, plates with low numbers issued to officials, registration disks, and homemade or kit plates are areas of particular interest to me. I will gladly answer all correspondence. Photographs or photocopies will help identify plates. If you have any license plates for sale, I am a serious buyer.

Trent Culp
P.O. Box 550
Misenheimer, NC 28109
(704) 279-6242

LIL' ABNER AND DOG PATCH

Who could forget Al Capp's Lil' Abner, Daisy Mae, Mammy and Pappy Yokum, Sadie Hawkins, and all the other Dog Patch gang who entertained America via the funny paper and comic books for so many wonderful years? Lil Abner is no longer seen in the funnies, but I know he and his associates are still out there in newspapers, comic books, toys, and what-nots.

If you have memorabilia relating to the Dog Patch characters that you want to sell or trade, let's get together. Please state your asking price for one item or your collection.

Kenn Norris
P.O. Box 4830
Sanderson, TX 79848-4830

LINENS

I am interested in buying the fancier grade of old linens from baby bonnets to bedspreads. If you have any old and unusual item in good repair, please let me know. I am always interested in hearing about what you have, whether one piece or many.You may send photos, descriptions, or approval boxes (please drop a note first), and I will return photos, boxes, etc. within three days or send a check for what I keep. If I buy nothing, I pay your postage. A few examples of items I am looking for are listed below.

Jan Spencer
1701 Orange Tree Lane
Redlands, CA 92374
(714) 798-7865

We Pay

Battenburg Pieces	**10.00+**
Crochet, Tatting Scrap Bag	**Your Price**
Red Work Embroidery	**10.00+**
White on White	**10.00+**
Quilts, pieced or appliqued	**50.00+**
Quilt Blocks	**Your Price**
Other Fancies	**Your Price**

I buy good quality lace, linens, and textiles. I'm interested in all types except crochet. I don't buy things with rips or holes, but I can safely and professionally remove stains myself. Price ranges are listed, but exact prices depend upon size and workmanship. The fancier and finer an item, the more it is worth. All letters enclosing a SASE will be answered. I will buy by the piece or box lots.

Pahaka September
19 Fox Hill
U Saddle River, NJ 07458
(201) 327-1464

We Pay

Lace Curtains, older or lace on net	**10.00-75.00**
Other Curtains, older brocade, velvet, etc.	**5.00-50.00**
Lace Bedspreads or Other Large Fancy Spreads	**10.00-75.00**
Pillow Shams, large (prefer fancy)	**5.00-45.00**
Pillowcases, fancy	**3.00-15.00**
Sheets w/Fancy Work	**5.00-45.00**
Tablecloths, w/lace, embroidery, cutwork, etc.	**10.00-75.00**
Tablecloths, banquet size (144" long)	**20.00-100.00**
Tablecloths, large round w/work or lace	**25.00-100.00**
Figural Linens, items w/dancers, cupids, ladies, etc.	**5.00-150.00**
Napkins & Cocktail Napkins, mint condition	**1.00-5.00**
Bridal Veils & Headpieces, 1800's–1930's	**10.00-75.00**
Lace Yardage or Lace Box Lots	**Write**
Lace Collars (no common)	**10.00-75.00**
Yardage of Material, 1800's-1940's	**Write**
Paisley Shawls (see my clothing list also in this book)	**25.00-200.00**
Victorian Needlepoint w/Petitpoint or Beads	**10.00-50.00**

Most antiques originated in Europe, but hand-sewn quilts are one of the few collectibles that are unique to America. Quilts were created by pioneers as practical and pretty decorations to an otherwise humble and sometimes colorless home. Quilts were originally designed with many pieces of solid-color fabric, as printed material was not yet available. There are several hundred patterns of quilts attesting to the imagination and time involved in producing this art of bygone days.

I collect hand-stitched quilts and will pay up to $100.00 for these. Also wanted are woven coverlets, samplers, cross stitch, needlepoint (the more colorful, the better), lace, hankies, linens, crocheted or tatted doilies, tablecloths, napkins, pillowslips, etc. Single pieces or collections with no rips or stains are wanted. Please write with description of the item, your price, and your phone number.

Also wanted are decorative **tole-painted items, Quimper pottery, Belleek china, and cookbooks or booklets.**

Lori Hughes
253 Magda Way
Pacheco, CA 94553

LUNCH BOXES

I am buying metal or vinyl lunch boxes and metal thermoses from 1950 to 1985. Listed below are only some of the ones I am seeking. Prices vary due to condition.

Terri L. Mardis
1104 Shirlee Ave.
Ponca City, OK 74601
(405) 762-5174

We Pay

Jetson's 1963 Dome Top Lunch Box or Thermos	100.00
Bullwinkle or Atom Ant Lunch Box or Thermos	20.00+
Munsters Lunch Box	35.00+
Cartoon Zoo Lunch Chest Lunch Box or Thermos	35.00+
Addams Family Lunch Box	15.00+
Smokey the Bear Lunch Box	15.00+
The Monroes Dome Top Lunch Box	25.00+
Buccaneer Dome Top Lunch Box	25.00+
Rifleman Lunch Box	20.00+
Wild, Wild West Lunch Box	20.00+
Annie Oakley 1955 Lunch Box	18.00+
Lone Ranger 1954–1955 Lunch Box	40.00+
Howdy Doody 1954 Lunch Box	35.00+
Bozo 1963 Lunch Box	35.00+
Paladin Lunch Box	15.00+
Jungle Book Lunch Box	15.00+
Flintstones Lunch Box	15.00+
Superman 1954 or 1967 Lunch Box	25.00+
Supercar 1962 Lunch Box	25.00+
Beatles Lunch Box, any	20.00+
Monkees Lunch Box, any	20.00+
Casey Jones Lunch Box	40.00+

Cable Car Lunch Box .... **40.00+**
Hometown Airport Lunch Box.. **40.00+**

_____

MAGAZINES

    I am interested in all types of paper ephemera, especially items with a visual format. This includes books, advertising items, calendars, photos, prints, posters, magazines, scrap and trade card albums, and catalogues. I am also very interested in collections of old letters and business correspondence from before 1900. Lots of valuable paper items pertaining to business are still being thrown out every day! If you come across large or small amounts of paper goods in an attic, garage, store, or warehouse — please write to us! Even if condition is not good, you may be pleasantly surprised. If it is old and paper, I'm interested. Here are some prices I will pay for old paper items.

Hugh Passow
306 Main St.
Eau Claire, WI 54701

Magazines   **We Pay**

Ladies' Home Journal .... **up to 50.00**

Magazines

McCall's	up to 15.00
Life	up to 25.00
Pictorial Review	up to 35.00
Designer	up to 30.00
Delineator	up to 15.00

Magazines, bound   We Pay

Harper's Weekly	up to 400.00
Leslie's Weekly	up to 100.00
Collier's	up to 100.00
Harper's Bazaar	up to 150.00
Puck or *Judge*	up to 150.00

Other Paper   We Pay

Trade Card Albums	up to 150.00
Scrap Albums	up to 100.00
Books of Old Store Receipts	up to 100.00
Old Store Receipts, loose	Write
Collections of Old Letters	Write

Here are just a few of the magazines I buy. Please quote your asking price for any that you have to sell that were printed before and up to about 1960. I buy any quantity. Prices below are for clean, complete magazines. In many cases I buy coverless issues as well. This is just a partial listing. I buy many others and those with other dates as well. These are just my minimum prices.

Bob Havey
P.O. Box 183
W Sullivan, ME 04689
(207) 422-3083

We Pay

Ladies' Home Journal, 1910–1920's	10.00
Vanity Fair, 1910–1920's	10.00
Vanity Fair, 1930's	4.00
Vogue, 1910–1920's	10.00
Vogue, 1930's	5.00
Pictorial Review, 1910's	8.00

Pictorial Review, 1920's	5.00
Harper's Bazaar, 1910-1920's	10.00
Woman's Home Companion, 1910's	8.00+
Esquire with Varga Foldouts, 1940's	12.00
Saturday Evening Post, 1910-1920's	4.00+
Saturday Evening Post, 1930's	2.00
Cosmopolitan pre-1921	3.00+
Cosmopolitan, 1921-1932	4.00+
Good Housekeeping, pre-1921	3.00+
Good Housekeeping, 1921-1932	4.00+
Good Housekeeping, 1933-1939	2.00
Movie Magazines, 1930's	5.00+
Movie Magazines, 1940's	4.00+

Pulp Magazines, 1910-1930's   **We Pay**

Horror	15.00+
Mystery	8.00+
Weird	10.00+
Detective	3.00+
Western	1.00+

Wanted: *Life* magazines from 1936 to 1960. Especially wanted are top star or baseball covers. Many, many other magazines besides those listed below are wanted (car, movie, sports, news, men's, etc.). They must be in fine condition with no clipped or missing pages or any major damage.

Glen Arvin
P.O. Box 107
Celestine, IN 47521

                                                     We Pay

Life, 1930's	1.00
Life, 1940's	75¢
Life, 1950's	50¢
Life, *Time*, or *Newsweek* w/Baseball Covers, 1930's or 1940's	5.00+
Life, *Time*, or *Newsweek* w/Baseball Covers, 1950's	3.00+
Esquire or *Fortune*, 1930's or 1940's	3.00+
Street-Smith, 1950's	10.00+
Sport or *Sports Illustrated*, 1940's-1960's	50¢-25.00
Teen Magazine, pre-1970	1.00+

Magazines

Other Teen or Music Magazines, pre-1970 .... **1.00+**
Playboy, Dec. 1953 issue, Dec. 1954 issue, or Jan. 1955 issue .... **25.00+**
Playboy, Dec. 1953 issue .... **250.00+**

I am always buying magazines needed to complete my collection. **Sporting magazines** are my main interest. *Field & Stream* before 1920, *Outdoor Life* before 1922, and *Sports Afield* before 1932 are especially wanted. I will pay $3.00 and up for *Ducks Unlimited* before 1973. I also collect **Smokey the Bear memorabilia.**

Thomas McKinnon
P.O. Box 86
Wagram, NC 28396
(919) 369-2367

We Pay

1930's **4.00**
1920's **5.00**
1910's **5.00-10.00**
1900's **8.00-12.00**
1890's .... **20.00+**

I wish to buy **Cream of Wheat ads in color** from *Needlecraft Delineator, Pictorial Review, Ladies' Home Journal, Woman's Home Companion*, etc., from 1900 through early 1925. I will pay $2.00 each for ads or $3.00 for the complete magazine in good condition.

Carol J. Beattie
3374 Ver Bunker Ave.
Port Edwards, WI 54469

The Railway Mail Service is a member of the American Philatelic Reasearch Library as well as other philatelic societies that study postal markings and history. As with most philatelic libraries, the principal efforts are being directed toward organizing and cataloging the collection. To expand the coverage and variety of materials available for the use of postal historians, I also seek to purchase or swap documents which pertain to post office operations.

There is a wide spectrum of **postal artifacts** that we are interested in finding. Listed below are prices for periodicals that are clean, complete, and show only minor wear. For specific items, please write to the Rail Mail Service Library with a complete description. Send a #10-size SASE for a free set of illustrated want lists of all postal artifacts wanted. Also, I will provide free, direct referrals to other collectors if someone writes me about a postal item and it happens to be something I do not collect; so finders and pickers should use me as a first point of reference for these items. Because my work requires extensive travel, please allow two weeks for a reply.

Dr. Frank R. Scheer, Curator
Railway Mail Service Library
12 E Rosemont Ave.
Alexandria, VA 22301-2325

We Pay

Post Haste, all issues	50¢
Postal Service News, all issues	25¢
Postal Life, all issues	10¢
R.M.S. Bugle, Railway Mail, single issue, all dates	4.00
R.M.S. Bugle, Railway Mail, bound volume, all dates	50.00
Harpoon, single issue, all dates	1.00
Harpoon, bound volume, all dates	20.00
Railway Post Office, 1949–1940, single issue	25¢
Railway Post Office, 1939–1930, single issue	35¢
Railway Post Office, 1929–1920, single issue	50¢
Railway Post Office, 1919–1910, single issue	1.00
Railway Post Office, 1909–1899, single issue	2.00
Railway Post Office, 1949–1899, bound issues	Write
The Postmark (Canadian), prior to 1940, single issue	2.00
The Postmark (Canadian), 1941–1950, single issue	1.00
The Postmark (Canadian), 1951–1960, single issue	60¢
The Postmark (Canadian), 1961–1970, single issue	50¢
The Postmark (Canadian), pre-1940–1970, bound issues	Write
The Transit Postmark, 1940's–1950's, single issue	1.00
The Transit Postmark, 1940's–1950's, bound volumes	20.00
The Transit Postmark Collector, H.P.O. Notes, 1950's–1970's, single issue	10¢
The Transit Postmark Collector, H.P.O. Notes, 1950's–1970's, bound issue	5.00
Journal of the T.P.O. & Seapost Society, single issue, all dates	25¢
Journal of the T.P.O. & Seapost Society, bound issue, all dates	10.00
High-Railer (AmeRPO), prior to 1960, single issue	25¢
High-Railer (AmeRPO), 1960 to end, single issue	10¢
R.M.A./N.P.T.A. Branch Newsletter, prior to 1950, single issue	50¢

R.M.A./N.P.T.A. Branch Newsletter, 1951–1960, single issue .... **40¢**
R.M.A./N.P.T.A. Branch Newsletter, 1961–1970, single issue .... **25¢**
R.M.A./N.P.T.A. Branch Newsletter, 1971 to end, single issue .... **10¢**
The Traveler (Great Britain), all issues **3.00**
The Post Office Magazine (Great Britain), prior to 1940 .... **2.00**
The Post Office Magazine (Great Britain), 1941–1950 .... **1.00**
The Post Office Magazine (Great Britain), 1951–1960 .... **75¢**
The Post Office Magazine (Great Britain), 1961–1970 .... **60¢**
The Post Office Magazine (Great Britain), 1971 to date .... **50¢**

I am a collector interested in purchasing small **pocket-sized magazines**. They usually are 4" x 6" in size. Magazines must be in near-mint condition and date from 1948 until 1968. I pay 50¢ to 75¢ each depending on quality and quantity. Listed below are some titles wanted.

Bold	*Inside*	*Sensation*
Brave	*Male Life*	*She*
Brief	*News*	*Show*
Carnival	*People*	*Slick*
Celebrity	*Picture Life*	*Swank*
Dare	*Picture Week*	*Star*
Exclusive	*Point*	*Tempo*
Fame	*Pose*	*That Girl*
Focus	*Preview*	*Topps*
Glance	*Pulse*	
He	*Quick*	

I also collect *Modern Man* magazines from 1953 until 1970 in near-mint condition and will pay $2.00 to $10.00 each.

Charles F. Nardi
1400 Craneing Rd.
Wickiffe, OH 44092
(216) 944-6536

I am purchasing **all magazines published exclusively for Blacks**. I want any magazine from 1969 and earlier and will buy a single magazine or hundreds!

Jerry Bland
P.O. Box 6205
Kinston, NC 28502
(919) 522-5377

Magazines for Blacks   **We Pay**

1960's .... **2.00+**
1950's .... **3.00+**
1940's .... **4.00+**
1930's .... **6.00+**
1920's & earlier .... **7.00+**

As a long-time dealer in new and out-of-print sporting books, the past decade has been spent in accumulating what well may be the nation's largest stock of outdoor magazines. Our stock includes magazines on hunting, fishing, hunting dogs, archery, guns, gun collecting, and related subjects. If you are interested in purchasing magazines, let us know which titles you want, and we will send you a priced listing of them. Similarly, we are in the market for old sporting periodicals. I am interested in purchasing the materials listed below.

American Rifleman, 1923-1930
Arms & the Man, all issues
Handloader Magazine, 1966 to date
Rifle Magazine, 1969 to date
Recreation, 1888-1920
Outdoor Recreation, Outer's Recreation, Hunter-Trader-Trapper, Outer's, Outing, 1800's–1949
Fly Fisherman, The American Fly Fisher
Gun Dog, early issues
Sporting, any prior to 1900
Gun Digest, #1 through #10
Stoegers Shooters Bibles, 1924–1950

Highwood Bookshop
P.O. Box 1246
Traverse City, MI 49685
(616) 271-3898

I am buying *Life* magazine (2 copies) from August 8, 1955. I will pay $5.00 and up.

Alice E. Marson
1667 Glenmount Ave.
Akron, OH 44301
(216) 724-1887

MAGIC

I eagerly seek magic memorabilia of all types, particularly paper relics of magic's 'golden age' (1890 through 1920). Prices paid will depend on scarcity, historical significance, content, and condition of the item. It is almost impossible to list suggested prices here without seeing a particular item. So call or write, and we can talk specifics. Depending on the item, I might go below or above the ranges listed here. A free swap list is also available to other magic collectors.

Ken Twombly
5131 Massachusetts Ave.
1-800-673-8158 or (301) 320-2360

We Pay

Vintage Posters	25.00-500.00
Houdini Posters	500.00+
Other Houdini Items	5.00-500.00
Other Children's Magic Sets	25.00-125.00
Magic Books	5.00-500.00
Scrapbooks of Magicians	20.00+
Photos & Articles Dealing with Magic	5.00+
Prints & Engravings of Magicians	10.00+
Magic-Themed Premium Items	5.00+
Magicians' Sheet Music, Pin-backs, You-Name-It	10.00+

MARBLES

Private collector is buying old marbles and related items. I am looking for quality sulphides, Lutz, swirls, onionskins, clambroths, and unusual marbles.

Also wanted are awards, medals, and trophies from marble tournaments or contests. Photos are appreciated. Marbles must be of first quality and not polished or reproduced.

Lynn Christian
P.O. Box 22
Ames, IA 50010
(515) 232-2222

I am interested in any handmade glass marble in mint condition only. Please send a photo and give the size — the bigger the better!

Don R. Williams
150 E Lakeview Ave.
Columbus, OH 43202
(614) 261-8549

We Pay

Slag w/Pontil Marks... **30.00+**
Sulphides .... **40.00+**

Clambroths .... **50.00+**
Clouds .... **50.00+**
Onionskins .... **50.00+**

MASONIC MEMORABILIA

    I want to buy for my collection any Masonic, Knights Templar, Scottish Rite, Shriners, Eastern Star, or other related organization memorabilia. Items wanted are pins, medals, badges, books, paper items, or gold, silver, and plated jewelry. Older items are preferred, but I will consider items of any age. I also collect Kansas merchant tokens, 'good for' tokens, memorabilia from Kansas State Agricultural College (K.S.A.C.), and older items from Manhattan, Kansas. Coins, tokens, and related items from other places are also considered. Please write with a description of your item.

David Sies
P.O. Box 522
Manhattan, KS 66502

MATCH SAFES

I am an advanced collector interested in purchasing quality pocket match safes. I collect all categories including figural, advertising, sterling, enameled, and combination types. I am interested in one or an entire collection. Please send picture and/or description along with requested price. Listed below are some of the items I am interested in purchasing.

George Sparacio
P.O. Box 139C
Newfield, NJ 08344

We Pay

Advertising, celluloid wrapped	**40.00+**
Arm & Hammer, gutta percha	**50.00+**
Art Nouveau, sterling	**55.00+**
Enameled, on brass, French type	**125.00+**
Enameled, on sterling	**135.00+**
Knapsack, tin	**10.00**
Oriental, brass	**130.00**
Pabst Beer, brass	**30.00**
Pants, figural, pewter	**75.00**

Match Safes

President Cleveland, figural, plated brass.. 175.00
President McKinley, figural, plated brass... 175.00
Skull, figural, brass or white metal 100.00
Tartan, go-to-bed 125.00

MEDICAL MEMORABILIA

    We have been buying **rubber syringe outfits, hot water bottles, bulbs, enamel can irrigators, etc.** for the past several years. Pre-1965 items are wanted, whether common or unusual. Please send in 'as is' condition. Items may be boxed or or unboxed. Related items such as books, films, manuals, magazines, photos on use, accessories (especially those made of hard black rubber), boxes, instructions, catalogs, etc. are wanted as well. Listed below are samples of items and prices paid. If your item is not listed here, write for a price. Prices will vary with the item's condition.

Brunswick
P.O. Box 9729
Baltimore, MD 21204

We Pay

Rubber Fountain Syringes, Folding & Combination Syringes **12.00-25.00**
Rubber Bulb Syringes (adult or infant) **5.00-15.00**
Enamel Can Irrigators **12.00-35.00**
Pewter & Hard Rubber Antique Syringes... **Write**

Rubber Hot Water Bottles **5.00-20.00**
Accessories (clamps, tubing, hard rubber fittings, etc.) **1.00-10.00**
Old Wooden Dovetailed Syringe Boxes **8.00-25.00**
Old Wooden & Cardboard Syringe Boxes w/Contents 'As Is' **20.00-50.00**
Related Books, Manuals, Magazines, Photos, Etc. **5.00-25.00**
Related Instructional Films, 16mm, 35mm or 8mm (basic nursing, treatments
    & procedures, home nursing, baby & child care) **10.00-20.00**

I am buying **early medical and quack medical devices and scientific items from the 1800's to the 1920's**. Listed below are some of the items I am interested in finding.

Richard Cane
8391 NW 21st St.
Sunrise, FL 33322
(305) 741-6838

We Pay

Violet Ray Machines .... **20.00+**
Induction Coil Type .... **15.00+**
Hand-Crank Type .... **100.00+**
Whimhurst Rotating Glass Disc Type .... **100.00+**
Microscopes .... **50.00+**

I buy any type of **antique veterinary medicine memorabilia** including old animal medicine bottles and tins, advertising signs and calendars, store display cabinets, trade cards, pamphlets, puzzles, giveaways, surgical instruments, balling guns, portable stable medical cases, etc. Anything relative to Dr. Daniels, Dr. Claris, Dr. Lesure, Pratts, Humphrey, etc., is wanted as well.

Susan Genecco
4410 Lakeshore Dr.
Canandaigua, NY 14424
(716) 394-9188

We Pay

Dr. Daniels Medicine Cabinets .... **400.00+**
Dr. Daniels Paperweight .... **150.00+**
Pratts Medicine Cabinets .... **400.00+**
Pratts Wheel of Success Game .... **25.00+**

Militaria

I am buying **WWI military items** from the 1914 through 1918 war. I am particularly interested in items from the **American Ambulance Field Service and the French Foreign Legion**. The types of items I am looking for are uniforms, helmets, insignia, documents, medals, ambulance plates, etc. — practically anything which would be related to these two volunteer groups. Please let me know if you have anything in this area. I will pay generous prices for such items.

Dennis Gordon
1246 N Ave.
Missoula, MT 59801
(406) 549-6280

I am interested in buying any material which was connected with the **9th and 10th U.S. Cavalry or the 24th and 25th U.S. Infantry or any Black militia, local military, lodge, or fraternal groups**. I am interested in any photos or books showing Black soldiers in uniform. I will buy one piece or an entire collection. Some typical prices are listed below. I will pay higher prices for unusual items or for items in excellent condition. I will buy any and all items connected with the groups wanted — no matter what it is.

David L. Hartline
P.O. Box 775
Worthington, OH 43085

We Pay

9th & 10th U.S. Cavalry Hat Insignia **25.00**
24th & 25th U.S. Infantry Hat Insignia **20.00**
Identified CDV Photos **40.00**

Identified Tintype Photos **50.00**
Identified Paper Photos **45.00**
Outside Group Photos.. **85.00**
9th & 10th or 24th & 25th Uniforms, complete....................... **150.00**
Civil War Discharge Papers **75.00**
Military Discharge Papers 1870–1920...................................... **50.00**
Military Equipment, marked to these units **50.00**
Identified Civil War Swords.. **250.00**
Black Regimental History Books **60.00**

I am looking for **German and Japanese military items prior to and through WWII**. Especially wanted are edged weapons, medals, or uniform parts (helmets, tunics, visor hats, etc.). Listed below are some of the items I seek with prices I will pay.

Tom Winter
817 Patton
Springfield, IL 62702
(217) 523-8729

We Pay

Japanese Samurai Swords.. **100.00+**
German S.S. Daggers .... **100.00+**
German Medals .... **25.00+**
German Helmets... **30.00+**
German Tunics.. **40.00+**
German Visor Hats.. **35.00+**

Uniform insignia of R.O.T.C. units from high schools, colleges, and universities are needed for my collection. Also needed are the same types of items from private military schools. These are distinctive insignia or crests and are of the enamelled type worn on the shoulder loops of the uniform or in some cases on the coat lapels. I will pay up to $5.00 for these for my collection. If you have this type of insignia and are unable to determine their exact identity, please feel free to send me a sketch or photocopy of the item, and I will identify it for you. I also have other insignia for sale or trade.

Arthur J. Grau, Jr.
1935 Quincy Ave.
Racine, WI 53403

We collect **military badges (insignia)**. Distinctive insignia are usually enamelled and multicolored, often with a scroll reflecting a motto or other logo. These abstractions from a unit's coat of arms were first authorized in 1922, and there are several thousand varieties.

Although we are willing to pay from $1.00 to more than $100.00 for an acceptable piece, we cannot make an offer or accept an asking price until we are fairly sure of the item's identity and condition. We buy one or more pieces. If you do not know the unit that your insignia represents, describe it as best you can. Mention whether or not there is a scroll (logo), color composition, pertinent charges (e.g., animal, star, arrow, etc.), and severity of any defects (e.g., cracks, gouges, scratches, smudges, etc.). If you have an asking price, please state it.

Albert E. Baker
2776 41st Ave.
San Francisco, CA 94116

Wanted from your attics: all kinds of **German, U.S., and Japanese militaria of WWI and WWII**. We pay postage both ways. Listed below is a sampling paid for German items.

Dora Lerch
P.O. Box 586
N White Plains, NY 10603

We Pay

Daggers	**20.00-500.00**
Swords	**20.00-500.00**
Lugers	**250.00-1,000.00**
Badges	**5.00-1,000.00**
Documents	**5.00-150.00**

I am buying military items of all types. I prefer **medals, hats, emblems, insignia, and all types of small collectibles.** Military items from all wars are wanted. Also purchased are **guns, swords, knives bayonets,** etc. Send a description and list any make, name, or marking on the item, and a quote to buy will be given. Items must be seen to be evaluated.

C.E. Packer III
5614 Lyons View Dr.
Knoxville, TN 37919
(615) 588-9399

We Pay

German Daggers, reproductions .... **25.00+**
German Daggers, originals... **75.00+**
M.P.-38s or M.P.-40s... **500.00+**
P.-38s .... **100.00+**
Lugers .... **200.00+**

As a veteran of this war, I am collecting **any and all items from the Korean War**. Listed below are some of the items I seek. I will pay fair prices plus UPS charges. Write, describing the item, and include your price.

Special Unit Patches (K.M.A.G., etc.)
Awards (all orders)
Flags or Banners (North or South)
Cigarette Lighters w/Crests
Photographs
Souvenirs
Unit Items

Edward B. Smith Sr.
2541 S State
Springfield, IL 62704
(217) 744-4201

I am a collector buying **trench art and shell art**. I will buy anything made out of shell casings or plane skins. Any amount will be bought, and I will travel anywhere for large collections. Trench art items of interest include vases, lamps, letter openers, airplanes, hats, powder and stamp containers, shaving and drinking mugs, lighters, ash trays, pipe racks, tumblers, flatware, displays, matchbox holders, picture frames, watch bands, cigarette cases, anything! I pay $150.00 and more for larger items and those with extra-fine detail or silver inlay. Average buying prices are $10.00 to $50.00. Plain shells are not wanted.

Gene J. Oakley
2614 York Rd.
South Bend, IN 46614
(219) 233-7783

Mississippi — we are always buying **military and non-military items from or about Camp Shelby**. Please send price and description or photocopy. The price paid depends on the item and its condition. The following are only a few of the items we are interested in buying.

Post Cards
Brochures
Photographs
Unit Histories
Souvenirs
Propaganda Leaflets
WWII Correspondence (U.S. soldiers & German POW at Camp Shelby)
Fringed 'Mother' Pillows

Treasure Hunt
416 Walnut St.
Hattiesburg, MS 39401

Nazi, German and Japanese items are especially wanted. Nazi uniforms, helmets, books, flags, band instruments, silver, porcelain, gorgets, swords, daggers, standards, presentation items, plaques — nearly anything German with a swastika is wanted. Large accumulations are welcomed. Also wanted are Japanese flags, uniforms, swords, and other militaria items. Please describe and be sure to include your price.

Kurt Miller
Box 331
Cedarburg, WI 53012-0331

MIRRORS

I am seeking brass hand-held mirrors with porcelain scenes of flowers, cupids, ladies, etc., on the back. The handle of the mirror should unscrew so the glass can be replaced. Porcelain decoration should be perfect. I will pay your asking price.

Andra Behrendt
6321 Joliet Rd.
Countryside, IL 60525

MISCELLANEOUS

I have been both a collector and a dealer since 1971. I buy, sell, trade, and consign items and run estate, house, and garage sales. I clean attics as well. Listed below are items I'm seeking that are pre-1970. Please price your item for resale. I spend several months in Florida, but mail is forwarded.

Robin's Nest
P.O. Box 549
Syracuse, NY 13201

Pre-1970 Collectibles   **We Pay**

Advertising Signs (metal, paper, or neon)	up to 50.00
Black Americana	up to 50.00
Cartoon Glasses	up to 30.00
Cartoon, Comic, Cowboy, Space, & TV Character Items	up to 50.00
Firefighting Items ($200.00 for 2-color Lantern)	up to 30.00
Holiday Items (even artificial trees from Germany)	up to 50.00
Knick-Knacks	Write
Metal Lunch Box & Thermos	up to 50.00
Musical Instruments	up to 25.00
Railroad Items	up to 50.00
Scouting Items	Write
Viewmaster Reels	Write
Erotica	up to 25.00
Funeral Home Items (embalming tables, examining tables, etc.)	up to 50.00
Jewelry & Furs	up to 50.00
Medical Quack Machines, Instruments, Skulls, Etc.	up to 50.00

Taxidermy.. up to 100.00
Odd, Unusual, Strange, & Gaudy Items .... **Write**

MISSION FURNITURE

I am always interested in buying Mission furniture by Gustav Stickley, Limbert, Roycroft, and others. I prefer pieces with the original finish intact. Not all pieces are signed, so you should check before you sell something that could be an original. Below are some of the prices I will pay for items in good shape. I also buy hand-hammered copper, sterling, and brass, as well as art pottery from the same period.

Keith Browne
P.O. Box 1592
Rockford, IL 61104
(815) 398-7137

We Pay

Gustav Stickley Wastebasket .... **650.00+**
Gustav Stickley Bookcase, 2-door .... **2,000.00+**
Gustav Stickley Morris Chair .... **2,500.00+**
Gustav Stickley Settle (Sofa) .... **3,000.00+**
Limbert Stand, trapezoidal cutout .... **800.00+**
Limbert Library Table, square cutouts............................... **1,200.00+**
Limbert Bench, square cutouts, single seat....................... **1,500.00+**
Roycroft Side Chair, 1 slat... **350.00+**
Roycroft Bookshelf, tapering... **2,000.00+**
Roycroft Lamp w/Helmet Shade .... **800.00+**
Roycroft Table Lamp .... **1,500.00+**

MOTORCYCLES

Collecting motorcycles is a relatively new hobby. Generally speaking, enthusiasts are young and old, and most are mechanically oriented. We appreciate the artistry involved in the manufacture of pre-1970 motorcycles. I am interested in purchasing motorcycles and related items from 1895 to the late 1970's. I will consider any American or European make (no Japanese). I like original (not repainted) motorcycles best — but I will consider all, running or not running, incompete or only parts in any condition. Also wanted are sidecars, scooters, unique home-built motorcycles, and steam motorcycles built prior to 1970. The following is a partial list of makes I would be interested in buying.

Ariel	Indian
BMW	Matchless
BSA	Norton
Crocker	Royal Enfield
Cushman	Simplex
Excelsior	Triumph
Harley Davidson	Whizzer

I also buy new or old stock parts, tools, used parts, clothing, memorabilia, etc. Since there are a great many related items I am interested in, I can only give a general list.

Service Manuals	Kidney Belts
Repair Manuals	Boots
Dealer Literature	Breeches
Advertising Items	Scarf Hats
Posters	Riding Caps
Photographs	Gloves
Tank Badges	Jackets
Lapel Pins	Uniforms
Oil Cans	Tool or Saddle Bags

I will buy large collections or will broker the same or will buy only one piece. I have years of experience, and references are available. If writing, please send a complete description of the item (including its age and condition) and a picture, if possible, along with a SASE. Please feel free to call for information.

Bruce Kiper
Ancient Age Motor Co.
21301 Coakley Lane
Land O'Lakes, FL 34639
(813) 949-9660

MOVIE MEMORABILIA

I pay the higest prices for movie posters, lobby cards, 1-sheets, glass slides, window cards, etc. Please send me photos, photocopies, or lists including film title, star, date (if any), condition, and dimensions. I will give a prompt response and will pay cash.

Dwight Cleveland
1815 N Orchard St. #8
Chicago, IL 60614-5136
(312) 266-9152

Lobby Cards (11" x 14")   We Pay

Casablanca 1,000.00
Blond Venus 750.00

Window Cards (14" x 22")   We Pay

Frankenstein 1,000.00
King Kong 950.00

1-Sheets (27" x 41")   We Pay

Dracula 2,000.00
Flying Down to Rio 1,500.00

Snow White **1,250.00**
Wizard of Oz **2,200.00**

3-Sheets (41" x 81")   **We Pay**

Robin Hood **2,500.00**

Wanted: Movie star covers on *Look*, *Time*, *Newsweek*, and other news-type magazines. Many pre-1960 movie magazines are wanted. Of special interest are covers of Marilyn Monroe, Elvis, John Wayne, Gale Storm, Shirley Temple, Lucy, Judy Garland, Mickey Rooney, Dick Clark, Bobby Darin, Joan Collins, Jayne Mansfield, Mamie Van Doren, Lili St. Cyr, Irish McCalla, Brigitte Bardot, Sophia Loren, Roy Rogers, Gene Autry, etc. I will pay $3.00 and up for most issues with these stars on their covers. Magazines all about a particular star from the '50s as well as from other years are wanted. Please contact me if you have any western magazines on stars, any Hollywood annuals, yearbooks, or who's who type magazines, movie posters, lobby cards, pressbooks, or stills. Magazines and related items need to be in nice condition with uncut pages and no major damage. Below is an example of some of the magazines sought with prices I pay.

Glen Arvin
P.O. Box 107
Celestine, IN 47521

                                                                        We Pay

Look w/Marilyn Monroe Cover, 1950's .... **5.00+**
Look or *Time* w/Hopalong Cassidy Cover, 1950 .... **10.00**
Any Movie Magazine w/James Dean Cover, 1950's **15.00**
Magazines w/Patti Page Covers, 1950's **5.00**

I am buying movie posters and lobby cards from 1900 through 1960, from one piece to a thousand or more. All the various sizes are wanted: one-sheet (27" x 41"), window card (14" x 36"), 3-sheet, 6-sheet, etc. I am also looking for studio annuals, exhibitor's books, motion picture heralds, and other movie-related ephemera.

Sam Sarowitz
23 E 10th St.
New York, NY 10003
(212) 477-2499

I'm a collector of old movie memorabilia. My main area of interest centers about movie trade publications including both studio publicity books and magazine publications. These date from the 1900's to the 1940's. Both hardcover and softcover books were used to describe and picture upcoming movies from each of the various studios such as M.G.M., Paramount, etc. Some were very colorfully illustrated, while others were not. I'm interested in all of these publications. Write or call if you have any material related to the above. I also trade for my wants. Prices quoted are conservative.

George Reed
7216 Kindred St.
Phil., PA 19149
(215) 725-3003

We Pay

Happy Omen for Happy Showman, Fox, 1931–1932	100.00
Your Lucky Star, M.G.M., 1930–1931	125.00
Parade of Hits, M.G.M., 1926–1927	125.00
Greater New Show World, Paramount, 1930–1931	100.00
Advertising the Motion Picture, Quigley Pub., 12½" x 9½"	125.00
Pathe, 1930–1931	100.00
Paramount 15th Birthday Group, 1926–1927	125.00
United Artists, 1926–1927	100.00

MUSICAL INSTRUMENTS

The tradition of the organ grinder and his monkey can be traced back hundreds of years to Europe. Early immigrants brought the organ-building trade with them, and the organ grinder was a familiar sight in many American cities in days gone by. It was often the only live music heard by working-class people.

I am an organ grinder and help to keep this tradition alive today. I collect **monkey organs and virtually anything old that depicts or is related to organ grinders**. The value of an old organ depends greatly upon its origin and condition. Following are prices that I will pay for organs that are working. I pay similar prices for organs that are not playing but have no missing parts. I pay less for organs that are broken or incomplete.

Hal O'Rourke
Box 47
Lanexa, VA 23089
(804) 966-2278

Organs
We Pay

25 Keys or Less	**2,000.00+**
35 Keys or Less	**3,000.00+**
More Than 35 Keys	**5,000.00+**

Related Items
We Pay

Post Cards, any type	**1.00-10.00**
Trade Cards	**3.00-10.00**
Sheet Music	**1.00-10.00**
Prints	**5.00-50.00**
Etchings	**10.00-100.00**
Statues or Figures	**10.00-500.00**

We are interested in buying **all unrestored mechanical musical instruments**. Our prices are flexible and depend upon the condition of the individual instrument.

Dell Urry
920 Jewell Ave.
Salt Lake City, UT 84104
(801) 972-3197

We Pay

Player Pianos	**350.00+**
Reproducing Pianos	**1,000.00+**
Music Rolls	**1.00+**
Other Instruments	**Call or Write**
Record Players	**50.00+**
Advertising Fliers	**1.00+**

NILOAK

We buy Niloak pottery and Ouachita pottery — both swirl and glazed pieces. Prices paid are determined by the height of the item and are calculated by giving a price per inch. I will also buy Niloak animals; glazed animals are $12.00 to $15.00.

Pat Monton
2326 Willow
Portland, TX 78374
(512) 643-5843

	We Pay
Swirl Niloak, 1" through 10" tall, price per inch	10.00
Swirl Niloak, 10" tall or taller, price per inch	15.00-20.00
Glazed Niloak, per inch in height	2.00-3.00
Ouachita, per inch in height	10.00

NORTH DAKOTA POTTERY

I am interested in North Dakota potteries such as W.P.A. nursery figurines and Rosemeade pottery. Please also see my listing under Rosemeade in this book.

George P. Williams
R.R. 1, Box 24
Cleveland, ND 58424

W.P.A. Nursery Rhymes	We Pay
Little Jack Horner	200.00
Little Miss Muffet	200.00
Tom Tom the Piper's Son	200.00
Jack Be Nimble	200.00
Humpty Dumpty	200.00
3 Little Pigs & Bad Wolf	200.00
Little Red Riding Hood & Wolf	200.00
Old King Cole	200.00
Little Mouse Brown	200.00
Little Boy Blue	200.00
Other W.P.A. Nursery Rhymes	75.00-200.00

NOVELTY ITEMS

I am buying the following novelty-type items in good to mint condition.

The Boxed, Locket Dollars: These were made by using 1873–1879 U.S. trade dollars. They are hinged and open like a locket, often holding a picture. They are also made using 1892–1893 Columbian half dollars.

The Mini-Pinfire Guns: These were made between 1800 and 1900 in Austria and Germany, and between 1930 and 1950 in Japan. Some may be found as tie tacks or cufflinks. Most are 1½" to 1¼" long and shoot a mini-pinfire blank cap-type cartridge.

Send a full description, photocopy, and price of the item.

John Rex
P.O. Box 6384
Lynnwood, WA 98036

We Pay

Boxed, Locket, Trade Dollar	**65.00+**
Boxed, Locket, Columbian Half Dollar	**80.00+**
Mini-Pinfire Austrian Derringer	**25.00+**
Mini-Pinfire German Derringer	**25.00+**
Mini-Pinfire Japan Derringer, Revolver, or Rifle	**20.00+**

NUTCRACKERS

I am an advanced collector of nutcrackers and am always in the market for unusual items. I prefer cast iron or brass figural nutcrackers in the shape of animals or people. These normally have a lever to crack the nut between two moving parts, usually the mouth. Mechanical nutcrackers are of interest also. Serrated jaws actuated toward each other through some sort of mechanical movement perform the goal of cracking a nut. I would appreciate hearing from anyone with nutcrackers for sale as described.

Earl E. MacSorley
823 Indian Hill Rd.
Orange, CT 06460
(203) 387-1793

NUTS AND BOLTS

I am in the process of accumulating nuts and bolts-related items. I want jewelry, promotional items, old wooden boxes, and other antique storage containers. I am paying the following for perfect-condition items. I'll buy almost anything related to the fastener industry that is pre-1960. Pre-1900 things command the highest prices you can imagine.

Melvin Kinsmer
726 Deal Ct.
San Diego, CA 92109

We Pay

Tie Pins	2.00+
Cuff Links	2.00+
Earrings	2.00+
Tape Measures	3.00+
Knives	2.00+
Wooden Box, sides printed only	5.00+
Storage Cabinets, prior to 1920	200.00+
Circular Bins	200.00+

OCEAN LINERS

I am buying ocean liner memorabilia and prefer pre-1920 material, especially nineteenth century top-marked china and silverplate. I'm interested in all categories of shiplines — rivers, lakes, coastal, and transatlantic/transpacific, as well as cups and saucers from modern freighter lines. I also buy material relating to the S.S. Normandie and books illustrating house flags as well as shipline histories. Prices vary with condition and age, but here are some examples of prices I pay.

Karl D. Spence
108 Rue D'Azur
Slidell, LA 70461
(504) 649-5653

We Pay

1904 or 1912 Lloyd's House Flag Books	**75.00**
19th-Century Top-Marked China	**50.00+**
S.S. Normandie Interior Booklets	**35.00+**
S.S. Normandie Menus	**15.00+**
White Star Line China	**50.00+**
White Star Line Silverplate Hollowware	**50.00+**
Pre-1900 Passenger Lists	**10.00+**
Pre-1900 Interior Booklets	**30.00+**
Pre-1900 Silverplate Hollowware	**50.00+**

With the turn of the century and the advent of new forms of sea travel and luxury on the high seas, great ocean liners such as the Titanic, the Olympic, the Queen Mary, the Elizabeth, and the U.S.S. United States came into being. They all claimed to be the fastest and to have the ultimate in gracious accommodations.

These vestiges of the past are part of our heritage, and items related pictorially or otherwise are part of our collecting interest. We are anxious to obtain any item related to sea travel prior to 1940. I am looking for items from the following categories.

E.S. Radcliffe
3732 Colonial Lane SE
Port Orchard, WA 98366

We Pay

Ship Cards .... **2.00+**
Menus .... **2.00+**
Baggage Labels .... **2.00+**
Souvenirs .... **2.00+**
Flatware .... **2.00+**
Dinnerware .... **3.00+**
Travel Brochures **2.00-10.00**
Travel Posters .... **10.00+**
Linens .... **3.00+**
Pictures .... **1.00+**
Candy Tins .... **7.00+**
Ship Models .... **5.00+**
Ship Toys .... **5.00+**
Books .... **2.00+**
Passport Covers .... **3.00+**
Pins .... **5.00+**
Tickets .... **5.00+**
Match Covers .... **1.00+**
Match Boxes .... **1.00+**
Ash Trays .... **2.00+**
Badges .... **5.00+**
Medals .... **5.00+**

OLYMPIC GAME MEMORABILIA

We are buying Olympic game memorabilia. We buy quality, good condition items either individually or as a collection from any Olympiad, winter or
summer. Material prior to 1976 is preferred. We are also interested in any
unusual or unique Olympic souvenir item. Listed below are some of the
things we are seeking.

John & Virginia Torney
P.O. Box 2387
Huntington Beach, CA 92647

We Pay

Athlete Award Medals .... **1,000.00+**
Torches .... **400.00+**
Diplomas .... **100.00+**

Athlete Participation Medals.. **90.00+**
Official Badges .... **50.00+**
Official Reports .... **50.00+**
Commemorative Medals... **30.00+**

PAPERWEIGHTS

We are buying glass paperweights. We prefer paperweights from the 1840's through the 1970's, whether a single piece or a collection. We like paperweights from all over the world, from both factories and artists. Listed below are some of the paperweights we would like. Any old or unusual paperweight is wanted as well.

Joyce & Max Knight
101 Victory
Ponca City, OK 74604
(405) 765-5974

Antique   **We Pay**

Baccarat, St. Louis, or Clichy .... **100.00+**
Whitefriars or Bohemian .... **75.00+**
American or English .... **50.00+**

Contemporary   **We Pay**

Factory (St. Clair, Zimmerman, Degenhart, etc.)..................................... **10.00+**
Stankard, Kaziun, Trabucco, Banford, Ysart, Etc. .... **100.00+**

I am buying antique glass paperweights circa 1845 through 1900. French, American, English, and Bohemian types are sought. Types desired are mille-fiori, flowers, sulphides, fruit, animals, etc. I don't mind some surface wear, small nicks, etc. Large chips may be a problem. Please describe condition when you write to me.

I pay anywhere from $50.00 to $1,000.00 and up depending on rarity, size, and condition. I will purchase collections of paperweights of all types if at least part of the collection consists of the antiques mentioned above. Send a close-up, distinct photo of each paperweight, if possible, or at least an accurate description of your item. Indicate size, condition, price, etc. State whether or not you wish photos returned. I reply to all correspondence.

Tom Bradshaw
325 Carol Dr.
Ventura, CA 93003

_____

We are interested in purchasing all top-quality antique and contemporary glass paperweights, particularly French weights from the classic period, 1845 through 1870. We pay $50.00 to $50,000.00 depending on maker, beauty, rarity, and condition. We are interested in single items and entire collections.

The Dunlop Collection
P.O. Box 82370
Phoenix, AZ 85071-2370
(800) 227-1996
(602) 995-3550

_____

PATTERN GLASS

238

I am seeking pattern glass in the **Colorado** pattern. I prefer Dewey blue (cobalt) or green with the gold flashing and beading. However, I would consider amethyst flashed or ruby stained, with or without the gold. Also wanted is **King's 500** (not King's Crown) pattern of early pattern glass in Dewey blue (cobalt) with gold. This is illustrated in Heacock's book *Victorian Colored Pattern Glass*, on the cover and page 37. Pieces wanted are cruets, syrups, butter dishes, spooners, covered sugars, toothpicks, oil lamps, footed bowls, perfume bottles, etc. I will pay market values and up for items. I am a private collector. These items will not be resold.

Jean E. Carlson
2982 Mission St.
San Francisco, CA 94110

I am buying **old pattern glass with historical significance**. Pieces have animal, people, fish, or bird motifs. Absolutely no reproductions will be accepted. Listed below are some examples.

Gerald S. Oswald
R.R. 1, Box 112
Aurora, NE 68818

We Pay

Colored Log Cabin	50.00-500.00
Dragon	20.00-200.00
Fiery Opalescent Monkey	40.00-500.00
Gibson Girl	10.00-100.00
Jumbo	40.00-400.00
Fighting Cocks Covered Dish	250.00+
Two Black Boys Bathing Covered Dish	400.00+
Indian Chief Tan Creamer	100.00+
Frosted U.S. Coin 1892	38.00-500.00
Original Chocolate Slag Animals Dishes	100.00+
Hanging Bust Match Holders	50.00+
Child's Turtle Covered Dish	300.00+

I am buying early American flint and non-flint pressed glassware. Some items of particular interest are listed below.

Calvin L. Hackeman
8865 Olde Mill Run
Manassas, VA 22110
(703) 368-6982

Hawaiian Lei (non-flint) by Higbee | We Pay

Water Tumbler	25.00+
Square Compote	50.00+
Candlesticks	75.00+
Lamp	75.00+
Banana Stand	50.00+
Mug	25.00+
Cup & Saucer	20.00+
Square Plate	20.00+
Covered Round Compote	30.00+
Octagonal Compote	40.00+
Square Covered Honey	30.00
Goblets, except cordials	30.00+
Champagne Glasses	35.00+
Castor Set	100.00+
Bread Tray	25.00+
Ice Cream Set	100.00+
Platter	35.00+
Sugar Cover	15.00+
Water Pitcher	50.00+
Water Tray	30.00+
Syrup	75.00+
Sanitary Toothpick	40.00+
Cruets	45.00+
Punch Bowl	85.00+
Punch Cup	25.00+
Any Piece in Color or Carnival	Call

New Hampshire (Bent Buckle) | We Pay

Covered Sugar	20.00+
Spooner	15.00+
Biscuit Jar, covered	60.00+
Carafe	45.00+
Celery Vase	25.00+
Compote, large	35.00+
Water Goblet	20.00+
Milk Pitcher	60.00+
Water Pitcher, bulbous, ¾-gallon	70.00+
Plate	10.00+

Relish Tray .... **15.00+**
Water Tumbler .... **15.00+**
Flared Wine.. **20.00+**
Lemonade Cup .... **10.00+**
Custard Cup .... **10.00+**
Any Piece w/Ruby Stain.. **25.00-200.00+**

New Jersey   We Pay

Water Bottle .... **40.00+**
Cake Stand .... **40.00+**
Covered Compotes .... **40.00+**
Cruet.. **40.00+**
Butter Dish on High Standard .... **50.00+**
Water Goblet .... **25.00+**
Dinner Plate, 8" .... **10.00+**
Salt & Pepper Shakers.. **25.00+**
Syrup... **70.00+**
Wine Goblet .... **30.00+**

Virginia (Galloway)   We Pay

Basket .... **60.00+**
Water Bottle .... **25.00+**
Rectangular Bowl.. **20.00+**
Waste Bowl .... **20.00+**
Cake Stand .... **45.00+**
Champagnes.. **40.00+**
Celery Vase.. **40.00+**
Covered Compote .... **50.00-90.00+**
Cracker Jar **100.00**
Egg Cup .... **20.00+**
Water Goblet .... **45.00+**
Jelly, handled .... **15.00+**
Lemonades .... **20.00+**
Mug.. **20.00+**
Pickle Castor .... **50.00+**
Pitchers, other than medium tankard .... **40.00-60.00+**
Plates .... **15.00-25.00+**
Rose Bowl.. **20.00+**
Salt Dips .... **15.00+**
Squatty Salt & Pepper Shakers .... **25.00+**
Footed Sherberts .... **12.00+**
Covered Sugar Bowls.. **25.00+**
Sugar Shaker .... **25.00+**
Water Trays .... **50.00+**

Pattern Glass

Teepee   We Pay

Stemware, other than champagnes .... **10.00-20.00+**
Wine Decanter/Carafe .... **35.00+**
Water Pitcher .... **45.00+**

Balder   We Pay

Water Pitcher .... **25.00+**
Covered Sugar .... **20.00+**
Spooner .... **15.00+**
Salt & Pepper Shakers .... **45.00+**
Toothpick .... **20.00+**
Covered Butter .... **30.00+**

Punch Cups (pressed glass)   We Pay

Alabama .... **20.00+**
Lion's Leg .... **25.00+**
Big Diamond .... **25.00+**
California (Beaded Grape) .... **20.00+**
Connecticut .... **20.00+**
Dakota, etched or plain .... **20.00+**
Florida Palm .... **15.00+**
Florida Herringbone .... **20.00+**
Illinois .... **20.00+**
Louisiana .... **25.00+**
Maine .... **15.00+**
Maryland .... **15.00+**
Mississippi (Magnolia) .... **25.00+**
Missouri .... **20.00+**
Nebraska (Bismark) .... **15.00+**
Nevada .... **15.00+**
New Jersey .... **25.00+**
Ohio .... **20.00+**
Oregon (Beaded Loop) .... **20.00+**
Tennessee .... **20.00+**
Texas .... **15.00+**
Utah (Twinkle Star) .... **15.00+**
Vermont, any color .... **20.00+**
Late Washington .... **15.00+**
Early Washington .... **25.00+**
Wyoming (Engima) .... **20.00+**

Dakota (Fern & Berry)   We Pay

Water Pitcher .... **50.00+**

Covered Sugar .... **40.00+**
Spooner .... **30.00+**
Salt & Pepper Shakers... **45.00+**
Cruet .... **45.00+**

Other Patterns   **We Pay**

Carolina Water Tumblers.. **15.00+**
Illinois Candlestick, ea .... **25.00+**
Loop & Petal Compote/Vase, canary, flint .... **200.00+**
Other Colored Flint Pieces (salts to candlesticks)...................... **20.00-250.00+**

I am a serious collector of pattern glass. I collect the following patterns: **Westmoreland (Gillinder), Palm Leaf Fan (Bryce), Two Panel (Richards & Hartley) in amber, Moon & Star (many companies), and Geneva Custard in red and green.** I especially need the following pieces and will pay fair retail values for them.

Covered Compotes (except Moon & Star)
Lamps (all)
Wines (all)
Pitchers & Creamers (all)
Odd-Shaped Bowls (all)
Salt & Pepper Shakers (pairs)
Covered Cheese (Westmoreland)
Cracker Jar (Westmoreland & Palm Leaf Fan)

Mugs (all)
Tumblers (all)
Honey Dish (Westmoreland)
Plates (Westmoreland & Palm Leaf Fan)
Covered Sugar Bowl (2 pieces)
Sauce Dishes (all)
Odd Lids & Stoppers

Robert E. Boal
503 E Alder St.
Oakland, MD 21550

PEANUT BUTTER PAILS

Wanted: early tin peanut butter pails. I will pay $100.00 and up for mint tins with children, animals, movie stars, cartoon characters, or great graphics. Please send a photo.

Donald R. Williams
150 E Lakeview Ave.
Columbus, OH 43202
(614) 261-8549

PERSONALITIES

As a serious collector and fan of **Andrew Stevens**, son of actress Stella Stevens, I am willing to pay for items about him and of him. This includes articles or photos of him from magazines and books, 'live' photos or pictures from professional photographers, scrapbooks about him, scripts, autographed items, and addresses as to where to write him. Sought are items from his birth in 1955 — which may include his mother, Stella — to the present. Prices will be negotiable due to various items offered. Photocopies of articles or photos are very helpful.

Pamela M. Schott
10 Longview Dr.
Newark, DE 19711
(302) 368-5984

PHOENIX GLASS

I am reasearching the Phoenix Glass Company of Monaca, Pennsylvania, in an effort to write a detailed and accurate history of the company since its beginning in 1880. Besides recording the story of this great glass company, the resulting book would be a tribute to my grandfather, who was a glass blower at Phoenix from the 1920's until the 1950's.

Over the years, Phoenix has produced a wide variety of utilitarian and decorative glassware, including art glass by Joseph Webb, colored cut glass, gas and electric light shades, hand-decorated Gone-with-the-Wind style oil lamps, hotel and barware, pharmaceutical glassware, and their line of Sculptured Artware vases, bowls, etc., for which they are best known among collectors today. Lighting glass has been their main product since the beginning.

Besides the items already listed, I am especially hunting original company catalogs and advertising brochures, magazine ads showing Phoenix glassware, and anything else which will provide positive identification of the glassware that Phoenix produced. I'd also like to hear from retired Phoenix employees and other people who are willing to share their knowledge and love of Phoenix glass with me. Mini-biographies of 'the Phoenix family' will be included in my book.

The price I can pay varies, depending on the pattern, color, and condition of each item. Please price and fully describe each item. Photos are always helpful. I answer all letters and will reimburse you for postage and photos. Listed are specific patterns and items I am hunting.

Strawberry, 2-part console bowl & candle holders
Pine Cone, vase (does not have actual pine cones)
Bachelor Button, vase
Water Lily, candle holders
Primrose, vase
Zodiac, vase
Thistle, vase, 18" (except plain milk glass)
Dancing Nymphs, dark blue or other color on crystal, especially 17¾" platter
    or triangular candle holders (Note: dealers sometimes call this pattern
    Dancing Nudes)
Ormolu, any piece in fancy metal framing
Reuben Line or Selden Line (these have small orange oval stickers w/black
    lettering, found on Sculptured patterns)
Vollenden Ware, circa 1890–1910 (usually milk glass w/hand-painted scenes
    or portraits, Phoenix name stamped in block letters on base)
Ruba Rombic, fish bowl, vaseline glass with Phoenix in raised letters
Joseph Webb, art glass made 1883–1894 (Mother-of-Pearl, Diamond Quilted
    satin glass, etc.)
Original Catalogs or Brochures
Phoenix Ads From Trade Journals or Magazines
Book, *Pennsylvania Glassware 1870–1904*, by Pyne Press
Post Cards of Monaca, PA (usually circa 1890–1917)

Kathy Kelly
1621 Princess Ave.
Pittsburgh, PA 15216
(412) 561-3379

PHONOGRAPHS

We will purchase Victor Automatic Orthophonic phonographs and other huge-size phonographs such as Capehart, etc. We are paying $300.00 each and up, depending on the model and its condition. A few of the model numbers we wish to purchase are listed below.

No. 8-30
No. 9-40
No. 9-54
No. 9-55
No. 9-56
No. 10-35
No. 10-55

This is a sample of model numbers; others are wanted as well. We buy Victor Models 5-horn and 6-horn phonographs and are paying $500.00 each and up. We also buy many other types of horn phonographs with outside horns. Phonograph and radio combinations will be considered as well. We will purchase individual items or large collections. Please see our listings under 'Player Pianos' and 'Coin-Operated Machines' in this book for additional wants.

Our catalog, *A.M.R. Publishing Company Jukebox*, lists over 400 different jukebox and service manuals, radio and phonograph instruction manuals, player piano and organ service manuals, etc. It is available from us for $2.00. However, you need not buy our catalog for us to be interested in your item or collection.

A.M.R. Publishing Company
P.O. Box 3007
3816-168th Place NE
Arlington, WA 98223
(206) 659-6434
FAX (206) 659-5994

We Pay

Victor Models I through IV, outside horn.................................... **150.00-800.00**

Edison Diamond Disk	**100.00-600.00**
Edison Amberola Models 50 through 75, cylinder	**100.00-400.00**
All Outside Horn Styles	**100.00-2,000.00**
Capehart	**300.00-1,500.00**
Victor Orthophonica Models 10-50, 8-30, 10-35, or others	**200.00-1,200.00**
Victor Automatic Orthophonic Types	**Call or Write**
Columbia Gramophone in Elaborate Cabinet	**Call or Write**

We are collectors of **outside horn phonographs, disk music boxes, paper roll organs, and slot machines.** We also buy incomplete or broken machines or parts plus any advertising or books on the above subjects. Original condition brings top money, but we are interested in all machines.

Jack Brown
193 Roselawn NE
Warren, OH 44483
(216) 394-3201

We Pay

Phonograph, Victor VI, wooden horn	**3,000.00**
Phonograph, Victor V, wooden horn	**2,500.00**
Phonograph, Edison Opera, wooden horn	**3,000.00**
Music Box, Regina, 15½" double comb	**4,000.00**
Music Box, Regina, 15½" changer	**15,000.00**
Player Accordion, Hohner	**2,000.00**
Nickelodeon, Seeburg L	**4,000.00**

I am buying **early outside horn, cylinder, and disk phonographs in excellent condition.** Examples of prices paid are below.

Richard Cane
8391 NW 21st St.
Sunrise, FL 33322
(305) 471-6838

We Pay

Edison Cylinder	**250.00+**

Columbia Cylinder & Disk.. 250.00+
RCA Victor Disk .... 350.00+

PHOTOGRAPHICA

SARONY,   686 BROADWAY.
BUFFALO BILL

Charles has been buying old photographs for the past twelve years. His interests are American subjects from the 1800's to the early 1950's. Only original photos (no reprints) in excellent condition are purchased. When writing, please indicate subject, size, condition, identifying markings, any known historical information, and type of photo (tintype, CDV, cabinet card, real-photo post card, etc.). A photocopy is essential in evaluating the photograph's desirability. Items sent on approval will not be accepted. In the listings below, items marked by (+) indicate those subjects for which only photos from before the early twentieth century are wanted.

Charles L. Haffield.
1411 S State St.
Springfield, IL 62704

We Pay

Civil War Soldier Tintype	25.00
Civil War Solder CDV	10.00
Abe Lincoln CDV	12.00
Horace Greeley CDV	12.00
U.S. Grant CDV	10.00
Grover Cleveland Cabinet Card	8.00
Benjamin Harrison Cabinet Card	7.00
William Jennings Bryan Cabinet Card	8.00
William McKinley Cabinet Card	7.00
Black Person Tintype	9.00
Black Person Cabinet Card	7.00
Fireman Tintype	15.00
Fireman Cabinet Card	10.00
Fire Company Cabinet Card or Real-Photo Post Card	8.00
Lawman w/Badge Tintype	12.00
Lawman w/Badge Cabinet Card	10.00
American Indian Tintype	15.00
American Indian CDV or Cabinet Card	10.00
Baseball Player Tintype	15.00
Baseball Player Cabinet Card	12.00
Baseball Player Real-Photo Post Card or Regular Photo	4.00
Baseball Team Real-Photo Post Card or Regular Photo	10.00
Child w/Toy Tintype	10.00
Child w/Toy Cabinet or Any Other Type	5.00
Meat Market Interior or Exterior (+)	6.00
Telegraph Office Interior or Exterior (+)	6.00
Country Store Interior or Exterior (+)	5.00
Dry Goods Store Interior or Exterior (+)	5.00
Western Town Street Scenes w/People (+)	4.00
Circus Parades (+)	4.00
War Scenes w/Blimps	4.00
Non-Soldier Subjects w/Guns (+)	3.00

I am looking for those old pictures in your attic! Please use the following list as a guide. Subject matter determines price.

Daguerreotypes: very small or large portraits, unusual poses in any size, any exterior scenes, post-mortems.

Ambrotypes: anything unusual.

Cartes de Visite or Tintypes: military, political, exteriors, people with photographic items, toys, tools — anything different!

Stereoviews: early cards (these are larger and flatter than the curved gray ones usually seen).

Daguerreotype Cases: hard plastic, inlaid mother-of-pearl, or cases with a stereoviewer built in.

I will be glad to answer any questions. Top prices paid for the right item.

Robin Doty
7407 W Ridge Rd.
Brockport, NY 14420
(716) 637-7181

I am buying old photographs (1800's to early 1900's) and prefer American (5" x 7" or larger, mounted on cardboard) interior or exterior views of stores, shops, saloons, businesses, factories, street scenes, etc. I especially want pre-1920 family photos showing children with toys, decorated Christmas tree views or other holiday decorations, family outings, etc. I will also buy any variety of stereoview cards and photo (black and white) post cards but prefer American. I will pay premium prices; but price depends on condition, subject, and quantity in a lot. Please ship items for courteous, fast offer and payment. I'll reimburse your postage. Thank you!

Mr. Joseph F. Loccisano
2264 Nicholson Square Dr.
Lancaster, PA 17601

Collector buying hand-tinted photographs signed 'Frederick Martin' would prefer matted scenes of California missions, exteriors, and landscapes in excellent condition. Also wanted are other early California photographs circa 1850 to 1940. Prices paid depend on condition, subject, and desirability.

William L. Thompson
P.O. Box 4333
Carlsbad, CA 92008

I am interested in all types of paper ephemera, especially items with a visual format. This includes books, advertising items, calendars, photos, prints, posters, magazines, scrap and trade card albums, and catalogs. Please write to us describing your item even if the condition is not good.

Hugh Passow
306 Main St.
Eau Claire, WI 54701

We Pay

Albumen Outdoor Scenes.. 10.00+
Tintype Occupational .... 15.00+
Daguerrotypes Occupational .... 50.00+
Trade Catalogs, pre-1940's... 5.00+

PICKLE CASTORS

Pickle castors were a popular piece on the Victorian table. They consist of a decorated, silverplated frame that held either a fancy, clear pressed-glass insert or a decorated art glass insert and a pair of silverplated tongs. I prefer pieces in very good to excellent condition; glass jars must be mint. A close-up photo is most helpful. Prices can range from $50.00 to $750.00. I will make offers and answer all replies.

Bill Sinesky
7228 McQuaid Rd.
Wooster, OH 44691

PIE BIRDS

I avidly collect pie birds (pie funnels) and would like to enlarge my collection of the older pie birds of the U.S., England, and other countries. Also, I write a newsletter for pie bird collectors and would appreciate any photos or information you may be willing to share. I am seeking pie vents such as Donald Duck, Dopey, birds trimmed with gold paint, pink canary, seal, advertising pie funnels, the Pie Boy, Gaucho, etc. I will pay up to $50.00 or higher, depending on condition.

Lillian M. Cole
14 Harmony School Rd.
Flemington, NJ 08822
(908) 782-3198

PLAYER PIANO AND PLAYER ORGAN ROLLS

The first roll-playing machines were small hand-cranked organettes. These either played by means of a wooden cob with pins sticking out or by paper rolls. Around 1896 the Aeolian Company introduced a paper roll-playing organ. This early model played by means of a 44-note paper roll with end flanges that had pins sticking out to fit in the slot of the player. Later models played by means of 58-note rolls, and more elaborate models were introduced at a later date, mainly the Aeolian-Duo-Art Pipe Organ, and these played 116-note rolls. Wurlitzer and others also manufactured various roll-playing organs.

The first roll-playing devices for player pianos were built into a machine that was pushed up to a piano and had many fingers sticking out to play the keys. These early roll-playing machines used 65-note rolls with pin ends. Shortly after the turn of the century, the roll-playing mechanisms were installed within pianos by many manufactuers. These first models also played 65-note pin end rolls — many other models were introduced that played rolls of all sizes. Around 1912 an agreement was reached to make most rolls 11¼" wide. These early machines played the piano without expression; most were foot pumped. In 1906 M. Wlete introduced a new type of system that incorporated full expression by means of extra punched holes at each end of the paper rolls. The Ampico followed around 1912 and the Duo-Art at about the same date. Some other manufacturers introduced players with limited expression. With the great depression that began in October 1929, most player piano companies folded. After that, few other models were introduced until about the 1960's, when a few companies again began to produce player pianos that played 88-note rolls without expression.

We are willing to purchase most types of piano rolls except 88-note rolls. We will pay from $3.00 and up each.

We purchase most jukeboxes from 1900 to 1960. We pay $300.00 to $6,000.00.

We are paying $2,000.00 to $12,000.00 and up for Mason-Hamlin and Steinway Grand player pianos. We purchase roll-playing nickelodeons and pay $2,000.00 to $15,000.00 for these. Our price paid for original player piano, organ, or jukebox literature (brochures, photos, etc.) is $3.00 and up each. Please also see our listings under 'Coin-Operated Machines' and 'Phonographs' in this book.

A.M.R. Publishing Company
P.O. Box 3007
3816-168th Place NE
Arlington, WA 98223
(206) 659-6434
FAX: (206) 659-5994

POLITICAL ITEMS

Political buttons of all kinds, new and old, are collectible; but the most desirable are the celluloid-coated pin-backs ('cellos') produced between the 1890's and the 1920's. Many of these are attractively and colorfully designed, which enhances their value as historical artifacts. Most but not all buttons since then have been produced by lithography directly on metal discs ('lithos').

Collectors generally favor presidential buttons — especially picture pins from 1960 or earlier. 'Jugates' featuring presidential and vice-presidential candidate photos are even more desirable, but there are numerous other specialties within the hobby including state and local, third party, and 'cause' types.

Value depends on scarcity, historical significance, design, and condition — buttons with cracked celluloid, deep gouges or scratches, and/or rust-colored stains ('foxing') are not collectible. Reproductions exist, and many are marked as such; but a certain amount of expertise is needed to distinguish real from fake.

Although my own specialty is celluloid state and local buttons from 1925 or earlier, I am interested in purchasing all kinds of buttons in nice, clean condition only. Send me a clear photocopy of whatever you have, and I will either make an offer to purchase or, if not, give an informal appraisal. I will respond promptly to any and all inquiries, whether one button or a thousand. Prices below are for picture pins unless stated otherwise.

Michael Engel
12 Truehart Dr.
Easthampton, MA 10027
(413) 527-8733

Presidentials, 1896–1960   **We Pay**

Alton B. Parker, James Cox, John W. Davis .... **20.00+**
Theodore Roosevelt, Woodrow Wilson, Herbert Hoover........................ **10.00+**
William J. Bryan, William McKinley, Charles E. Hughes, Truman (all) ... **5.00+**
W.H. Taft, Harding, Coolidge, Al Smith, Willkie, Landon, F. D.R., J.F.K.,
    smaller pins .... **up to 5.00**

W.H. Taft, Harding, Coolidge, Al Smith, Willkie, Landon, F.D.R., J.F.K.,
  larger pins.. **5.00+**
Name Buttons, 1896–1932 .... **up to 10.00**

Third Party   We Pay

Socialist, Communist, Prohibition Candidates............................... **10.00-50.00**
Eugene V. Debs.. **35.00+**

State & Local   We Pay

Early Celluloid Pins for Governor, U.S. Senator, or Congress **2.00-25.00**
Other Early State & Local .... **up to 10.00**

Cause   We Pay

Early Labor Union Items... **5.00+**
Civil Rights or Vietnam **2.00-10.00**

I'm a private collector of **political campaign buttons as well as older advertising buttons and miscellaneous political items**. I will pay top prices for single items or an entire collection. Send a photocopy of what you have, and I will send my offer by return mail; or send your price, and I'll send a check by return mail. You may call nights and weekends or write. Listed below are a few items I seek and the prices I pay.

Ronald E. Wade
229 Cambridge
Longview, TX 75601
(903) 236-9615

                                                                  We Pay

Davis-Bryan Word Pin .... **50.00+**
Davis-Bryan Photo Pin... **350.00+**
Draft Bush US Senate Word Pin... **200.00+**
Eugene Debs Convict Pin.. **500.00+**
Eugene Debs Pennants, Posters, Etc. .... **100.00+**
FDR w/Young LBJ Photo Pin... **500.00+**
Garfield Collar Box .... **75.00+**
Honest Days w/Davis Teapot Dome Pin .... **400.00+**
James M. Cox Photo Pin, from 1920.. **75.00+**

Political Items

James Cox w/FDR Photo Pin .... **2,000.00+**
JFK for U.S. Senator Poster .... **200.00+**
JFK for Vice President Photo Pin **400.00**
JFK/LBJ Photo Pin .... **15.00+**
Lincoln Campaign Ribbons .... **200.00+**
Lincoln Tintype Photo Medal Pins .... **100.00+**
McGovern Pin w/Barbara Streisand Photo .... **100.00+**
McKinley or Bryan 'Soap Babies' .... **25.00+**
McKinley or Bryan Photo Umbrellas .... **150.00+**
McKinley/Teddy Roosevelt Photo or Dinner Bucket Pins .... **50.00+**
McKinley Mechanical Gold Bug, Flag, Etc. .... **50.00+**
Teddy Roosevelt w/Hiram Johnson Photo Pin .... **1,000.00+**
Teddy Roosevelt in Rough Rider Uniform Pin, small .... **15.00+**
Teddy Roosevelt in Rough Rider Uniform Pin, 1¼"+ .... **50.00+**
Teddy Roosevelt Rough Rider Bandanas .... **50.00+**
Teddy Roosevelt Rough Rider Beer Trays .... **100.00+**
Truman/Barkley Photo Pins .... **75.00+**
William Jennings Bryan Mechanical Silver Bug, Etc. .... **50.00+**
Woodrow Wilson 'Man of the Hour' Photo Pin .... **150.00+**
19th-C Presidential Campaign Flags .... **100.00+**

From 1840 until the appearance of celluloid buttons in 1896, American voters showed support for Presidential candidates and their platforms by wearing sulphide brooches, ferrotype pins, mechanical badges, silk ribbons, and other lapel devices. I am looking for nice quality examples of **nineteenth century political memorabilia**. The sample buying prices listed are for the more common varieties in undamaged condition. Scarcer candidates and artifacts will naturally bring higher prices.

Larry Leedom
7217 Via Rio Nido
Downey, CA 90241

We Pay

1840 W.H. Harrison Log Cabin Brooch	500.00
1840 M.Van Buren Portrait Brooch	1,500.00
1844 J. Polk Portrait Ribbon	600.00
1848 L. Cass Portrait Ribbon	2,500.00
1856 Buchanan/Breckinridge Portrait Ribbon	1,200.00
1860 Lincoln/Hamlin Jugate Portrait Ribbon	3,500.00
1860 S. Douglas Portrait Ribbon	2,400.00
1864 G. McClelland Portrait Ribbon	2,000.00
1868 U.S. Grant Ferrotype Pin	150.00
1872 Grant/Wilson Jugate Pin	750.00
1872 H. Greeley Ferrotype Pin	400.00
1876 R.B. Hayes Ferrotype Pin	200.00
1880 Hancock/English Jugate Pin	750.00
1884 Blaine/Logan Jugate Pin	150.00
1884 Cleveland/Hendricks Wooden Medallion	100.00
1888 Harrison/Morton Jugate Pin	100.00
1896 McKinley/Hobart Mechanical Flag Pin	200.00

I'm interested in **all Presidential campaign items from 1948 and earlier**. It's difficult to list prices for individual items since a plain and common pin may sell for $5.00, while an unusual one of the same candidate may sell for $50.00. If interested in selling your item, write or call, and we will decide on the best way to proceed.

Dave Beck
P.O. Box 435
Mediapolis, IA 52637
(319) 394-3943

Political Items

Pin-Back Buttons   We Pay

Lincoln Ferrotype .... 125.00+
McKinley/Teddy Roosevelt.. 10.00-100.00
Teddy Roosevelt Rough Rider 50.00
William Jennings Bryan... 10.00-100.00
Cox, picture 100.00
Wilson/Marshall .... 15.00+
Hoover, picture .... 15.00+
Truman For Judge 200.00

Miscellaneous Items   We Pay

License Attachments.. 10.00+
Ribbons.. 20.00+
Bandanas .... 30.00+

I am always looking for **Richard M. Nixon** related materials to add to America's largest Nixon collection. Sought are Eisenhower-Nixon, Nixon-Lodge, Nixon-Agnew, and Watergate-related items. A photocopy and a price are essential. SASE brings a response to every offer. No paper items are wanted, please. What do you have?

Eldon J. Almquist
975 Maunawili Circle
Kailua, HI 96734

                                                                 We Pay

Pin-Back Buttons .... 50¢-100.00+
Jewelry .... 2.00-25.00+
Medals or Coins .... 2.00-50.00+
Toys or Novelties... 5.00-100.00+
Ceramics or Glassware.. 5.00-25.00+
Textiles.. 5.00-25.00+
Inaugural or White House .... 10.00-50.00+
Anti-Nixon or Watergate .... 2.00-25.00+

I am interested in **rare and unusual presidential campaign items** — buttons, ribbons, banners, posters, bandanas, post cards, torches, canes, etc. I also collect campaign items of **Tennessee gubernatorial and senatorial races**.

Peggy A. Dillard
P.O. Box 210904
Nashville, TN 37221

We Pay

Post Cards, issued by the Nashville Tennessean, ca early 1900's, feature TN
  Politicians.. **35.00+**
Poster, I Am a Man, Memphis, ca 1968 .... **100.00**
Campaign Ribbons, Bob (Welcome Bob) & Alf Taylor (Our Alf) for
  Governor.. **200.00**
Button, F.D.R. & Lyndon Johnson together... **1,000.00**
Teddy Roosevelt Cane **150.00**
Poster, William Jennings Bryan w/octopus **500.00**
Buttons of the following TN gubernatorial candidates: Henry Clay Evans,
  Henry Horton (also jugate button w/Hannah), Jesse Littleton, Hill
  McAlister, John McCord, G.N. Tillman, Tom C. Rye, or E.W. Carmack
  for Senator.. **75.00+**
Buttons, Posters, Bandanas (featuring more than 2 candidates)....... **Top Dollar**

I am a twenty-year collector and dealer of political memorabilia with wide interests. Also wanted are all types of **buttons from fast-food chains and police** to any other kind — old or new. Just send a photocopy or mail your pins (insured, in a strong mailing box) for a fast offer. I am interested in buying your items (priced by you, or I will make a fair offer). Prices paid range from 50¢ to $1,000.00, depending on the item. Some sample prices are listed below. Thanks in advance for writing us!

Fred Swindall
Plaid Rabbit Button Exchange
111 NW 2nd St.
Portland, OR 97209

We Pay

Any Woodrow Wilson Picture Pin.. **10.00+**
Any Cox Presidential Pin, 1920 .... **15.00+**
Any Davis Pin, 1924 .... **35.00+**
Any Truman Pin .... **7.50+**
Inaugural Medal, 1933 .... **175.00**
Ike Playing Cards .... **10.00+**

Political Items

Lincoln Silk Ribbon, any .... **50.00+**

Charles began collecting **U.S. presidential campaign paper memorabilia** twenty years ago and has been at the forefront of this hobby since. Widely known as a top collector of the material in the U.S., he collects paper ephemera used to promote candidates to the U.S. presidency. Pamphlets, leaflets, flyers, tickets, electoral ballots, and hand cards are examples of his collecting pursuits. All campaigns are of interest, but he especially searches for nineteenth century and early twentieth century items. When writing to him, indicate the candidate, the year (if known), size, condition, inscription, and any picture on the item. A photocopy is helpful. Items sent on approval will not be accepted. Buttons, bumper stickers, or daily newspapers are not wanted.

Charles L. Hatfield
1411 S State St.
Springfield, IL 62704

We Pay

Henry Clay Electoral Ballot	**20.00**
Abe Lincoln Electoral Ballot	**25.00**
U.S. Grant Electoral Ballot	**15.00**
James Blaine Campaign Trade Card	**4.00**
Grover Cleveland Leaflet	**12.00**
Benjamin Harrison Leaflet	**12.00**
William Jennings Bryan Campaign Post Card	**8.00**
William McKinley Leaflet	**10.00**
Theodore Roosevelt Sheet Music	**8.00**
William Howard Taft Campaign Hand Card	**5.00**
Woodrow Wilson Leaflet	**7.00**
James Cox Brochure	**15.00**
Warren Harding Pamphlet	**8.00**
Calvin Coolidge Booklet	**6.00**
John W. Davis Brochure	**10.00**
Alfred E. Smith Leaflet	**8.00**
Herbert Hoover Pamphlet	**5.00**
Franklin D. Roosevelt Flyer	**6.00**
Alf Landon Brochure	**4.00**
Wendell Willkie Pamphlet	**4.00**
Thomas Dewey Ticket	**3.00**
Harry Truman Campaign Card	**5.00**
Dwight Eisenhower Pamphlet	**3.00**
Adlai Stevenson Leaflet	**3.00**

John F. Kennedy Brochure **3.00**
Barry Goldwater Pamphlet **2.00**

POST CARDS

I am the post card collector who signs his letters 'With Hot Fudge.' I have been collecting ice cream memorabilia for over fifteen years and, for most of that time, **ice cream-related post cards**. While my collection ranges from scoops to trays to signs to trade cards to freezers, I most enjoy collecting post cards because they are historically interesting, graphically pleasing, easy to store, and may be bought through the mail. Ice cream-related post cards show a fun slice of our world. My favorite post cards are pre-1920 real photo post cards that show an ornate soda fountain with a soda jerk behind it and people and children in front waiting to be served. These post cards really capture life as it was.

I would be happy to hear from anyone who collects ice cream-related post cards. I am one of the founders of the Ice Screamers, the association of ice cream memorabilia collectors, and a foremost collector of ice cream and soda fountain-related real photo post cards. If you have post cards to sell, think of me first. The following list will give you an idea of what I am looking for.

Allan 'Mr. Ice Cream' Mellis
1115 W Montana
Chicago, IL 60614
(312) 327-9123

Real Photo Ice Cream or Soda Fountain-Related   **We Pay**

Interiors w/People & Children Eating Ice Cream.................................... **20.00+**
Exteriors of Fairs, Street Vendors, Parlors.. **10.00+**
People Making or Eating Ice Cream .... **15.00+**
Animal-Drawn Ice Cream Trucks, especially in front of factories........... **20.00+**
Ice Cream Trucks Showing Company Name .... **30.00+**
Foreign, especially street vendors... **15.00+**
Ice Cream Carts w/Vendors & People Eating .... **10.00+**
Advertising.. **20.00+**

For as long as post cards have been printed and sold, there have been views of **post offices**. The attraction to the post card printer was that there was a post office in every community of significance; it was the federal presence at a personal service level. Before the phone, it was the focal point of communication with the outside world. Money orders were bought here to pay for mail-order catalog purchases. Aliens had to register their addresses here once a year; neighbors met each other every day to chat, even if there was no mail to be picked up or posted. Such a focal point of the village, town, or city was the post office, the ideal subject for a post card which for many years was a popular mode of writing.

Aside from local residents who often took pride in sending a picture of their local post office, these views were also popular among early post card collectors. There were units of post card clubs whose members specialized in them. Fortunately for collectors today, many of those people built large collections, so post office views are very abundant, especially from the large cities. The Railway Mail Service Library will buy any post office-view post cards at the following prices. Also, if you have more than one hundred post office views, I will discuss a group price to avoid the time and effort of evaluating each card individually. I accept any quantity of views, but I will purchase no more than five of any identical cards in one transaction. However, I will buy an unlimited number of cards of the same post office if they are different views by various manufacturers. Deduct five cents for used post cards missing their postage stamps. I will pay a premium of ten cents per card for any small town post office other than those described as 'smallest post office.' I will pay a fifty-cent premium for any interior post office view showing the sorting area (not the post office lobby) or one showing a railway or highway post office close-up (not as part of a train). I will trade duplicate cards at the values shown below for any post office-view card you have of equal value. I do not purchase any unused linen post cards produced by the Asheville Post Card Company. I will buy used views.

Railway Mail Service Library
12 E Rosemont Ave.
Alexandria, VA 22301-2325

I buy **many types of post cards as well as calling cards**. I desire that cards and post cards be clean and without damage. I prefer items produced from about 1890 to 1920. I am happy to have you send your items on approval and for examination. Postage and insurance charges are paid both ways. I am interested in, collect, and buy the following types of cards and post cards.

Homer Neel
4213 Westridge Dr.
N Little Rock, AR 72116

We Pay

Post Cards w/Blacks (chrome, linen or real photo), each	**up to 5.00**
Post Cards w/Santa Claus (in suits other than red), each	**up to 12.50**
Real Photo Post Cards (midgets, giants, sideshow people), each	**up to 12.50**
Calling Cards (black & white or color), each	**up to 30¢**

I am buying **pre-1920 Nebraska real photo post cards**. I will also buy certain selected color or printed cards of Nebraska with historical or social significance. Those relating to small towns are much preferred and bring good prices.

Gerald S. Oswald
R.R. 1, Box 112
Aurora, NE 68819

Pre-1920 Real Photos of Nebraska   **We Pay**

Main Streets	**10.00+**
Sod Houses	**10.00+**
Solomon D. Butcher Cards	**5.00+**

Post Cards

Farming or Ranching .... **2.00+**
Celebrations or Parades .... **4.00+**
Disasters or Fires... **3.00+**
Train or Auto Wrecks .... **4.00+**
Multi-Views... **4.00+**
Baptisms.. **5.00+**
Business Interiors... **10.00+**
Business Exteriors... **5.00+**
Business Wagons or Early Trucks .... **5.00+**

Pre-1920 post cards from Tampa, Miami, and Key West, Florida, are wanted by a student of the history of this area of Florida. Black and white real photo post cards are preferred. These must be in very good condition. **Any other old memorabilia of Tampa, Florida** is wanted as well. Write first with description and give your price.

Frank Garcia
13701 SW 66th St B-301
Miami, FL 33183

One of the best and least expensive ways to learn about an area is by collecting old post cards. A wealth of information can be learned about a favorite vacation spot or home town. I collect **old post cards from Lake Bomoseen, Vermont**. I am especially interested in a series of post cards that were made around 1905 that are each numbered and marked with an 'F'. For example, the post card of our house reads 'Reed's Lake View Cottage, Lake Bomoseen, VT, 81-F.' There are approximately 110 in this series. I have purchased or located almost thirty of these and usually pay $5.00 to $10.00 each. I would like to purchase any that I do not have at their full retail price. I am currently offering a 10% (of the actual selling price) reward just for information that leads me to an 'F' card that I do not have. If you have any of these 'F' series post cards from Lake Bomoseen, Vermont, please contact me immediately, and I will send you a list of the numbers that I do not have. If you know of a good lead toward finding these post cards, please let me hear from you. If as a result I find a card, I'll send you a reward. I also want general post cards from Lake Bomoseen, Vermont, as well. I will pay a premium price for a stereo view card of this lake, if any exist. I am willing to buy, sell, or trade cards in order to enhance my collection.

Charles S. Knight
1608 Delmar Dr.
Charlottesville, VA 22901

I am interested in buying **amusement park post cards with roller coasters or any park rides or park scenes**. Any date is fine, but only post cards in good condition are wanted — whether a collection or a single piece. Also sought are skee ball tickets and all unusual amusement park items.

Douglas A. Fink
9 Kenalcon Dr.
Phoenixville, PA 19460

I am buying **pre-1930's post cards of the Mississippi gulf coast, from Bay St. Louis, and from Camp Shelby**. Also wanted are **pre-1960 cards from small towns in Mississippi**. Please send price and description or photocopy. Price paid depends on the location and condition.

Treasure Hunt
416 Walnut St.
Hattiesburg, MS 39401

POSTAL ARTIFACTS

The Railway Mail Service Library is a member of the American Philatelic Research Library as well as other philatelic societies that study postal markings and history. As with most philatelic libraries, the principal efforts are being directed toward organizing and cataloging the collection. To expand the coverage and variety of materials available for the use of postal historians, I also seek to purchase or swap documents which pertain to post office operations.

There is a wide spectrum of postal artifacts which includes obsolete items that were issued and used by the Post Office Department or U.S. Postal Service. Most of these were marked 'Property of the Post Office Department' or had similar wording to that effect. Some of the major categories are listed below with price ranges. As with most historical objects, the price will vary depending upon age, condition, usage, and origin. Prices quoted are for U.S. artifacts; those from other countries may command an additional premium. For example, Canadian artifacts in each of these categories are generally scarcer than their U.S. counterparts. This is not true across the board, however, as in the case of street letter boxes from Great Britain. These have been imported in abundance, so they may be priced equal to or less than U.S. letter boxes. For specific items, please write to the Railway Mail Service Library with a complete description. Send a #10-size SASE for a free set of illustrated want lists of all postal artifacts wanted. Also, I will provide free, direct referrals to other collectors if someone writes me about a postal item and it happens to be something I do not collect; so finders and pickers should use me as a first point of reference for these items. Because my work requires extensive travel, please allow two weeks for a reply.

Dr. Frank R. Scheer, Curator
Railway Mail Service Library
12 E Rosemont Ave.
Alexandria, VA 22301-2325

We Pay

Books	**10.00-35.00**
Post Cards	**10¢-60¢**
Magazines	**50¢-5.00+**
Street Letter Boxes, pre-1880	**150.00+**
Street Letter Boxes, pre-1920, brass	**100.00**
Street Letter Boxes, after 1920, iron or steel, obsolete styles only	**50.00**
Badges, pre-1920 P.O.D./U.S.P.O. or any Post Office organization in the world	**Write**
Mail Locks & Keys, pre-WWI, P.O.D., U.S. Mail, Reg'd U.S. Mail, steel or brass, obsolete only	**Write**
Schedules of Mail Routes & Schemes, 1882-1972	**Write**
State Post Route Maps	**Write**
General Orders	**Write**

POSTERS

Long-time veteran collector wants to buy for his personal collection pre-1931 calendars, posters, signs, envelopes from these companies:

Austin Cartridge Co.
Austin Powder Co. (Cleveland, OH)
The Black Shells
Deadshot Gunpowder
Dominion Cartridge Co.
DuPont Gunpowder
Harrington & Richardson Arms Co.
Hazard Powder Co.
Hopkins & Allen Arms Co.
Hunter Arms Co. (L.C. Smith Shotguns)
Infallible Gunpowder
Ithaca Gun Go.
King Powder Co.
Laflin & Rand Powder Co.
Marble Arms & Mfg. Co.
Marlin Firearms Co.
Miami Powder Co. ('Alarm' Gunpowder)

Oriental Powder Co.
Parker Bros. Gunmakers (Meriden, CT)
Peters Cartridge Co.
Remington Arms Co.
Robin Hood Ammunition Co.
Robin Hood Powder
Savage Arms Co.
Selby Shotgun Shells
Selby Smelting & Lead Co.
Selby Smelting Works
J. Stevens Arms & Tool Co.
Union Metallic Cartridge Co.
U.M.C.
U.S. Cartridge Co. (The Black Shells)
Walsrode Gunpowder
Western Cartridge Co.
Winchester Repeating Arms Co.

Bill Bramlett
P.O. Box 1105
Florence, SC 29503
(803) 393-7390 (home)
(803) 665-3165 (office)

POTTERY

I am permanently interested in purchasing good examples of **American art pottery** with an emphasis on pieces produced during the **Arts and Crafts** movement. As pieces vary in quality of design and glaze, it is difficult to set ranges on everything. However, I am a committed collector and will pay for exceptional examples. Below are some prices I will pay for specific pieces.

Keith Browne
P.O. Box 1592
Rockford, IL 61104
(815) 398-7137

We Pay

Teco Vase, no handles, 6"..	**200.00+**
Teco Vase, 4 buttressed handles, 8"...	**800.00+**
Teco Vase, 4 handles, 12"..	**1,500.00+**
Grueby Vase, green, plain, 8"	**350.00+**
Grueby Vase, green w/leaves, 8"	**700.00+**
Grueby Vase, 2-color leaves & buds, 10"..	**2,000.00+**
Marblehead Vase, single color, 6"	**100.00+**

Marblehead Vase, multicolor design, 6" .... **800.00+**

As with most collections, I began collecting this particular type of pottery because of one piece (that my mother gave me). That one piece led me to buy another, and soon I was searching for this design at every opportunity. It is always a bright, light blue color with a dark blue tulip pattern. This pattern consists of a crude tulip with a smaller flower on each side. I have been unable to determine an 'official' name for this pattern, so I just refer to it as **Blue Tulip** pottery. So far I have discovered these pieces: a teapot, a relish dish, a sugar bowl with lid, a soup bowl with lid, a cookie jar, a serving tray, a round milk jug, a tall water pitcher, and a triangular flask.

This pottery is thought to be part of a supermarket promotion from the 1940's — possibly an A&P or ACME chain store. Different makers were undoubtedly involved, so some pieces have no mark on the bottom, some say 'USA', and others have 'Bake Oven USA' stamped on the bottom.

I am not certain that there are any more pieces in this set, but I suspect that there are others, and I dearly want to buy them. I have paid $10.00 to $20.00 each for the items I have but would consider any reasonable request for a piece that I need. Any information about this design would be most appreciated.

Charles S. Knight
1608 Delmar Dr.
Charlottesville, VA 22901

I collect **American art pottery**. I am especially interested in buying early dated **Van Briggle** pottery since my grandfather was a good friend of Artus Van Briggle, and Mrs. Van Briggle was my mother's godmother. Pieces dated before 1908 are preferred, but I will also consider buying high quality pieces dated in the teens and undated pieces with a number below the words 'Colo Spgs.'

I also buy decorated **North Dakota School of Mines** pottery with good color contrast, **signed Rookwood, Newcomb, Marblehead, Hylong, and other fine or unusual pieces of American art pottery.** Prices paid will be fair.

Scott H. Nelson
P.O. Box 6018
Santa Fe, NM 87502
(505) 986-1176

I would like to buy **unusual pottery from any period up to the 1950's.** It does not need to be signed — but I buy signed pieces also. Mint condition pieces only are wanted.

Beth Nehez
1414 Gordon Rd.
Lyndhurst, OH 44124

We Pay

Italian or European Pieces	10.00+
Figural Animals	5.00+
Flower Frogs	10.00+
Pennsbury, Royal Copely, Royal Haeger, or Hull	8.00+
Cookie Jars	10.00+
Teapots	12.00+
Roseville, Weller, or Coors	18.00+

I am buying the following pottery and pottery-type china listed below. Prices should be reasonable enough for resale. Please send a description and price. All prices must be in mint condition — free of cracks, chips, nicks, bruises, glaze crazing, or any other imperfections.

Hull	Franciscan
Roseville	Fiesta
Weller	Russel Wright
Red Wing	Lu Ray
Frankoma	Currier & Ives, by Royal China
Van Briggle	Memory Lane, by Royal China
Purinton	Liberty Blue, by Staffordshire
Shawnee	Vernon Kilns
McCoy	Blue Ridge
Watt	Friar Tuck Hummels

Bill Ogden
The Glass Pack Rat
3050 Colorado Ave.
Grand Junction, CO 81504

I would like to buy **art pottery with a preference for the Arts and Crafts era**. Although I will consider any art pottery of importance or of unusual origin. I will buy both signed and unsigned items. I will also purchase **metalwork** from the Arts and Crafts era. Listed below are some company names for potteries I seek.

Arc-En-Ciel	Fulper
Arequipa	Gay Head
Batchelder	Greuby
Biloxi	Grand Feu
Brouwer or Middle Lane	Halcyon
California Faience	Keramis
Cambridge	Marblehead
Cowan	Merrimac
Clewell	Overbeck
Clifton	Rookwood
Dayton	Redlands
Dedham	Weller
Frackelton	

Tim Ward
3232 #8 Denver Ave.
Merced, CA 95348

Pots Wanted: I will pay strong book values for the American pottery listed below.

ROSEVILLE

Rozane	Dahlrose	Ixia
Azurean	Victorian Art Pottery	Dawn
Olympic	Futura	Bleeding Heart
Mara	Sunflower	Fuchsia
Mongol	Jonquil	Bittersweet
Woodland	Pine Cone	Cosmos
Fudji	Ferella	Columbine
Fujiyama	Falline	White Rose
Della Robbia	Primrose	Foxglove
Crystalis	Blackberry	Freesia
Pauleo	Baneda	Snowberry
Aztec	Cherry Blossom	Zephyr Lily
Crocus	Morning-Glory	Apple Blossom
Carnellian II	Clemana	Bushberry
Mostique	Wisteria	Gardenia
Panel Nudes	Teasel	Silhouette Nudes

I am also seeking wall pockets, hanging baskets, tea sets, planters, book-ends, and jars and peds in most patterns. I will also pay strong book values for the following lines of Weller:

Weller

Louwelsa	Eocean	Glendale
Auroro	Sicard	La Sa
Dickens Ware 1st Line	Perfecto	Lamar
Dickens Ware 2nd Line	Jap Birdimal	Hudson

I also seek **figurals in Brighton, Muskota, Hobart and Lavonia, Copper-tone and Woodcraft pieces with animals, pop-eye dogs, and the Mammy Line**. I am buying other American art pottery including **Biloxi, Fulper, Greuby, Newcomb College, Rookwood, Teco, and dated Van Briggle.**

Antique Artware
369 Forest St.
Columbus, OH 43206
(614) 444-1588

Wanted are vases and ewers made in the following countries and marked:

Austria

Amphora	Karthago
Templitz	BB
RS&K	JBD
EW	Heliosine Ware
PD	

Hungary

Zsolnay	Fisher J

Prices depend on condition, size, and desirability. Please send description including any factory or artist's marks, your phone number, and a photograph, which will be returned.

Les Cohen
5530 Floral Ave.
Verona, PA 15147
(412) 793-0222 or leave message (412) 795-3030

Do you have a beautiful or unusual piece of pottery, but it's not marked, and you have no idea who made it? I buy **old and unusual pieces of unmarked pottery** — any type glaze, texture, or design will be considered. Just send me a photo or a detailed description, and I will try to pay your asking price or will make you an offer. No phone calls, please.

Edna Zemites
3543 Lawnview
Corpus Christi, TX 78411

PRINTS

I am interested in **all types of paper ephemera, especially items with a visual format.** This includes books, advertising items, calendars, and catalogs. Please write to me, describing your item. Listed are some examples with prices paid.

Hugh Passow
306 Main St.
Eau Claire, WI 54701

Prints	**We Pay**
Grand Canyon, by Moran	100.00+
Maxfield Parrish Prints	50.00+
McKenny Hall Indian Prints	30.00+
Travel Posters, 1920's	50.00+
Audubon Elephant Folio Prints	250.00+

Other Paper	**We Pay**
Trade Card Albums	**up to 150.00**
Scrap Albums	**up to 100.00**
Books of Old Store Receipts	**up to 100.00**
Old Store Receipts, loose	**Write**
Collections of Old Letters	**Write**
Edison-Mazda Calendars by Maxfield Parrish	**100.00+**

I am buying **old lithographic color prints of Santa**. I prefer these to be larger than a post card and date from 1890 through 1920. I like them to be with children; if they have advertisements on them, it is all the better. I do not want pages from magazines or magazine covers. Santa prints wanted often say 'printed in Germany' and are diecut. Sometimes these prints were used on calendars. Depending on size, condition, and rarity, these old prints of St. Nicholas will fetch a price from $10.00 to $50.00 or more.

Mike Newell
2113 Nottingham
Cape Girardeau, MO 63701
(314) 334-5153

I am looking for **prints from old magazine covers, posters, calendars, etc**. Especially wanted are prints by Bessie Pease Gutmann, Annie Benson Muller, Zula Kenyon, Maxfield Parrish, and Wallace Nutting. Guardian Angel prints, Black memorabilia prints and items, and Cupid prints are sought. Prints titled

Spring Song (girl watching bird) and *Found* (dog and lamb) are specifically wanted for my collection. Please send a complete description, including condition, size, frame, etc., along with your price.

Carol J. Beattie
3374 Ver Bunker Ave.
Port Edwards, WI 64469

I am interested in buying **Harrison Fisher, Howard Chandler Christy, and Bessie Pease Gutmann prints** in good condition and unstained.

Sachs Antiques
2433 Nicholson Rd.
Sewickley, PA 15143

We Pay

Prints, original, old & unmatted .... **20.00+**
Prints, w/original frames .... **30.00+**
Magazine Covers .... **10.00+**

I buy old prints (etchings, engravings, lithographs, etc.) and original artwork (oils, watercolors, pastels, etc.) whether framed or unframed. Being from Spartanburg, South Carolina, I am particularly interested in subject matters (maps, views, wildlife, etc.) and artists pertaining to the Carolinas and, more specifically, the Piedmont area of South Carolina. Please send a photo and description. Thank you.

Henry Barnet
516 Maverick Circle
Spartanburg, SC 29302

PURSES

The purse was first and foremostly used for that wonderful formal occasion, ball, wedding, or honeymoon and complimented the outfit being worn. Beaded bags have been around for more than 200 years. Early bags, called reticules, had drawstring tops and were made in fine fabrics such as silk, satin, and velvet. They were embroidered or beaded and had room enough to carry a handkerchief, fan, perfume bottle, and money pouch. Other common purse materials were tapestry and metal mesh. Leather took over in the early 1900's, but beaded and mesh bags came back for a time in the 1920's. Misers purses (also called stocking purses) were elongated bags first worn by men in the eighteenth century to hold coins. By the nineteenth century, they were crocheted, knitted, or netted and were carried by both men and women. Chatelaine bags hung from hooks attached to the waists of full-skirted dresses and were fashionable from the 1860's on. The gate-top purse was first introduced in the 1880's and had an expanding metal neck. At the end of the nineteenth century, mesh and metal purses were manufactured by the Whiting & Davis Co. of Plainville, Massachusetts, and their operations continue today. Mesh purses were also made by the Mandalian Manufacturing Co. from 1922 to around 1935. Other manufacturers, none of whom ever became a force in the industry, are Evans, Napier, or those unknown manufacturers whose products simply say 'Made in France' or 'Made in Canada.'

I collect the **ornate Victorian, Art Nouveau, and Art Deco** purses. Of special interest are the enameled mesh purses with painted designs. Some are elaborately designed with ornate or jeweled frames, sport big tassels in exciting colors, or have unique designs with scenes of birds, flowers, houses, country scenes, geometric patterns, and others.

Condition is important with respect to the fringe being original, a pattern that is clear and intact, no missing beads, a good frame, and a good closure. The handle must be original and in good to excellent condition. If the bag is very rare and very lovely, a defect in one place will not be a problem. The frame must be in alignment and should open and close easily. The design must be bright, clear, not flaking, without dents, scratches or chipping. Normal wear is acceptable, but the bag must be in good to excellent condition. The chain handle and tassels should be intact and original. In conclusion, price is determined by uniqueness, condition, elaborateness of design, age, and size of beads (smaller beads are preferred).

Veronica Trainer
P.O. Box 40911
Cleveland, OH 44140
(216) 871-8584

We will purchase painted **metal mesh purses made by the Whiting & Davis Co. and the Mandalian Manufacturing Co. in the 1920's and early 1930's**. There are three basic types of mesh: Dresden or chain-link type, Armor-Mesh or flat-link type, and Bead-Lite which is a flat link-and-bubble mesh. Especially wanted are purses featuring figural designs; scenic or landscape designs; elaborate geometric or floral patterns; ornate frames with polished stones, faux jewels, or enameled decorations; painted frames; and Art Deco frames with painted inserts.

We are interested only in purses in mint or near-mint condition. The uniqueness of the design and condition of the paint on the mesh are the most critical factors in determining desirability. On mint condition bags, the paint must be virtually perfect. Near-mint purses will have few or no missing fringe chains or drops and will show only minor paint wear.

Sherry & Mike Miller
303 Holiday Dr.
R.R. 3, Box 130
Tuscola, IL 61953
(217) 253-4991

Flat Mesh, Dresden, or Bead-Lite   **We Pay**

Child's Size (2¼" x 3", 2½" x 3½" or 3" x 4¾") **40.00-65.00**
Small Size (3¼" x 5¾", 3½" x 6¼" or 4" x 7") **50.00-75.00**
Medium Size (4½" x 7¾", 5" x 6¼" or 5¼" x8") **70.00-125.00**
Large Size (4½" x 10", 5" x 9" or 6" x 9¾") **90.00-165.00**
Extra Large (7" x 12", 8" x 9" or 9¼" x 12") **125.00-200.00**

I am buying **vintage Victorian purses and purses made up to and through the 1930's.** Especially wanted are unusual mesh or beaded examples. Purses should be in good condition, showing little wear. Listed below are minimum prices paid for the right purse. Please note that compacts are part of the frame.

The Curiosity Shop
P.O. Box 964
Cheshire, CT 06410
(203) 271-0643

We Pay

Purse/Compact.. **75.00-150.00+**
Purses w/Fancy Frames .... **45.00+**
Unusual Purses .... **35.00+**
Enamel Mesh (3 or more colors)... **40.00+**
Glass Beaded Scenes on Frames... **50.00+**

Purses

Glass Beaded w/Castle... **75.00+**
Glass Beaded w/People... **75.00+**
Glass Beaded w/Houses... **50.00+**
Glass Beaded w/Animals... **60.00+**

I am buying for my collection **hard plastic pocketbooks of the 1940's and 1950's**. I prefer colored ones over clear Lucite examples. Signed purses will have more value than unsigned ones, but I'm interested in them all. The fancier or funkier the better. Below is a sampling of prices I pay. Prices listed are for very good to better condition.

Kathy Alexander
124 Grandview St.
Bennington, VT 05201
(802) 447-1309

We Pay

Clear Lucite .... **15.00+**
Plain, unsigned .... **20.00+**
Plain, signed.. **25.00+**
Fancy (filigree or rhinestone) .... **35.00+**
Unusual .... **40.00+**

We are currently buying **metal mesh purses by Whiting & Davis or Mandalian, circa 1870's through the 1940's**. Purses must be in mint condition and stamped with the manufacturer's mark. We are always seeking the more unusual type bag. We would also like to correspond with other collectors.

Terri & Dennis La Mothe
P.O. Box 40421
St. Petersburg, FL 33743
(813) 343-9100

We Pay

Enameled Bags, simple design .... **25.00+**
Bags, large .... **35.00+**

Original Boxes & Tags w/Above an Additional	**5.00**
Old Ads for Mesh Bags, black & white	**2.00**
Old Ads for Mesh Bags, color	**3.00**
Intact Jewelry Catalog	**25.00+**

QUILT TOPS AND VINTAGE MATERIAL

I am buying quilt tops — finished, unfinished, worn, damaged. Also wanted are quilt blocks, pieces, and yardage made before 1960 only. No synthetics or blended fabrics are wanted. Cottons and linens are primarily of interest. Also bought are aprons made of pre-1960 cotton organdy, broadcloth, gingham, or linen. I collect apron patterns also. Please send descriptions, colors, condition (no mildewed or musty items are wanted), age, etc. Photos would be helpful and will be returned. Uniqueness, lace, or embroidery influence price. All letters will be answered.

Bianca Hoekzema
7670 Iron Ct.
Boise, ID 83704

We Pay

Quilt Tops, complete, good condition .... **35.00+**
Quilt Tops, less than good condition... **10.00+**
Quilt Blocks, Pieces, or Yardage (depends on condition, quantity, etc.). .**Fair Prices**
1950's Aprons, good condition .... **1.00+**
Pre-1950 Aprons, good condition .... **3.00+**

QUIMPER

I am interested in buying Quimper made before World War II — whether a single piece or a collection. I most desire interesting, unusual molds with naive painting. Listed below are some pieces sought. I will pay what the market commands for top quality examples and less for more ordinary ones.

Jardinieres
Vases
Candlesticks
Platters
Plates (in croiselle, geometric, or naive patterns)
Miniatures (e.g., doll tea set)
Snuffs
Cruet Sets
Teapots (especially donut shaped)

Helaine Lesnick
9 Stratton Rd.
Scarsdale, NY 10583

RADIO PREMIUMS

During the 1930's and 1940's, every radio adventure show gave away hundreds of premiums such as rings, decoders, badges, etc. Sometimes they came in cereal boxes, but most often the sponsors asked us to send in box tops along with ten or twenty-five cents. Then we would wait with great anticipation for our latest treasure to arrive in the mail. It would be enjoyed, used until it wore out, or proudly displayed. Some of the most memorable progams were: The Lone Ranger, Green Hornet, Sky King, Jack Armstrong, The Shadow, Tom Mix, and Roy Rogers. Over the years most of these premiums were broken, lost, or thrown away. I have been spending my second childhood rebuilding my original collection and adding to it, and I've included television programs' premiums as well. Since thousands of these trinkets were mailed all over the United States, they often turn up in old boxes, drawers, and other unexpected cubbyholes. A photo, sketch, or rubbing can help identify the piece. They may not be clearly marked. Prices listed are for examples in very fine condition. We prefer not making offers, and if a SASE is not enclosed, we will only answer on items of interest.

Jan & Bruce Thalberg
23 Mountain View Dr.
Weston, CT 06883
(203) 227-8175

We Pay

Lone Ranger Film Strip Saddle Ring... **35.00**
Lone Ranger Flashlight Gun (secret compartment in handle) **30.00**
Lone Ranger Secret Compartment Ring (4 versions: Army, Navy, Air Force,
    Marines), each **35.00**

Sky King Aztec Indian Ring 35.00
Sky King Mystery Picture Ring 50.00
Sky King Radar Signal Ring.. 30.00
Sky King Electronic Television (1949).. 25.00
Sky King Navajo Treasure Ring (1950) 30.00
Sky King Teleblinker Ring... 35.00
Sky King Signal Scope (1947) 15.00
Space Patrol Plastic Club Badge.. 25.00
Space Patrol Binoculars... 30.00
Space Patrol Major Mars Rocket Ring 35.00
Straight Arrow Golden Nugget Cave Ring 25.00
Straight Arrow Rite-a-Lite Arrowhead... 30.00
Superman Cornflakes F-87 Airplane Ring 30.00
Superman Crusaders Ring 35.00
Superman Secret Compartment Initial Ring.. 65.00
Tennessee Jed Look-Around Ring 35.00
Capt. Video Photo Ring.. 25.00
Capt. Video Flying Saucer Ring 35.00
Capt. Video Space Gun Ring 20.00
Capt. Video Purity Bread Tab.. 5.00
Capt. Video Secret Seal Ring.. 25.00
Tom Mix Lucky Charm.. 20.00
Tom Mix Good Luck Spinner.. 15.00
Tom Mix Straight Shooters Ring 25.00
Tom Mix Branding Iron 20.00
Tom Mix Glow-in-the-Dark Medal.. 25.00
Tom Mix Look-Around Ring 20.00
Tom Mix Signature Ring... 35.00
Tom Mix Magic Light Tigereye Ring... 35.00
Terry & the Pirates Gold Detector Ring 25.00
Terry & the Pirates China Clipper Ring.. 15.00
Capt. Midnight Initial Printing Ring 15.00
Capt. Midnight Mystic Sun God Ring 35.00
Capt. Midnight Commander Ring 20.00
Capt. Midnight Whirlwind Whistle Ring... 25.00
Capt. Midnight Sliding Secret Ring.. 25.00
The Shadow Blue Coal Glow-in-the-Dark Ring 100.00
Buck Rogers Ring of Saturn Ring 50.00
Roy Rogers Saddle Ring, signed 25.00
Roy Rogers Hat Ring, signed.. 25.00
Roy Rogers Microscope Ring 20.00
Roy Rogers Iron Ring 25.00

I am a cash buyer for radio premiums relating to the personalities listed below. This is only a partial list; I may be interested in others as well.

Amos & Andy	Frank Buck	Nick Carter
Babe Ruth	Fu Manchu	Operator 5
Buck Jones	Gabby Hayes	Red Ryder
Buck Rogers	Gene Autry	Rin Tin Tin
Buster Brown	Green Hornet	Roy Rogers
Capt. America	Green Lama	Secretary Hawkins
Capt. Midnight	Hop Harigan	Sgt. Preston
Capt. Video	Hopalong Cassidy	Shadow
Chandeau the Magician	Howdy Doody	Skippy
Charlie McCarthy	Howie Wing	Sky King
Davey Adams	Jack Armstrong	Space Patrol
D.A.S.C. (Shipmates Club)	Jimmy Allen	Spider
Detectives Black & Blue	Junior Justice Society	Straight Arrow
Dick Steel	Kayo	Super Circus
Dick Tracy	Lassie	Superman
Dizzy Dean	Orphan Annie	Tennessee Jed
Don Winslow	Lone Ranger	Terry & Ted
Sunbrite Nurses	Lone Wolf	Terry & the Pirates
Fibber McGee & Molly	Mandrake	Thurston the Magician
Flying Family	Mel Purvis	Tom Corbett
		Tom Mix

Many other radio and cereal personality premiums are wanted as well. Send your list with prices desired. Please be sure to state condition. Listed are samples of prices paid.

Bob Richardson
38600 5th Ave.
Zephyrhills, FL 33540
(813) 783-9342

We Pay

Buck Rogers Badges	**30.00+**
Chandeau the Magician	**15.00+**
Capt. Midnight Decoders	**25.00+**
Davey Adams Rings	**100.00+**
Dick Tracy Items	**3.00-100.00**
Frank Buck Items	**10.00-100.00+**
Hopalong Cassidy Items	**10.00-100.00**
Lassie Rings	**25.00+**
Lone Ranger Rings	**30.00+**
Pep Pins	**2.00+**
Orphan Annie Decoder & Manuals	**12.00-50.00**
Roy Rogers Rings	**20.00-100.00+**
Sky King Rings	**25.00-200.00**

RADIOS

I buy unusual and Art Deco radios! Look for RCA table-top and console radios in black and chrome, Sparton, Troy, and other radios with mirrored exteriors. Also sets with colored Bakelite (red, yellow, blue, etc.) are bought. Look for names such as Dewald, Crosley, Garod, Kadette, Sentinel, and others. Radios with novelty cases (Charlie McCarthy, Walt Disney characters, globes, baseballs, etc.) are wanted. And sets made with Lucite or Plexiglas, such as Cyart, are bought. Plus, I buy any electronic item in an ususual Bakelite or metal cabinet. Also bought are early transistor radios (mid and late 1950's) and novelty transistor radios. Regency Models TR-1 to TR-6, Sony TR-63 and TR-84, and Raytheon, Mitchell, and Belmont are some early sets.

Harry Poster
P.O. Box 1883
S Hackensak, NJ 07606

We Pay

Sparton Mirror Table-Top Radios **700.00-3,000.00**
Sparton Console Nocturne Model 1186 .... **10,000.00+**
RCA Black & Chrome Radios **1,000.00-8,000.00**
Air King Skyscraper-Shaped Radios **1,000.00-12,000.00**
Colored Bakelites: Fada, Emerson, Motorola **400.00-4,000.00**
Zenith Bakelite Nurse Radio-Intercom .... **400.00+**
Novelty Radios: World's Fair, Mickey Mouse, Etc. **400.00-3,000.00**
Early Transistor Radios **50.00-150.00**
Novelty & Advertising Transistor Radios **20.00-150.00**

I am interested in purchasing plastic radios from the 1930's and 1940's. These radios were made by Addison, Air King, Arvin, Crosley, Dewald, Emerson, Fada, Garod, G.E., Motorola, RCA, Sentinel, Sonora, Sparton, and others. The radios are different from the dark, grainy Bakelite radios in that they are made from a colorful liquid resin called Catalin. Common colors are yellow, green, blue, and red. Many have swirls or mottling which make them even more interesting. After 1950 the radio makers began substituting a cheaper plastic for Catalin. These later radios are not yet of much value, and I am not purchasing them at this time. It is easy for me to tell from your description whether you have a prized Catalin radio or not. Condition is very important. Cracks in the case will detract from the value, as will missing or 'wrong' knobs or handles.

William K. Holland
1708 E Lancaster Ave.
Suite 133
Paoli, PA 19301
(215) 648-0369 or (215) 647-7099
FAX (215) 647-4448

We Pay

Addison, Air King	500.00+
Emerson, prewar	800.00+
Fada, prewar	750.00+
Fada, postwar	300.00+
Motorola	1,000.00+
RCA	250.00+

RAILROADIANA

Railroad china and glassware are sought by collector. One piece or an entire collection is wanted. Dishes are commonly stamped on the bottom with a china company's name and the railroad's name. Items from various railroads will command various prices. Photos are invaluable in determing price. Chips and cracks render china and glassware valueless.

Lisa Nieland
1228 W Main St.
Red Wing, MN 55066
(612) 388-4027

We Pay

Plates	**5.00+**
Platters	**20.00+**
Butter Pats	**10.00+**
Cups & Saucer Sets	**15.00+**
Soap Dishes	**15.00+**
Children's Dishes	**25.00+**
Castor Sets	**50.00+**
Glasses, Tumblers, Etc.	**8.00+**
Salt & Pepper Shakers	**20.00+**

I am purchasing railroad china made by Trenton companies such as Lamberton and Scammel. Other companies will be considered. Prices paid are based on quality and quantity.

Richard Conti
6 Beverly Pl.
Trenton, NJ 08619
(609) 584-1080

RAZORS

I buy ornate, fancy-handled straight razors in excellent condition. Of special interest are ornate sterling silver handled straight razors. Also wanted are carved mother-of-pearl handles and figural celluloid handles with color. Condition of the handle and blade are important. I will pay more for straight razors in excellent condition with original blades. Also of interest are straight razor advertising signs — especially porcelain signs with good, original colors. One piece or an entire collection will be bought. Listed below are examples of the items I want and the prices I will pay.

Russ Palmieri
27 Pepper Rd.
Towaco, NJ 07082

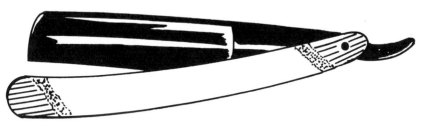

We Pay

Straight Razors .... **200.00+**
Ornate Sterling Silver .... **100.00+**
Ornate Aluminum.. **100.00+**
Carved Mother-of-Pearl... **100.00+**
Figural Celluloid w/Color... **75.00+**

I am a serious collector of fancy-handled straight razors and related items. I prefer sterling, cast aluminum, and mother-of-pearl razors. However if you have figural celluloid handles, please contact me. Please see the listing below for more information. I will pay a minimum of $50.00 for any razor not listed, based on quality and pattern. Please send a photocopy or your razor itself by insured mail. I pay postage both ways.

Len Calinoff
11 Sandra Dr.
Hauppauge, NY 11788
(516) 724-2193

We Pay

Sterling Razors .... **100.00+**
Cast Aluminum Razors .... **75.00+**

Mother-of-Pearl Razors .... 75.00+
Shotgun Handle .... 100.00+
Barber Pole Handle .... 100.00+
Fish Handle .... 100.00+

I am looking to buy **ladies' boudoir safety razors**. These razors were produced for about thirty years for the express use of women. Being very tiny (1" to 3" overall), they allowed women to discreetly shave mustache and facial hair as they could be easily hidden. These razors were produced in Germany and the United States. I have examples in metal, celluloid, and Bakelite. Razors came packed in square tins and bicycle-shaped holders complete with blades. I will pay up to $25.00 each, depending on age and condition.

Dawn V. Ricker
39145 Marne
Sterling Heights, MI 48313

I collect **early, unusual safety razors, blade banks, mechanical sharpeners, and stroppers, as well as shaving-related catalogs, instruction sheets and booklets, store advertising and display materials, and manufacturers' giveaways**. Prices will vary, depending on the particular item, its age and condition. But my price will reflect a collector's interest, not a dealer's who might expect to pay less in order to be able to resell.

Lester Dequaine
155 Brewster St.
Bridgeport, CT 06605
(203) 335-6833

RECORDS

Listed below is a small portion of the records I am seeking to buy, along with prices I will pay. Records should be in nice, playable condition: not cracked, badly worn, or scratched. I buy thousands of records by mail each year and travel to purchase large, worthwhile collections. For the convenience of sellers by mail, I offer (for $2.00, refundable when I buy) *Shellac Shack's Want List of 78 rpm Records*, a 72-page, fully-illustrated catalog listing thousands of 78 rpm records on commonly-found labels (Bluebird, Columbia, Decca, Victor, etc.), individually listed with specific, bona fide buying prices for each disc. It also contains information on scarce and preferred labels (78s and 45s), shipping instructions, etc. This want list is a 'live' offer to buy, backed by enough cash to handle any possible offering, and not just a vague reference.

It is not necessary, however, to buy anything from me in order to sell me records. Lists of records are welcome, but should include record labels and numbers, names of artist/bands, and song titles. Return postage should accompany lists.

My Book *American Premium Record Guide*, may be useful to those seeking to learn more about popular record collecting. It identifies and prices more than sixty thousand records (78s, 45s, and LPs) in the major categories of popular record collecting: dance bands, jazz, blues, hillbilly, rhythm and blues, rock 'n roll, rockabilly, etc. Ask your bookseller, or write for further information.

L.R. 'Les' Docks
P.O. Box 691035
San Antonio, TX 78269-1035

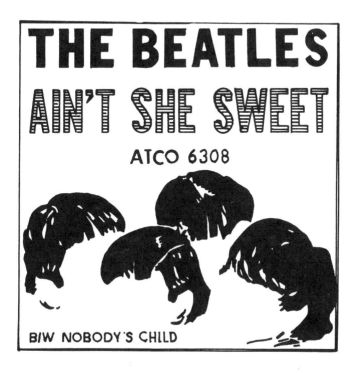

78 rpm   We Pay

All Star Quartet, Perfect 14513 .... 5.00
All Star Quartet, Perfect 14525 .... 5.00
Danny Altier, Vocalion 15740 .... 50.00
Arcadia Peacock Orch. of St. Louis, Okeh 40264, 40272, 40372, 40440,
    each 10.00-20.00
Arcadian Serenaders, Okeh 40503, 40517, 40538, each 10.00
Arcadian Serenaders, 40562 .... 20.00
Autograph Label (Chicago), any .... 3.00+
Gene Autry, Champion Label, any .... 6.00+
Gene Autry, Superior 2561 .... 60.00
Gene Autry, Victor 23630, 23707, each 20.00
Black Patti Label (Chicago), any .... 20.00+
Bolton & Cipriani's Orch., Columbia 93-P 10.00
Broadway Bell-Hops, Harmony 140-H, 355-H, 450-H, 546-H, each 3.00
Hale Byers' Orch., Brunswick 3108 .... 5.00
Hale Byers' Orch., Vocalion 15370 .... 10.00
California Ramblers, Edison 11042 .... 50.00
Joe Candullo's Orch., Gennett 3385, 3405, each 10.00
Jack Chapman's Orch., Victor 19775 .... 25.00
Chicago Loopers, Perfect 14910 .... 30.00
Jerome Conrad's Orch., Harmony 738-H 3.00
Bob Deikman's Orch., Gennett 3196 .... 10.00
Jerry Fenwyck's Orch., Clarion 11503-C 10.00
Frankie & Johnnie Orch., Bluebird 6499 .... 7.00
Jack Gardner's Orch., Okeh 40501, 40518, each .... 10.00+
Lou Gold's Orch., Harmony 98-H 4.00
Lou Gold's Orch., Perfect 14496, 14549, 14584, each 5.00
Golden Gate Orch., Perfect, 14500, 14542, each 5.00
Jean Goldkette's Orch., Victor 20469 .... 15.00
Ross Gorman's Virginians, Gennett 6132 .... 10.00
Fred Hall's Sugar Babies, Okeh 40410, 40437, 40482, 40496, each .. 5.00-10.00
Mal Hallett's Orch., Edison 14080 .... 20.00
Henry Halstead's Orch., Victor 19513, 19514, each 10.00
Harmonians, Harmony 123-H, 185-H, 503-H, 774-H, each 3.00
Hightower's Night Hawks, Black Patti 8045 .... 300.00
The Hottentots, Vocalion 15161 .... 10.00
Gordon Howard's Multnomah Chieftains, Gennett 6381 .... 10.00
Jimmy Joy's Orch., Okeh 40627 .... 20.00
Art Kahn's Orch., Columbia 624-D, 769-D, each 3.00
Kirby's Kings of Jazz, Bell 589, 591, 592, 598, each 10.00
Ernest Loomis' Orch., Victor 20755 .... 25.00
Bert Lown's Loungers, Harmony 892-H, 974-H, each 6.00
Original Indiana Five, Perfect 14601 .... 5.00
Original Memphis Five, Perfect 14539, 14746, each 5.00
Original Memphis Five, Vocalion 15712, 15805, 15810, each 15.00-30.00
Glen Oswald's Serenaders, Victor 19733 .... 10.00

Jack Pettis' Pets, Vocalion 15703, 15761, each **20.00**
Q.R.S. Label, any... **4.00+**
Red Hot Dogs, Banner 6069 .... **10.00**
Willard Robison's Orch., Perfect 14905 .... **20.00**
Stillman's Orioles, Perfect 14508 .... **5.00**
Hank Williams, any on Sterling Label (not MGM), each .... **25.00+**
Bill Wirges' Orch., Perfect 14443 .... **5.00**
Yankee Six, Okeh 40335, 40348, each **15.00**

As a private collector, I am seeking pre-1970 blues, rock, and rockabilly 45 rpm and 78 rpm records, or 33⅓ rpm albums. I prefer records by small little-known companies by Black artists, but I will consider major stars if prices are reasonable. Also collected are **magazines, books, sheet music, and picture sleeves featuring artists.** I will pay cash or will trade with other collectors. I can travel to see large collections. When you write, please send lists of titles and artists and the price wanted. I will respond to all letters. No collect calls, please.

Greg Wade
1320 Ethel
Okemos, MI 48864-3009
(517) 349-8688

RED WING

I am interested in purchasing Red Wing stoneware. Pieces may be marked Red Wing Stoneware Co., Minnesota Stoneware Co., or North Star Stoneware Co. I am especially interested in salt-glazed pieces which are hand decorated with butterflies, birds, leaves, etc. Most Red Wing products are wanted, including churns, water coolers, bowls, crocks, and jugs. If you have any Red Wing stoneware I would be happy to hear from you. Listed below are examples of prices paid. Please note that some common pieces could be worth less than prices below, and some not so common ones command much higher prices.

R.V. Chase
121 2nd Ave. N
Onalaska, WI 54650

	We Pay
Churns	75.00+
Water Coolers	100.00+
Crocks	50.00+
Jugs	50.00+

I am actively seeking and buying quality pieces of Red Wing stoneware for my personal collection. I am looking for items in mint or near-mint condition and will buy one or several pieces. The following list includes some of the items I am seeking, but I would be interested in any piece of Red Wing stoneware in mint condition.

Bill Harned
1036 E Wilson Ave.
Salt Lake City, UT 84105
(801) 466-7056

	We Pay
Refrigerator Jars, blue & white, bailed handle	90.00+

Refrigerator Jar, bailed handle, w/advertising .... **140.00+**
Refrigerator Jar, stacking, w/advertising .... **85.00+**
Any Bail-Handled Jar w/Advertising .... **95.00+**
Beater Jars w/Logo (eggs, cream, salad dressing) & Advertising .... **85.00+**
Butter Churns, any size.. **75.00+**
Any Crock w/Advertising.. **100.00+**
Any Jug w/Excelsior Springs Advertising .... **100.00+**
Spongeband (Greyline) Pitchers w/Advertising .... **140.00+**
Greyline Pantry Jars w/Advertising, any size .... **200.00+**
Union (Red Wing) Stone Mason Fruit Jars.. **80.00+**
Churn Lid, any size.. **20.00+**
Crock Lid, any size .... **20.00+**
Jar Lid, any size.. **10.00+**

RELIGIOUS ITEMS

A study of the art forms of any people must essentially take into consideration the cultural background from which art springs. Therefore, the Museum of Classical Antiquities and Primitive Arts (MOCAPA) is interested in acquisitions of religious art from the following areas: Mexico, Guatemala, Venezuela, Brazil, the United States, etc. We are not searching for pieces that were created for airport sale, tourists, or export. The works of art must have been used by their makers for religious, social, or ceremonial rites. Our business transactions are handled in a professional, judicious, and discreet manner.

MOCAPA
P.O. Box 2162
Medford Lakes, NJ 08055

We Pay

Bultos .... **45.00+**
Retablos .... **35.00+**
Santos .... **45.00+**
Ex Votos .... **25.00+**
Crucifixes .... **35.00+**
Vestments.. **35.00+**
Altar Items... **20.00+**
Chalices .... **35.00+**
Linens... **10.00+**

Religious Items

I collect large, metal antique **crucifixes**, either free-standing, for the wall, or large ones worn by clergy men and women. The more ornate and older, the better. Please send clear, color photos if at all possible. However, always include a concise description including height or length, type of metal (if known), and any history (if known). I am most interested in crucifixes that are undamaged and still have all original features such as the Christ figure or INRI inscription piece. The following is a list of the most common types of metals and a range of how much I will pay.

Marshall Watson
1101 Montego Rd.
Ft. Worth, TX 76116

Crucifixes   We Pay

Chrome or Pewter **20.00-50.00**
Brass **25.00-80.00**
Bronze **40.00-100.00**
Silver or Silverplate **50.00-150.00**
Other .... **Negotiable**

I primarily buy items relating to churches of Roman Catholic and Eastern Orthodox but will consider all other offerings including Judaica. **Statues, vestments, altar cloths, missals, candelabra, chalices, holy water fonts, censers, and crosiers** are some of the things I seek. Also wanted are books from all denominations.

Lillian Kaiser
419 Cedar St.
Santa Cruz, CA 95060-4304

JOHN ROGERS' STATUARY

John Rogers was born in America in 1829. He studied sculpture in Europe. One of his first plaster of Paris statues was 'The Checker Players' (done in Chicago in 1859). It is estimated that his studio's total production reached 100,000 pieces between 1860 and 1893. Many of his statues protrayed American life in humorous and sentimental ways. He also did several groups during and after the Civil War showing the bravery of the Union soldiers. The average issue price of these statues was about $14.00.

I will pay many times the original price for Rogers' statues in original condition. More will be paid for the following selected works. Please send picture with a description including condition of your item.

M. Hobbs
15 W 414 Fillmore St.
Elmhurst, IL 60126
(708) 279-7771

                                                          We Pay

School Days #152, 21½" .... **350.00+**
Fetching the Doctor #163 .... **375.00**
The Photograph #156 .... **375.00**

John Rogers' Statuary

Peddler at the Fair #157 .... **375.00**
Football #199 .... **400.00**
Slave Auction #58 .... **450.00**
Polo #158 .... **500.00+**

John Rogers' groups are wanted in any condition. Photos are helpful; but, if not available, write with detailed description about chips, breaks, and paint finish, or call collect evenings or weekends. I also have duplicates for sale.

Bruce Bleier
73 Riverdale Rd.
Valley Stream, NY 11581
(516) 791-4353

ROOKWOOD POTTERY

I want to purchase pre-1965 Rookwood pottery items for my collection. The two main types of Rookwood pieces that interest me are animal figural paperweights and hand-decorated, artist-signed pieces. I want only items in excellent condition, without damage, repair, or major kiln flaws.

For the paperweights, the main criteria are color (white or dark blue being more desirable than yellowish-green or purple) and type of glaze (matt or high-gloss). On these, simply list shape number, color, and glaze. On the artist pieces I need to know size, artist, type of glaze, subject matter, and date. A photo is very helpful. I have listed general prices which I will pay, depending on the aforementioned variables. I will buy any undamaged Rookwood pottery piece.

Jim Fleming
7941 State Rd.
Cincinnati, OH 45255

We Pay

Bear Paperweight	175.00
Double Rabbits	200.00
Mouse Paperweight	150.00
Squirrel Paperweight	150.00
Other Paperweights	75.00+
Scenic Vellum Plaques	600.00+
Vase w/Flowers	125.00+
Vase w/Scene	300.00+
Standard Glaze w/Cat or Kittens	800.00
Standard Glaze w/Rabbit	1,000.00
1920's High-Glaze Decorated Vase	200.00+

ROOT BEER COLLECTIBLES

Root beer has been around a long time. Companies such as Hires did a lot of advertising in the late 1800's. The country was flooded with trade cards and newspaper advertising. I am looking for pottery and stoneware mugs from many of these companies, trade cards, trays, signs (tin or paper, no newspaper please), openers, packet mirrors, pin-back buttons, or anything you may have with root beer advertising on it. I am a collector, not a dealer. If you have anything that you think I would be interested in purchasing, please send a description or picture if possible and price. I also collect Wisconsin and Minnesota etched beer glasses and mugs from the pre-prohibition era only. I will pay your price for any item I can use. Before you sell, please give me a try. I will be fair and honest with you.

Rollie Pataska
N 5718 CTH-OT
Onalaska, WI 54650

We Pay

Mugs	30.00-200.00
Glasses	10.00-150.00
Cards	5.00-20.00
Trays	50.00-400.00
Openers	5.00-20.00
Signs, tin	up to 500.00
Signs, paper	up to 300.00

I am a serious and advanced collector of pre-1930 Hires root beer memorabilia. I have spent over fifteen years buying Hires bottles, concentrates, watch fobs, mirrors, openers, dispensers, signs, mugs, trays, booklets, trade cards, letters, buckles, and a myriad of other Hires-related advertising.

My preference is to acquire items in good to mint condition only. Photos of items for sale will alleviate time delays. In light of my advanced collection, the items I am seeking are rarer and higher priced. Prices for rarer items may begin at $50.00, and the maximum could be $4,000.00 or more. Of course, condition plays a major role in pricing any item. Consultations and appraisals may be welcomed.

Steve Sourapas
1413 NW 198th St.
Seattle, WA 98177
(206) 542-1791

I am buying early pottery root beer mugs, bottles, and jugs. I'm looking for these brands as well as others:

American	Gehring	Paramount
Bardwell	Gold Bond	Richardson
Berry	Graf	S&H
Bowey	Hall & Lyons	Schuster
Cormor	Hennesey	Sterns
Croce	Hunter	Stite
Dr. Murphy	Jim Dandy	Wiedeman
Dr. Swett	Kravemor	Zarembo
Faust	Miner	Zipp
Graf	Papoose	

Unusual glass mugs and early advertising soda fountain glasses are also wanted. I buy a single piece or entire collections.

Jan Henry
Rte. 2, Box 193
Galesville, WI 54630
(608) 582-4290

We Pay

Pottery Root Beer Mugs **25.00-350.00**
Pottery Root Beer Bottles... **25.00-75.00**
Pottery Root Beer Jugs **75.00-150.00**
Glass Root Beer Mugs **5.00-40.00**
Early Soda Fountain Advertising Glasses.. **10.00-75.00**

ROSELANE SPARKLERS

From 1945 until 1952, Roselane Pottery (Baldwin Park, Pasadena, California) produced their line of Sparklers, consisting of twenty-nine different animals. These designs are made of porcelain bisque with jeweled eyes (usually rhinestones), and include owls, roosters, doves, cats, elephants, etc. They range from 2" to 8" tall and are sometimes marked with *U.S.A. Roselane* incised on the bottom. I will pay up to $6.00 for small figures and $10.00 for large ones.

Lee Garmon
1529 Whittier St.
Springfield, IL 62704

ROSEMEADE

I am buying Rosemeade pottery made by the Wahpeton Pottery Company of Wahpeton, North Dakota. The pottery was founded in 1940 and continued until it closed in 1961. Some items of interest are planters, TV lamps, shaker sets, serving pieces in the form of birds, animals, fish, figurals, etc. Listed below are some of the items I am seeking, but I will always consider items not listed as well.

Ron Giese
7300 Hunters Run
Eden Prairie, MN 55346
(612) 934-9730

Figurines	We Pay
Bear	85.00
Alligator	100.00
Coyote	85.00
Mountain Goat	95.00+
Panda	85.00
Pheasant, large	85.00+
Duck	85.00
Sailboat	95.00+
Buffalo	75.00+
Zebra	85.00

Shakers	We Pay
Birds	40.00
Flamingo	35.00
Puma	60.00
Badgers	60.00
Fish, multicolor	50.00
Coyotes	50.00
Chickens	35.00+
Buffalo	40.00
Mountain Goats	45.00
Cattle	45.00
Foxes	60.00
Pointer Dogs	65.00
Chickadee Heads	50.00

Other Items	We Pay
Figural TV Lamps	250.00+

Figural Banks .... **65.00+**
Spoon Rests .... **35.00+**
Covered Containers .... **45.00+**
Figural Planters .... **60.00+**

I am buying Rosemeade pottery. I prefer larger figurines and lamps, but I buy all pieces. Listed below are examples of items wanted with prices I'll pay.

Clayton Zeller
1115 26th Ave. S #4
Grand Forks, ND 58201

We Pay

Ash Tray Figurine, large **55.00**
Pointer Figurine **50.00**
Buffalo Figurine, brown **100.00**
Fighting Rooster Figurine **60.00**
Rooster Figurine, 14" **175.00**
Koala Bear Figurine **50.00**
Mallard Figurine, large **85.00**
Fish Plaque **50.00**
Pheasant Plaque **80.00**
Sea Gull Plaque **80.00**
Turkey Hors d'Oeuvres **60.00**
Peacock Bell **75.00**
Elephant Bell **50.00**
Bear Bank **80.00**
Buffalo Bank **100.00**
Fish Bank **80.00**
Hippo Bank **80.00**
Pony Bank **80.00**
Rhino Bank **100.00**
Chicken Lamp **400.00**
Dog Lamp **250.00**
Panther Lamp **300.00**
Pheasant Lamp **250.00**
Stag Lamp **250.00**
Rosemeade Dealer Sign **300.00**
Open House Souvenir **55.00**

ROSEVILLE

Some years ago, my mother sent me a piece of Roseville pottery as a gift. It was a brown Clematis vase, which I thought was rather hideous. I kept it, though, and my mother sent me another piece of Roseville, a white Gardenia vase. From that moment on, I was hooked. Now I have a modest collection to which I add to on a weekly (really!) basis. My appreciation for Roseville pottery only seems to grow as time goes on.

I buy all types of Roseville pottery except Clematis and Peony. Since I am a collector, I can usually afford to pay more than a dealer. If you have some Roseville or a piece of pottery that resembles Roseville, please write or call me with the number or description of your piece and your asking price. Or send me a photo if the piece is hard to describe and is unmarked. If you like, you can send me any written offers you've received, and I will do my best to beat them.

Leslie K. Ray
2000 Robyn Rd.
Springdale, AR 73764
(501) 750-2012

ROWLAND AND MARSELLUS

I am buying Rowland and Marsellus blue and white transfer or multicolored 10" rolled-edge plates, souvenirs of cities, towns, personalities, or events. I buy other Staffordshire, England, souvenirs imported by Bawo & Dotter, Royal Fenton, A.C. Bosselman, and British Anchor Pottery Company. Other souvenirs like metal tumblers or porcelain picturing U.S. and Canadian scenes from the early part of this century are wanted as well. Listed below are some of the things I am seeking. Please write for free information and want list of other things.

David Ringering
1509 Wilson Terrace
Glendale, CA 91206
(818) 241-8469

We Pay

Souvenir Plates, rolled edge, 10"... **40.00+**
Souvenir Plates, fruit & flowers, 9½" .... **30.00+**

Souvenir Plates, 9" .... **25.00+**
Souvenir Tumblers .... **50.00+**
Souvenir Cups & Saucers... **60.00+**
Souvenir Pitchers (R&M) .... **150.00+**
Souvenir Cobalt Porcelain (German)...................................... **8.00+**
Souvenir White Porcelain (German) .... **5.00+**
Souvenir Metal Tumblers (German).. **8.00+**
Porcelain Lobster Divided Dish w/Lobster handle, 10"-12".................... **40.00+**

ROYAL HAEGER

    The prestigious Royal Haeger line was introduced in 1928 by The Haeger Pottery in Dundee, Illinois. This line is mainly comprised of figurines, console/mantel sets, vases, and lamps. The designer of this line, Royal A. Hickman, also produced pottery other than Royal Haeger. Therefore, I will buy pieces marked 'Royal Hickman-Paris' and 'Royal Hickman-California Designed,' as well as Royal Haeger pieces. Basically, all pieces are signed and numbered on the bottom. I will pay reasonable prices for the following items: figurines, table lamps, TV lamps, vases, console/mantel sets, decanters, and miscellaneous.

Lee Garmon
1529 Whittier St.
Springfield, IL 62704

I am buying early Royal Haeger pottery. I prefer items designed by Royal Hickman between 1937 and 1944. I buy only pieces in mint condition and am willing to pay a fair price. The pieces I want will be signed on the bottom in raised lettering 'Royal Haeger by Royal Hickman.' I also buy figural Royal Haeger lamps with original shades in good condition and with original stickers attached. Most of the lamps I'm looking for will be in the form of animals or fish. Listed below are the major pieces sought. They will usually be marked with 'R' and a number as listed here.

David T. Bobenhouse
P.O. Box 1179
Des Moines, IA 50311

We Pay

R-495 Black Panther w/Tail Stretched Out, 26"	50.00
R-174 Oriental Head, Woman, ¾-face view, 11"	50.00+
R-175 Oriental Head, Man, ¾-face view, 11"	50.00+
R-153 Oriental Head, full face, 11"	50.00+
R-181 Nude, arms & hands covering face, 14"	75.00+
R-8040 Portable Table Fountain, 20" bowl w/nude on turtle's back over pump	75.00+
R-199 Nude, back arched on post, arms over head, 18"	75.00+
R-208 Sea Gull Vase, 16"	50.00
R-231 Floor Vase, prancing deer border in relief, 23"	85.00+
R-256 Jardiniere w/Curled Edge, 12"	75.00
R-279 Basket Vase, 21"	50.00+
R-305 Giraffe Head on Rectangular Base, 19"	100.00
R-144 Floor Vase w/Floral Base, 20"	75.00+
R-841 Flamingo Vase, tall	50.00+
R-830 Scroll Vase, 20"	40.00+
R-982 Pelican Vase, 20"	40.00+
R-247 Swan Vase, beak on breast in waves, 12½"	35.00
R-170 Ram's Head Vase, curling horns, 11"	50.00
R-174 Laughing Horse Head Vase, head down, 10"	30.00

R-633 Imperial Mongolian Man Figurine, 23".. **75.00+**
R-634 Imperial Mongolian Woman Figurine, 23½"................................. **75.00+**
R-1177 Neptune Riding Sailfish Figurine, 20" .... **65.00+**
R-1178 Mermaid Riding Sailfish Figurine, 20".. **65.00+**
R-1407 Thunder & Lightning (3 horses) Figurine, 17½"............................ **65.00**
R-596 Large Horse w/3 Riders Figurine, 14" long...................................... **75.00**
R-166 Greyhound Figurine, head down, 9" **35.00**
R-167 Greyhound Figurine, head up, 9" **35.00**
R-168 Nude Torso Figurine, 14"... **40.00+**
R-218 2-Giraffe Figurine, 15"... **40.00**
R-218B 2-Giraffe Flower Block, 15".. **45.00**
R-209 Console Bowl w/2 Pigeons, 19" across **45.00**
R-227 Lily Bowl w/3 Lilies, 13" across **30.00**

RUSSEL WRIGHT

I am a private collector of Russel Wright items. I primarily collect the Iroquois Casual china in all colors except Lemon Yellow, Sugar White, pink, and blue. I also collect some items in Sterling, Imperial (glassware), and Bauer art pottery lines designed by Russel Wright. I am willing to pay current book prices and up, depending on the rarity of the items. Specific pieces wanted are listed below.

Iroquois: 14" chop plates, redesigned covered butter dishes, covered saucepans, hostess plates, and pepper mills.
Sterling: redesigned water pitchers, coffee bottles w/lids, and ash trays.
Imperial: pinch and twist footed glassware.
Bauer: 5" corsage vase and 8½" flower vase.

Richard K. Claycomb
Apt. C
1122 Washington St.
Key West, FL 33040
(305) 294-3448

SALESMAN'S SAMPLES

Salesman's Samples

I am actively buying fine salesman's samples and anything small and well made — dollhouse items are not wanted, however. If the item is in miniature and is complete, I would be interested, whether it is a salesman's sample or not. Hundreds of different types of salesman's samples were made — too many to list. I see examples that are new to me constantly, so if you have something you think might be a sample or that is fine and well made, please feel free to contact me.

John B. Everett
P.O. Box 126
Bodega, CA 94922
(707) 876-3513

Salesman's Sample	We Pay
Barber Chair	3,000.00+
Gas Stove	1,500.00+
Bank Vault Doors & Deposit Vault Gates	2,000.00+
Store Display Cabinets	500.00+
Ladders	200.00+
Dental Cabinets	5,000.00+
Signs	500.00+

SALOON MEMORABILIA

The charming and most collectible saloon period is that between the Civil War and the coming of prohibition in 1919. There is a wide variety of smaller pieces from this Golden Age. While most people think of saloons as a place to drink beer or whiskey, the social life in a saloon went far beyond that. It included cigar sales, gambling, 'free lunch,' and all that went with these things.

We are interested in these pieces, from small coin-operated gambling machines to beer and liquor advertising and signs, and from display cases to cash registers. We have written a book that shows and gives values to many of these items called *Bueschel's Saloon Series: B.A. Stevens Billiard and Bar Goods.* This book (as well as several others) is available for $29.95 plus $2.00 postage per book from The Coin Slot (4401 Zephyr St.; Wheat Ridge, CO 800-33-3299; 303-420-2222). Please ask for a complete listing of books on arcade and slot machines, trade stimulators, etc.

Richard M. Bueschel
414 N Prospect Manor Ave.
Mt. Prospect, IL 60056
(708) 253-0791

We Pay

Glass Whiskey Sign	200.00
Glass Beer Sign	175.00
Cash Register	200.00
Table w/Stein Holders	150.00
Photograph of Saloon Interior	15.00
Photograph of Saloon Exterior	10.00
Card Playing Holdout	75.00
Etched Beer Stein	25.00
Framed Beer Advertisement	60.00
Cast Iron Coin Machine, payout	500.00
Wooden Coin Machine, payout	350.00
Cast Iron Coin Machine, non-payout	300.00
Wooden Coin Machine, non-payout	150.00
Floor Model Strength Tester	500.00
Bar-top Strength/Grip Tester	150.00
Dice Game Under Glass	150.00
Mechanical Cigar Cutter	75.00
Saloon Equipment Catalog, before 1900, per page	1.50
Saloon Equipment Catalog, 1900–1919, per page	1.00
Saloon Trade Magazines, each	2.00
National Police Gazette, before 1900, each	3.00
National Police Gazette, 1900–1919, each	1.50

Giveaways and nippers (nips) are saloon collectibles that date from about 1900 through the 1920's. They are small ceramic or glass figural bottles. They get the name giveaway from an occasion when a bar would give a small free drink or nip to good customers, especially at Christmas or New Year's. Ceramic nippers were made in Germany, France, America, or Japan (sorry, no Japanese nippers are wanted). Most are unmarked, but a few say Germany or Depose. Nippers are figurals such as dancers, girls with champagne, drunks, Scotsmen, or other humorous figures. Some are shaped as pigs with flowers, blindfolds, or with maps at their sides. Many are full figurals, but other nips may just have a figural raised on the surface of the bottle. Some are multicolored; some are only blue or brown. Many have a wood grain-like finish on the back. Other shapes are as diverse as eyes, shoes, shells, or octopi. Most nippers have a screw top with the glass ground at the opening. Listed below are some examples.

John Goetz
Box 1570
Cedar Ridge, CA 95924
(916) 272-4644

We Pay

Girl in Hand	75.00
One of the Boys	50.00
Various Dancers	50.00-200.00
Baseball Player	200.00
Girl w/Lobster	75.00
Girls w/Champagne	50.00+
Sailor w/Life Preserver	100.00
Red Cat	100.00
Devil on Front	125.00
Farmer	50.00
Giggle Soul	200.00
Octopus, milk glass	350.00
Clam, milk glass	75.00
Clam, cobalt	150.00

SALT AND PEPPER SHAKERS

I am buying **Hull's Little Red Riding Hood, Van Tellingen, and nodder** salt and pepper sets. Please state condition and your price.

Teresa's Treasures
3100 Country Place Dr.
Plano, TX 75075
(214) 964-2129

We Pay

Hull's Little Red Riding Hood, small .... **15.00+**
Hull's Little Red Riding Hood, large .... **25.00+**
Hull's Little Red Riding Hood, medium .... **Consider Your Price**
Van Tellingen .... **8.00+**
Nodder .... **10.00+**

Plastic **figural gasoline pump** salt and pepper shaker sets that stand approximately 2½" tall are just one example of the many specialty versions of novelty salt shaker collectibles. Produced for and distributed free by service stations from the early 1950's through the mid 1970's, these miniature replicas of actual gas pumps were made for almost every brand of gasoline during that era. Brands representing those with the most service stations thus are the most common and are less desirable, such as Esso, Texaco, and Phillips 66. I'm seeking to buy sets representing the gasoline brands listed below. Many may still be in in their original boxes; others will be unpackaged. Prices range from $10.00 to $25.00 a pair. Write with your find, and I'll respond immediately to your inquiry.

Aetna	Dixie	Leonard
APCO	El Paso	Lion
Amlico	Fleet-Wing	MFA
Ashland	FS (Farm Service)	Martin
Bay	Frontier	Pan-Am
Boron	Getty	Paraland
CALSO	Hancock	Rocket
Carter	Hudson	Skelley
Clark	Huskey	SOC
Cliff Brice	Hi-Speed	Tenneco
Crystal Flash	Imperial	UTOCO
Derby	Keystone	Zephyr

Peter Capell
1838 W Grace St.
Chicago, IL 60613-2724
(312) 871-8735

I collect salt and pepper shakers. I prefer those made by **Regal China signed by Van Tellingen or Bendel**. I need large green love bugs and small pigs and will pay up to $85.00 (and possibly more) depending on condition.

Rachel Lachance
15 Woodside Ave.
Saco, ME 04072

SALTS

I wish to buy lacy open salts made by the Boston and Sandwich Glass Co., New England Glass Co., Providence Flint Glass Co., and others. I will pay the most for those in excellent or mint condition but will consider battered examples if the price is right. Colored examples would be most welcomed. Where possible please use Neal reference numbers. McKearin, Heacock and Johnson, or Smith references are next best. Prices below are for salts in good to excellent condition and clear in color.

Jean Savchitz
5410 Ogletree Ct.
Dayton, OH 45424

	We Pay
Neal BF-1F	65.00
Neal CT-1A	70.00
Neal DN-1	150.00
Neal EE-1A	50.00
Neal EE-3A	95.00
Neal EE-7	125.00
Neal EE-8	110.00
Neal GA-5	80.00

Neal HL-4 .... **150.00**
Neal OP-1A.. **120.00**
Neal SC-7 .... **80.00**
Neal SL-18 .... **175.00**
Neal SH-1 .... **180.00**
Neal WN-1 .... **150.00**

SAMPLERS

Samplers of the eighteenth and nineteenth century usually included a verse, date, and name (or initials) of the maker along with an alphabet. Sometimes the locale of the maker was given. Often a school or teacher's name would be sewn in also. Sizes will vary. I pay according to condition, quality, uniqueness, etc. Depending on condition, I will pay $300.00 and up for samplers plus shipping costs. I would appreciate a clear color photo of the sampler as well as any history. These will be returned.

Sue Gobetz
Westview
Middletown Springs, VT 05757

SCIENTIFIC AND OPTICAL INSTRUMENTS

I collect scientific instruments made prior to 1920. I want old microscopes, surveying instruments, sextants, tripod telescopes, spectroscopes, and related books and catalogs. I don't want balance scales. Specific prices can't be stated because of the many factors involved — type of item, age, maker, condition, completeness, and complexity.

Don't polish the brass; I will pay more for items in untouched, original condition. Value depends on whether all parts, accessories, and case are present. However, I do buy incomplete instruments and individual parts such as microscope lenses and mirrors. Every maker made instruments ranging from small student models to complex research models. The latter are more valuable. A photo or sketch is helpful.

Paul Ferraglio
4410 Lakeshore Dr.
Canadaigua, NY 14424
(716) 394-7663

SCHAFER & VATER POTTERY

I am researching and collecting Schafer & Vater pottery. The pottery was produced by a German company from 1880 until around 1960. They were known for their bizarre figurines, figural pitchers, hatpin holders, and match holders in painted and/or glazed bisque. They also produced jasperware in several different colors, including pink and lavender. Many of the pieces are incised with an 'R' inside a 'Star' under a 'Crown' mark. I am interested in purchasing catalogs, books, and photos in addition to actual examples. Listed below are a few of the items I am seeking.

Dawn V. Ricker
39145 Marne
Sterling Heights, MI 48313

We Pay

Lavender Jasperware Teapot	100.00+
Lavender Tea Set Items	15.00+
Brown Bear Hatpin Holder	50.00+
Glazed Figural Creamers	30.00+
Glazed Figural Milk Pitchers	45.00+
Catalogs	20.00+
Post Cards	2.00+
Jasperware Vases	30.00+
Glazed Vases	25.00+
Figurines	45.00+

SCHOOLHOUSE COLLECTIBLES

Even though most all of us have some memento of our school days — yearbook, scrapbook, class picture, diploma, club pin, senior ring, letter sweater, etc. — as a rule, schoolhouse collectibles are not something one would deliberately set out to accumulate without good reason! Being a professional educator, I have a very exciting reason. I plan to establish a school-related musuem. Someone once said that 'school is a building that has four walls . . . with tomorrow inside.' I want to preserve some of those 'tomorrows' that have made us the great country we are today.

Education is essential to a free society. We associate certain items such as bells, books, and blackboards as being tools of educators. Just as educational methodology undergoes reformation, so does the educator's equipment. New innovative methods come and go; old equipment is replaced by the new. McGuffey's Readers were essential in the 1800's, just as computers are essential today. As you gather schoolhouse-related articles, let your imagination soar. Add to the list below; let me hear from you.

Kenn Norris
P.O. Box 4830
Sanderson, TX 79848-4830

We Pay

George Washington Print	**15.00**
Abraham Lincoln Print	**15.00**
Teacher's Hand Bell	**12.00**
Inkwells, desk	**8.00**
Inkwells, molded	**5.00**
Dip Pens	**2.00**
Diplomas, Announcements	**3.50**
Yearbooks	**2.50**
Maps	**2.50**
Map Holders, oak	**20.00**
Photographs	**1.00**
Slates, single	**12.00**
Slates, double	**23.00**
Pencil Sharpeners, student	**2.50**
Pencil Sharpeners, class	**7.00**
Mounted Bells	**37.50**
Lunch Pails	**5.00**
War Bond Posters	**5.00**
War Bond Stamp Books	**5.00**
Wartime Booklets for Paper, Scrap, & Metal Drives	**5.00**
Marbles, Jacks, Jump Ropes	**5.00**
Class Rings	**20.00**
Club Pins	**2.00**
FFA or FHA Articles	**3.00**
Athletic Equipment	**5.00**
Leather Football Helmets	**40.00**
Award Letters	**3.00**

Trophies	3.00
Ruler, Compass, Protractor	1.00
Pencil Boxes	6.00
Fountain Pens	4.00
Books	1.00
Tablets	1.00
Teaching Aids	5.00
Documents (Local, State, or Federal)	1.00
Print Stamp Sets	12.00
Eraser Dusters	7.50
Student Desk, single	20.00
Student Desk, double	50.00
Teacher Desk	100.00
Book Shelves, stackable	100.00
Potbellied Stove	200.00

I am buying old schoolhouse collectibles. I prefer items from the late 1800's until around 1930 — especially anything from old one-room schoolhouses. Please send a letter and a photo, if possible, along with your price.

Billy Haynes
Box 82
Hermleigh, TX 79526

We Pay

Pictures	2.00+
Books	2.00+
Desks	10.00+
Bells	15.00+
Lunch Pails	5.00+
Writing Materials	5.00+
Inkwells	5.00+
Lamps	50.00+

SCOTTIE DOG MEMORABILIA

The hobby of collecting Scottie dog memorabilia is not new, as some collectors have been engaged in this field for over thirty years. However, the popularity of Scottie collecting has been brought to the attention of dealers in recent years through the promotion of Donna and Jim Newton of Columbus, Indiana. In 1983 the Newtons began publishing the *Scottie Sampler*, a quarterly newspaper offering historical data, current market prices, features, photos, and ads. As a free bonus, subscribers of the *Scottie Sampler* are encouraged to participate in a collectors' fellowship called Wee Scots. This group holds an annual collectors' show and informal regional meetings across the United States. The aim of the unorganized group is to provide programs which include education, acquisition, and fellowship.

Donna and Jim Newton have been collecting over twelve years. They have a large, comprehensive collection and are currently looking for unique Scottie items. The Newtons do not make initial offers and request photos on all items before purchasing. They prefer items from the 1930's and 1940's. All prices paid depend on condition.

Donna Newton
c/o Wee Scots, Inc.
P.O. Box 1512, Dept. 91-1
Columbus, IN 47202-1512

We Pay

Advertising Tins	**4.00-10.00**
Big Little Books (Penny Brown series only)	**8.00-10.00**
Buster Bean Comic Strips	**1.00-4.00**
Black & White Scotch Ads or Displays	**5.00-30.00**
Frankart Bookends (Art Deco)	**30.00-50.00**
Greeting Cards	**50¢-1.50**
Magazine Covers	**1.00-6.00**
Post Cards or Trade Cards	**2.00-4.00**
Silhouette Pictures	**5.00-50.00**
Cambridge Glass	**Write**
Rosenthal Figures	**Write**

7-UP COLLECTIBLES

I am an active collector of 7-Up memorabilia and buy old advertising items. I prefer items that are pre-1960 and in excellent to mint condition; but, if I don't have them, I'm always interested — even if they're not in the best condition. Listed below are some of the things I am seeking, and the prices I will pay reflect near-mint to mint condition. Remember, I collect almost anything with 7-Up on it — the older the better!

Don Fiebiger
1970 Las Lomitas Dr.
Hacienda Hts., CA 91745

	We Pay
Calendars	35.00+
Tin Signs	45.00+
Cardboard Signs	20.00+
Neon Clocks	150.00+
String Holders	200.00+
Glass Signs/Menu Boards	75.00+
Figural Crossing Guard Sign	400.00+
Matchbooks	1.00+
Pencils	2.00+
Lighted Signs	75.00+
Lighted Clocks	85.00+
Mirrors	45.00+
Amber-Colored Bottles	35.00+
Salt & Pepper Shakers	25.00+
Bottles w/Paper Labels	10.00+
Tie Bars/Lapel Pins	8.00+

Service Pins.. **10.00+**
Drinking Glasses .... **8.00+**

SEWING MACHINES

The fact that Thomas Saint, an English cabinetmaker, invented the first sewing machine in 1790 was unknown until 1874, when Newton Wilson, an English sewing machine manufacturer and patentee, chanced on the drawings included in a patent specification describing methods of making boots and shoes. By the middle of the nineteenth century, several patents were granted to American inventors. Among them was Isaac M. Singer, whose machine used a treadle. After it was already in public use, Singer realized that he had forgotten to apply for a patent for the treadle.

1850's machines were ruggedly built, usually of cast iron. Once the sewing machine was accepted as the mechanical wonder, the ironwork became more detailed and ornate in the 1860's and 1870's.

I buy pre-1875 treadle, hand-operated sewing machines and cast iron toy sewing machines. I do not want any oak treadle machines or any of the following brands: Davis, Domestic, Home, Household, National, New Home, Singer (except machines using a flat belt), Weed, Wheeler & Wilson, or Willcox & Gibbs.

Sandra Edenhofer
P.O. Box 500
Brimfield, MA 01010-0500
1-800-942-8968

We Pay

Atwater, patent May 5, 1857 .... **1,200.00+**
Bartholf, patent April 6, 1858.. **2,500.00+**
Bartlett, patent October 10, 1865.. **350.00+**
Beckwith .... **600.00+**
D.W. Clark, latest patent June 8, 1858.. **1,400.00+**
Mme. Demorest, patent May 13, 1862... **800.00+**
Fetter & Jones .... **2,000.00+**
J.G. Folsom, patent March 1 & May 17, 1864.. **450.00+**
James E.A. Gibbs, patent August 10, 1858.. **3,000.00+**
Grover & Baker, latest patent May 27, 1856.. **1,200.00+**
Hancock... **500.00+**
J. Hendrick Sewing Shears, patent Oct. 5, 1858 .... **1,200.00+**

Sewing Machines

Albert H. Hook, patent Nov. 30, 1858 & May 17, 1859 .... **3,800.00+**
Du Laney, Little Monitor, patent May 2, 1872.................................... **3,000.00+**
McLean & Hooper .... **5,000.00+**
Ladd & Webster, Hunt & Webster, Hunt, patent Nov. 2, 1852 & May 9,
    1854 .... **3,000.00+**
Landfear's, patent Feb. 26, 1856... **5,000.00+**
Leavitt.. **1,800.00+**
Nettleton & Raymond, patent April 14, 1857 .... **5,000.00+**
Pratt's, Ladies' Companion, patent Feb. 3, March 3, 1857 & Feb. 16, 1858 **4,000.00+**
Shaw & Clark, latest patent Feb. 16, 1864... **900.00+**
Thompson .... **400.00+**
Watson, patent March 11, 1856 & December 8, 1857............................ **850.00+**
A.B. Wilson, latest patent Nov. 12, 1850 .... **5,000.00+**
Woodruff, patent July 3-10, 1855 & Sept. 7, 1858 .... **3,000.00+**

We are interested in buying any and all sewing-related memorabilia. Preferred are items in 'as found' condition. All prices depend on condition.

Dell Urry
920 Jewell Ave.
Salt Lake City, UT 84104
(801) 972-3197

We Pay

Black Domestic Sewing Machine Head .... **50.00+**
Other Treadle Machines .... **75.00+**
Instruction Books for Machines .... **5.00+**
Advertising Fliers .... **1.00+**

SEWING THIMBLES

I currently own approximately 160 thimbles and have been collecting only about three years. I wear size 10 or 11 but collect all shapes and sizes, when the price is right. I'm a 'frustrated seamstress' with a desire to have a collection of thimbles from every state, city, company, etc. As well as thimbles, I'm interested in buying old darners and other items related to sewing. I will answer all correspondence and would like to hear amusing stories concerning sewing. I'm also making a scrapbook of pictures, etc., for my senior years.

Recycled Memories
339 Foot-of-Ten Rd.
Duncansville, PA 16635
(814) 695-9653

Thimbles	We Pay
Old Plastic w/Advertising	1.00
Old Brass w/Advertising	2.00
Porcelain w/Hallmark	3.00
Sterling w/Mark	5.00
Miscellaneous Items	**Call or Write**

SEWING TOOLS

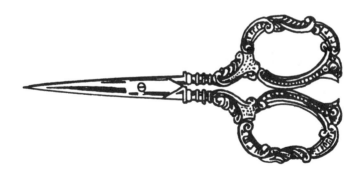

Sewing tools have played an important role in women's lives for centuries, beginning as strictly utilitarian devices and eventually, by the early 1800's, becoming highly decorative as well as functional. The popularity of fancy needlework during the nineteenth century gave middle and upper class women the opportunity to carry their tools with them when entertaining or paying visits. These tools, sometimes given as gifts or purchased as souvenirs, often became a woman's prized possessions.

As a collector, I am willing to pay top dollar for pre-1920 high quality sewing tools. Anything sterling, gold, figural, or within a matched set is highly desirable. I buy single items or entire collections. While condition, age, and rarity usually determine price, a general price listing (for items assumed to be in very good condition) is given below.

Wendy Burgener
701 E 3rd Ave.
Brodhead, WI 53520

We Pay

Sterling Silk Winder 35.00-85.00
Sterling-Capped Emery 30.00-40.00
Sterling Tape Measure 30.00-60.00
Sterling Knitting Needle End-Guards 55.00-85.00
Sterling Hem Gauge 50.00-60.00
Brass Nanny Pin w/Goldstone 75.00
Brass Figural Tape Measure (turtle, hat, shoe or whiskey flask) 65.00-75.00
Sterling Glove Darner 45.00-55.00
Steel or Brass Chatelaine w/3-4 Tools 50.00-125.00
Sterling Chatelaine w/4-5 Tools .... 200.00+
Flat, Wooden or Leather Casket-Shaped Case w/4 Tools 150.00

SHAVING MUGS

I am hungry for character shaving mugs and information about them. I will consider buying a single mug or a collection. These mugs can also be found with relief decoration. Listed below are some that I want.

David C. Giese
1410 Aquia Dr.
Stafford, VA 22554
(703) 659-5984 (after 8 pm) or FAX (703) 659-2329 (anytime)

We Pay

Daschund (entire dog) .... 300.00+
Man's Skull w/Ruby Eyes .... 200.00+
Rhino's Head .... 150.00+
Man's High Button Collar .... 140.00+

Owl .... **250.00+**
Rooster's Head .... **150.00+**
Tiger's Head .... **180.00+**
Goat's Head .... **160.00+**
Pig's Head... **130.00+**
Mug w/Razor Handle .... **90.00+**

SHIP MODELS

I am seeking to add to my collection of small wooden ship models made by Van Ryper. Most of the models range in size from about 6" to 17". They were produced in some quantity in a small shop on Martha's Vineyard, Massachusetts, from about 1937 to 1958. These models are branded on the bottom 'Van Ryper, Vineyard Haven, Mass.' I will pay $50.00 and up, depending on size and condition of models.

L.M. Rusitzky
P.O. Box 1051
Marco Island, FL 33969

SHAWNEE

I am buying figural (animals, people, etc.) and decorative kitchen items made by the Shawnee Pottery Co., such as cookie jars, pitchers, teapots, creamers, salt and pepper shakers, and figurines. I am especially interested in any pieces with gold trim, decals and hand decorating. I prefer pieces in excellent to mint condition (no cracks, chips or repairs) but will consider some examples with minor damage and will pay less accordingly. I buy Shawnee Corn Line dinnerware and some of their vases and planters as well. I do not buy any items with cold paint; colors must be under glaze only. Rare and unusual pieces of any Shawnee pottery line are always of interest to me. Listed below are some of the items I am seeking. Also, I would like to buy items relating to the company such as trade catalogs, dealer signs, and other advertising materials.

Stephanie Horvath
745 14th Ave. S
St. Cloud, MN 56301

Smiley Pig Cookie Jar.. 50.00
Smiley Pig Cookie Jar, gold decorated 85.00
Smiley Pig Water Pitcher... 35.00
Smiley Pig Water Pitcher, gold decorated................................. 50.00
Smiley Pig Water Pitcher, solid gold....................................... 150.00
Smiley Pig Creamer... 20.00
Smiley Pig Creamer, gold decorated 35.00
Winnie Pig Cookie Jar... 60.00
Winnie Pig Cookie Jar, gold decorated..................................... 95.00
Smiley or Winnie Pig Salt & Peppers, small............................. 12.00
Smiley or Winnie Pig Salt & Peppers, small, gold decorated 20.00
Smiley or Winnie Pig Salt & Peppers, large.............................. 25.00
Smiley or Winnie Pig Salt & Peppers, large, gold decorated.....45.00
Puss-N-Boots Cookie Jar 45.00
Puss-N-Boots Cookie Jar, gold decorated 85.00
Puss-N-Boots Creamer 10.00
Puss-N-Boots Creamer, gold decorated 35.00
Puss-N-Boots Salt & Peppers 8.00
Puss-N-Boots Salt & Peppers, gold decorated........................... 16.00
Muggsy Dog Cookie Jar 75.00
Muggsy Dog Cookie Jar, gold decorated.................................. 150.00
Muggsy Dog Salt & Peppers, small... 12.00
Muggsy Dog Salt & Peppers, small, gold decorated.................. 20.00
Muggsy Dog Salt & Peppers, large.. 35.00
Muggsy Dog Salt & Peppers, large, gold decorated................... 45.00
Granny Ann Teapot 30.00
Granny Ann Teapot, gold decorated 60.00
Tom Tom Teapot.. 25.00
Tom Tom Teapot, gold decorated 50.00
Bo-Peep or Boy Blue Pitcher 30.00
Bo-Peep or Boy Blue Pitcher, gold decorated 55.00
Lucky Elephant Cookie Jar, gold decorated 85.00
Lucky Elephant Creamer, gold decorated 40.00
Sailor Boy Cookie Jar, gold decorated..................................... 150.00
Owl Cookie Jar 35.00
Owl Cookie Jar, gold decorated 75.00
Clown Cookie Jar... 50.00
Clown Cookie Jar, gold decorated 75.00
House Cookie Jar.. 200.00
House Teapot 150.00
House Sugar w/Lid 50.00
Tumbling Bear or Bulldog Bank.. 30.00
Figurines (tumbling bear, teddy bear, Peke dog, puppy, rabbit, deer, or squirrel),
    each.. 8.00
Above Figurines, gold decorated, each 20.00

The Shawnee Pottery Company of Zanesville, Ohio, produced items from 1937 through 1961. I collect their Corn Line of dinnerware called Corn Queen, Corn King, and White Corn. I am interested in pieces that are in excellent condition and will pay extra for dishes with mint, original factory labels intact. I also collect a limited amount of other Shawnee salt and pepper shakers, creamers, and cookie jars. Prices depend on condition and availability. Please send SASE with correspondence. A photo is much appreciated and will be returned with SASE. Numbers listed are Shawnee company reference numbers that are often, but not always, embossed on the bottom of the piece. Given below is a partial listing of items wanted — please write.

Rosemary De Blieck
507 Irvine Ave. NW
Bemidji, MN 56601

We Pay

Butter Dish, covered, #72	17.00
Casserole, individual, 9-oz, #73	18.00
Cookie Jar, #66	50.00
Cup, 5-oz, #90	12.00
Platter, 12", #96	20.00
Teapot, individual, 10-oz, #65	35.00

SHIRLEY TEMPLE

I am buying all original Shirley Temple items — one piece or a whole collection. Prices paid depend on condition. Listed below are items that are especially wanted. Jewelry, clothes, press books — any thing on Shirley is wanted.

Frank Garcia
13701 SW 66th St B-301
Miami, FL 33183

We Pay

Book, *Little Miss Broadway*	25.00
Book, *Little Princess* #1783	20.00
Book, *Little Star* #1762	20.00

Book, *Christmas Book* #1770 .... **40.00**
Book, *Her Life in Pictures* #1734 .... **25.00**
1937 Hollywood Dance Folio #16 .... **25.00**
Sheet Music, *Curly Top's Birthday* **25.00**
Sheet Music, *Happy Birthday Curly Top* **25.00**

SHOTGUN SHELL ADVERTISING AND BOXES

I am interested in buying advertising and selling aids furnished by firearms manufacturers to their salesmen and dealers. I am also buying two-piece shot shell boxes. Listed below are some of the things I am seeking.

Bruce A. Bouma
P.O. Box 152
Dunkirk, NY 14048

We Pay

Sales Sample Sets .... **50.00+**
Window Shells .... **15.00+**
2-Piece Shot Shell Boxes .... **15.00+**
Shell-Related Advertising .... **10.00+**
Powder Cans .... **10.00+**
Brass Shot Shells .... **1.00+**
Aluminum Shot Shells .... **2.00+**
Flechette Shot Shells .... **10.00+**
Gun Posters **10.00**
Bullet Boards .... **35.00+**
Cartridge Boards **100.00**
28 GA Slugs **1.00**

Long-time veteran collector wants shotgun shell paper boxes which held 100 shotgun shells. These show colorful hunting, trap, or skeet shooting scenes on the top and sides of each box. These 100-round paper boxes would measure about 9" square. Brands sought are listed below:

Union Metallic Cartridge Co.'s 'CLUB' paper shot shells
Union Metallic Cartridge Co.'s 'NEW CLUB' paper shot shells
Winchester's 'RIVAL' paper shot shells

Bill Bramlett
P.O. Box 1105
Florence, SC 29503
(803) 393-7390 (home)
(803) 665-3165 (work)

SILHOUETTES

Silhouettes, cut-out profile portraits or shapes (usually in black and white), were first made about 1700; some are still being made today. They were first called silhouettes about sixty years after they were introduced. The cuttings were named for an unpopular Frenchman, Etienne de Silhouette; because he was laughed out of office as Controller General of Finances, the term silhouette came to mean a man reduced to his simplest form. (The man taxed by Silhouette was indeed reduced to his simplest form.)

Loretta Nowakowski
414 E Wallace Ave.
New Castle, PA 16101
(412) 652-2181

We Pay

Elaborate Cutouts .... **50.00+**
On Cloth w/Signature .... **50.00+**
Reverse Paintings on Glass of Children or Groups .... **20.00+**
Others Wanted .... **Call or Write**

SILVER AND SILVERPLATE

I am buying **all types of either sterling silver (.925 fine) or pure silver (.999 fine). I do not buy silverplate.** We are especially interested in any pieces made by these companies:

Alan Adler	Georg Jensen (Denmark)
Porter Blanchard	Old Newbury Crafters
Bucellati (Italy)	Stone
Cartier	Unger Bros.
Kalo	Tiffany
Lebolt	

We will pay more for these patterns:

Old Orange Blossom or Raphael by Alvin
Cupid or Labors of Cupid by Dominick & Haff
Versailles by Gorham
Love Disarmed by Reed & Barton
Georgian by Towle
Grande Baroque by Wallace

I will buy but pay less for damaged or monogrammed pieces. We buy napkin rings, candle holders, plates, bowls, and all types of hollowware. We will also buy Franklin Mint items, private mint items, solid silver coins, medallions, jewelry, bullion, and anything marked .925 or Sterling. Sample buying prices are shown below. Ship your silver to our address for a fast quote and check.

Coronado Coins
P.O. Box 181440
942 Orange Ave.
Coronado, CA 92178-1440
(619) 437-1435 (Monday-Friday 9 am-5 pm)

We Pay

Complete Sets of Flatware, not monogrammed	**up to 5,000.00**
Antique Tableware	**up to 10,000.00**
Serving Trays	**up to 1,500.00**
Tea Sets	**up to 4,500.00**

I want to buy **Redfield silverplate.** James H. Redfield was associated with a variety of silverplating companies between 1852 and 1872: Bray & Redfield, 1852–1857; Bancroft Redfield & Rice, 1857–1963; and Redfield & Rice, 1863–1872. They manufactured their own silverplated flatware and purchased hollowware pieces 'in the metal' from major manufacturers for decorating and plating. These wares range from plain and simple to ornately figural.

I want both flatware and hollowware by these manufacturers. Condition need not be perfect. Worn plating and minor dents are OK if priced accordingly. Never re-plate a piece before offering to me.

The wide variety of items and range of design and decoration make no simple price guide possible. I will pay fair market value for pieces based on design and condition — the price you could easily get for a similar item by any other manufacturer. If you find a piece priced higher than you want to pay for resale, send a detailed description and tell me where it is. If I purchase it, you will receive a 10% finder's fee.

Judy Redfield
216 E Pkwy. Dr.
Columbia, MO 65203

I am looking to buy **Lovely Lady** pattern silverplate that was made by Holmes & Edwards. Spoons (nut, olive, demitasse, citrus, and bouillon), lemon forks, sauce ladles, cheese servers, carving sets, youth sets, and hollowware are wanted. Please write or call.

Susan Rauckman
11 Cypress Point
Collinsville, IL 62234
(618) 344-2238

We are buying **silverplated hollowware and flatware**. Hollowware may be in need of being replated, but we prefer a better condition. Flatware must be in excellent to mint condition. We offer competitive pricing on all items. Send photo with information on the back about the hollowware item including manufacturer's marks, size, etc. Do not send the item without contacting us first. Please call about patterns of flatware — single pieces or complete sets are wanted. Price will be quoted at that time. We will clean and polish all pieces.

Bill & Beverly Rhodes
N 4820 Whitehouse
Spokane, WA 99205
(509) 328-8399

We Pay

Coffee or Tea Sets	50.00+
Coffee Servers	10.00+
Trays	10.00+
Serving Trays	5.00+
Iced Butters	20.00+
Spoon Holders	20.00+
Napkin Rings (figural pieces)	10.00+
Silverplated Novelties	3.00+

I would like to purchase **sets and serving pieces from all sterling and silverplate companies.** Some are listed here:

Tiffany	Samuel Kirk
Georg Jensen	Steiff
Alvin	Towle
Frank Smith	Tuttle
Gorham	Wallace
International	Whiting
Oneida	

Other **Tiffany silver, bronzes, lamps, jewelry, and pottery** are wanted as well. I buy **art pottery, coins, stamps, jewelry, orientalia of all types, china, crystal** and items from France and England. Items must be in mint condition.

Bill Simmons
315 SW 77th Ave.
N Lauderdale, FL 33068

We Pay

Tiffany, Audubon, Ladle	35.00
Tiffany, English Cing, Casserole Spoon	50.00
Georg Jensen Sterling, Acorn, Pierced Tablespoon	50.00
Georg Jensen Sterling, Acorn, Ladle	50.00
Gorham Sterling, Classic Bouquet, Casserole Spoon	25.00
Gorham Sterling, Golden Medici, Tomato Server	35.00
Rogers Silverplate, Vintage, Tomato Server	10.00
Rogers Silverplate, Vintage, Pie Server	10.00
Lunt Sterling, Rondelay, Cold Meat Fork	25.00
Most Sterling Dinner Forks	7.00+
Most Sterling Salad Forks	4.00+

Most Sterling Dinner Knives .... **4.00+**
Most Sterling Teaspoons .... **3.00+**
Any Silverplate Flatware... **25¢+**
Any Sterling Collector Spoon.. **3.00+**
Any Coin Silver Flatware .... **1.00+**
Any Silverplate Punch Ladle .... **10.00+**

SODA FOUNTAIN
COLLECTIBLES

Our interest is in the history of the industry, and we plan to publish a book on this subject in the near future. Consequently we seek written material which will help us. We look for trade catalogs showing equipment and supplies from such companies as Tufts, Matthews, Lippencott, Puffers, etc. Also of interest are trade magazines such as *Soda Fountain*, *Soda Dispenser*, pre-1910 issues of druggist magazines, and billheads from these companies, etc.

We also want to include historical information on potables — root beer, ginger ale, and many other beverages served at the fountain. Many companies, such as J. Hungerford Smith of Rochester, New York, played a major part in this industry. We seek information and sales aids made by them to promote their products. Photographs of interior views of the old fountains are also sought, so we can share our information with other collectors and interested parties.

Harold & Joyce Screen
2804 Munster Rd.
Baltimore, MD 21234
(301) 661-6765

We Pay

Advertising Fans w/Soda Fountain or Ice Cream Scenes 20.00
Soda Glasses w/Product Name, pre-1902 .... 25.00
Soda Glasses w/Product Name, post-1920.. 15.00
Root Beer Mugs, stoneware 35.00
Root Beer Mugs, salt glaze or Bristol glaze 80.00
Root Beer Mugs, cameo style.. 125.00
Eskimo Pie Magic Jar 450.00
Soda Fountain Magazine, 1902–1910.. 20.00
Soda Fountain Magazine, 1911–1920.. 15.00
Soda Fountain Magazine, 1921–1930.. 12.00
Soda Fountain Magazine, 1931–1940 .... 8.00
Soda Dispenser Magazine.. 15.00
Druggist Magazines, pre-1910 .... 10.00+
Equipment & Supply Catalogs, pre-1900, per illustrated page 1.00
Equipment & Supply Catalogs, post-1900, per illustrated page................. 50¢+
Billheads, pre-1900... 5.00+
Milkshake Mixers, mechanical... 250.00+
Photographs, interior views of soda fountains .... 15.00+
Post Cards, pre-1920 soda fountains... 10.00+
Spatula Soda Water Guides 40.00

J. Hungerford Smith Advertising   **We Pay**

Price Lists 15.00
Cardboard Signs.. 75.00
Tin Signs .... 150.00+
Paper Signs.. 50.00
Recipe Books 25.00
Cardinal Cherry Syrup Dispenser w/Pump 900.00

Syrup Dispensers w/Original Pumps   **We Pay**

Jersey Cream.. 500.00
Orange Julep... 600.00

Soda Fountain Collectibles

Grape Julep **600.00**
Cherry Julep **600.00**
Afri-Kola **900.00**
Buckeye Urn **600.00**

I have been collecting ice cream memorabilia for over fifteen years. My collection ranges from **scoops and trays to signs, trade cards, and freezers.** I am always looking for unusual soda fountain and ice cream-related memorabilia. The primary image must be soda fountain or ice cream-related and graphically interesting. All items should be in excellent condition. Please send a photocopy of the item along with your price.

Allan 'Mr. Ice Cream' Mellis
1115 W Montana
Chicago, IL 60614
(312) 327-9123

We Pay

Trade Magazines, pre-1930 *Soda Fountain, American Druggest* w/ice cream-related cover .... **20.00+**
Soda Fountain Supply Catalogs, pre-1920, except Mills #31 .... **30.00+**
Post Cards, especially real photos of soda fountains or advertising .... **10.00+**
Trade Cards, especially ice cream freezers & parlors .... **10.00+**
Booklets, pre-1930 w/colorful covers .... **10.00+**
Advertising Fans, picturing ice cream or people eating it .... **10.00+**
Pin-Back Buttons, pictorial, advertising ice cream companies .... **20.00+**
Ice Cream Scoops, extremely unusual ones (4 or 5 in Wayne Smith's book). **200.00+**
Ice Cream Trays, including tip trays in excellent condition (9 or 10).. **300.00+**
Salesman Samples, ice cream equipment .... **300.00+**
Toy Trucks, ice cream wagons .... **100.00+**
Watch Fobs, especially those showing ice cream .... **40.00+**
Tape Measures, usually celluloid .... **40.00+**
Ephemera, pre-1920 billheads, letterheads, covers, etc. .... **10.00+**
Sheet Music, ice cream on cover .... **10.00+**
Magazine Advertisements & Illustrations, especially pre-1900 woodcuts . **5.00+**
Printer's Cuts, especially showing soda fountain scenes or ice cream graphics . **5.00+**
Valentines, soda fountain scene .... **5.00+**
Photographs, especially old soda fountains or ice cream trucks .... **20.00+**
Matchcovers, only showing ice cream or soda fountain scene ....**1.00+**
Stock Certificates, vignette related to ice cream or soda company .... **30.00+**
Pocket Mirrors, ice cream image in excellent condition .... **50.00+**
Novelties (clickers, rulers, tops, etc.) .... **25.00+**

Old drugstore and apothecary items and collectibles have become increasingly sought after over the past ten years. Many people start out collecting straw jars and ice cream scoops to decorate their kitchens and recreation rooms. We have expanded from collecting these items to buying and collecting old drugstore show globes, candy display jars, medicine bottles of all types and shapes, and 'tools of the trade' of early druggists and doctors.

We are interested in buying any item that might have come out of an old drugstore, whether it had an old-fashioned soda fountain or not. We pay premium prices for early, unusual, complete, and undamaged items. We will buy one item, an entire collection, or the complete contents of a drugstore. We prefer pictures and prices be sent by anyone with items for sale. Please see our listings in this book under **Apothecary** and **Coca-Cola** for more information.

The American Museum of Apothecary
Science & Industries
18 Smith Acres
Northport, AL 35405
1-800-445-7811
(205) 556-1188 or (205) 339-2402

I am buying older soda fountain memorabilia. Anything that may have been used in a pre-1960 soda fountain, including advertising signs for products used there; unusual items are especially wanted. Top condition is a must. Send a photo and price or request an offer.

Rich Miller
144 E Main St., Box 203
Frostburg, MD 21532

We Pay

Heart-Shaped Ice Cream Scoops	**1,000.00+**
Heart-Shaped Ice Cream Dishes	**50.00+**
Unusual Ice Cream Scoops	**50.00+**
Syrup Dispensers	**100.00+**
Glass Label Syrup Bottles	**25.00+**
Ice Cream Trays	**25.00+**
Soda Trays	**25.00+**
Straw Holders	**25.00+**
Cone Holders	**20.00+**
Tin Advertising Signs	**20.00+**

Paper Advertising Signs .... **10.00+**

I want all items pertaining to soda fountains or grocery advertising — either unusual or common. I can use selling stock and items for my personal collection. No paper or cardboard items are wanted. And only items in excellent condition are needed. Please send information concerning age, condition, and price wanted.

Lois Wildman
175 E Chick Rd.
Camano Island, WA 98292

We Pay

Coca-Cola Trays .... **10.00+**
Pepsi-Cola Trays .... **15.00+**
Soda Thermometers, all brands.. **15.00+**
Tin Signs .... **15.00+**
Coca-Cola Button Signs, porcelain... **40.00+**
Soda Door Pulls.. **25.00+**
Picnic Coolers .... **25.00+**
Radios.. **15.00+**

I am searching for early soda fountain **advertising glasses and pottery root beer mugs.** Single pieces as well as entire collections are wanted.

Jan Henry
Rte. 2, Box 193
Galesville, WI 54630
(608) 582-4290

We Pay

Early Advertising Fountain Glasses... **10.00-75.00**
Pottery Root Beer Mugs **25.00-350.00**

SMOKEY THE BEAR AND WOODSY OWL

Wanted to buy: Smokey Bear or Woodsy Owl items that are from the 1970's or older — a single piece or a collection. I am not interested in items from the 1980's. Items wanted include stuffed toys, buttons, games, whistles, cookie jars, posters, and fire prevention items with Smokey or Woodsy on them. Good condition items are preferred. Also sought are Smokey the Bear lunch boxes and any kind of U.S. Forest dinnerware. This dinnerware is white with green line trim and a U.S. Forest Service emblem. I will buy plates, cups, bowls, pitchers, creamers, etc.

Joette R. Borzik
P.O. Box 1026
Fall City, WA 98025

Smokey the Bear and Woodsey Owl

Smokey the Bear and Woodsy Owl items as well things that were given away as public relations items at ranger stations, fairs, or schools are wanted. Examples are stuffed toys, posters, pins, pencils, pens, key chains, stickers, patches, rulers, jewelry, statues, books, stationery, etc. Please contact me regarding any U.S. Forest Service item also. I am interested in hearing what you have and will consider trading wants.

Noreen Stayton
P.O. Box 379
Doyle, CA 96109
(916) 827-2934

We Pay

Smokey the Bear **5.00-25.00**
Talking Smokey the Bear **25.00**
Smokey the Bear Jewelry **5.00**

SPARK PLUGS

I am a serious buyer of old and unusual sparks plugs as indicated by the prices below. It has been estimated that as many as four thousand different brand names have been placed on spark plugs since the inception of the internal combustion engine. As with most collecting fields, many of these are quite common — only a few hundred command a premium price. The spark plugs listed are only a small sample of the ones I looking for.

Special or unusual features found on a spark plug make it more valuable. Some of these features include an extra air gap at the top or an extra air valve in the base, a priming petcock on the side, a handle on the side for quick disassembly, and a ball bearing located in the base of the plug. Plugs with solid brass bodies and those that have colored or clear glass cores are also of special interest.

The prices listed below are for spark plugs in excellent used condition without rust and not broken or damaged. The same plugs in new 'old stock' condition and in original boxes are worth somewhat more. I will respond to all letters when a complete description and asking price is given.

Joseph F. Russell
455 Ollie St.
Cottage Grove, WI 53527

Plug Name   **We Pay**

Auto Marine 65.00
Su-Dig 40.00
Barney Google 50.00
Champion w/Priming Petcock.................................... 15.00
Affinity 8.00
All-In-One w/Priming Petcock 25.00
Vis Spark 10.00
James... 65.00
Twin-Double-Ended Plug 35.00
Hotstone Chicago 10.00
Packard... 8.00
Bull's Eye.. 40.00
Czar Top Primer 60.00
E.Z. Clean Prime 40.00
J.D. Visible... 15.00
Le Vac Air-O-Matic 20.00
Shurnuff 45.00
Maco Double Primer 50.00
Mulkeys w/Ball Bearing 65.00

SPRINGFIELD, ILLINOIS, MEMORABILIA

As a Korean War veteran living in Springfield, Illinois, I am collecting items relating to that war and to Springfield's history, commerce, banking, politics, advertising, etc. Listed below are some specific areas of interest. I will buy one item or one thousand. Write or phone with the description and price of your item. I pay fair prices plus UPS charges.

All Abe Lincoln Souvenirs, before 1960
All Post Cards
Police Memorabilia
Political Items
Sangamon Electric Badges, Posters, Etc.
Gulf Mobile Ohio Railroad Items
Allis Chalmers Badges, Posters, Advertising
Franklin Life Insurance Co. Items, before 1950
Illinois Watch Company Items
Beer, Milk, or Pop Items Marked Springfield
All Springfield Posters or Advertisements
Bank Checks, before 1900

Stock Certificates, any from above companies

Edward B. Smith Sr.
2541 S State
Springfield, IL 62704
(217) 744-4201

STAMPS

I am buying philatelic material from the United States and around the world. My main interests are better U.S. and foreign stamps (mint and used), postal covers, older post cards, view cards, and unusual philatelic items. Scott catalogs are used as a price guide. When a percentage is listed, it is the percentage of current Scott. The better the item, the better percentage is paid. Please write before sending large shipments.

Winfred Partin
414 Oak St.
Morristown, TN 37813

We Pay

Used U.S. Commemorative Stamps, off paper, undamaged, per 1,000 ..... **3.50+**
Used U.S. Se-Tenant Commemoratives, off paper, undamaged, per 1,000 . **4.50+**
Used U.S. Airmails & Back-of-the-Book, off paper, undamaged, per 1,000. **6.00+**
Used U.S. Definitives, off paper, undamaged, per pound .... **4.50+**
Used World Large Stamps, off paper, undamaged, per pound .... **8.00+**
Used World Small Stamps, off paper, undamaged, per pound .... **3.50+**
Used/Mint U.S. Singles or Sets, current value plus $5.00 ea .... **35%+**
Used/Mint World Sets or Singles, current value plus $5.00 ea................. **25%+**
Pre-1960 Post Cards, View Cards, Used/Mint, undamaged, per 100......... **7.00+**
Pre-1960 Postal Speciality Covers, clean, undamaged, per 100 .... **8.00+**
Pre-1985 First Day Covers, cacheted, unaddressed, undamaged, per 100.. **8.00+**

STANGL

I am interested in purchasing Stangl dinnerware in these patterns: Town and Country, Mediterranean, and Blue Caughley. All patterns should be in blue and in perfect condition with little wear.

Helaine Lesnick
9 Stratton Rd.
Scarsdale, NY 10583

We Pay

Cups & Saucers 10.00
Dinner Plates 10.00
Salad Plates 7.00
Hollowware .... 20.00+

STAR TREK

I am interested in purchasing the following Star Trek items in excellent or better condition. Also wanted are selected Star Wars figures, battery-operated space toys and robots, and all Lost in Space pieces. Send a listing with the item's condition and your price, or call for more information.

George J. Seiger
531 Hoyt St.
Pringle, PA 19704
(717) 287-1745

We Pay

Star Fleet Metal Detector 150.00
Star Trek Domed Lunch Box 150.00
Mr. Spock Porcelain Figure 75.00
Star Trek Collector Plates 25.00
Mego's Star Trek Aliens, 2nd Series, 8", mint on card 100.00
Mego's Star Trek Aliens, 2nd Series, 8", loose 50.00
Mego's Star Trek Aliens, 3rd Series, 8", mint on card .... 200.00+
Mego's Star Trek Aliens, 3rd Series, 8", loose .... 100.00+
Mego's Star Trek Decker Figure, 12", mint on card 75.00
Mego's Star Trek Klingon Figure, mint in box 40.00
Mego's Star Trek Communicators, mint in box 50.00
Mego's Star Trek Tricorder 50.00
Star Trek Next Generation Aliens, set of 4, 4" 50.00
Kenner Alien, 18" 125.00

Lost in Space Toys or Figures .... **50.00+**
Lost in Space Domed Lunch Box **200.00**
Star Wars Figures, mint on card or mint in box .... **10.00+**

STATUE OF LIBERTY

As early as 1876, ten years before the Statue of Liberty Enlightening the World was erected, souvenirs for this symbol of our country were being produced by the thousands. I collect the earliest memorabilia, including the items listed below.

Mike Brooks
7335 Skyline
Oakland, Ca 94611
(415) 339-1751

We Pay

Pre-1890 Books & Booklets .... **20.00+**
Donor Certificates .... **100.00+**
Inaugural Program **50.00**
Inaugural Invitation .... **100.00+**
Pin-backs **5.00-20.00**
Silk Bookmarks .... **25.00+**
Statues, Pre-1885, French or American **100.00-1,000.00**
Trade Cards **5.00-25.00**
Trade Handouts .... **10.00+**

STEINS

I'm a collector of antique beer steins. Character steins are my first choice, but other types such as Mettlach or brewery (Budweiser or Anheuser-Busch) are wanted as well. I have been in the antique restoration business for over thirty years and have special interest in making connections with fellow collectors and traders. Prices paid are determined by quality. If money doesn't interest you, maybe I could find something you might want in trade. I always have shelf room for another stein. Thank you.

Carl Guillot
1906 N Foster Dr.
Baton Rouge, LA 70806
(504) 357-6033

STOCK CERTIFICATES

Highest prices paid for old mining stock certificates (non-coal, issued pre-1920 certificates). Send photocopy of your mining stock certificate and the price you are asking, or we will make an offer. Listed below is only a partial listing of items wanted. A free descriptive list of old mining stock certificates is available upon request with large SASE.

Mineco
P.O. Box 487
Yucaipa, CA 92399
(714) 797-1650

We Pay

Ahumada Lead Co., circa 1921 .... **20.00**
Alaska Gold Mines, circa 1920 .... **18.00**
Arizona Copper Co., circa 1890 .... **50.00**
Batopilas Consolidated Mining Co., 1910 .... **20.00**
Belcher Divide Mining Co., 1919 .... **10.00**
Black Hawk Gold Mining Co., 1866 .... **45.00**
Brunswick Gold Mining Co., 1889 .... **20.00**
Bullion Consolidated Mining Co., 1870 .... **50.00**
California Nevada Copper Co., 1909 .... **10.00**
Durange Mapimi Mining Co., 1880 .... **90.00**
Emma Silver Mining Co., 1880 .... **90.00**
Erupcion Mining Co., 1920 .... **20.00**
Empire Zinc Mining Co., 1914 .... **19.00**
Flux Mining Co., 1919 .... **11.00**
Golconda Mining Co., 1880 .... **55.00**
Gould & Durry Silver Mining Co., 1875 .... **100.00**
Graphic Lead & Zinc Mining Co., 1906 .... **19.00**

I am buying stock **certificates, bonds, letterheads, pre-1900 vignetted checks, revenue stamped or revenue imprinted documents, and other vignetted documents.** Listed below is a sample of some items I am interested in buying. If you have something you think I may find interesting, send a photocopy or description, and I'll reply. All paper items will be considered.

William S. Knadler
33 Norwood Ave.
Norwalk, OH 44857

We Pay

Fire Insurance Policies .... **3.00+**
Fire-Related Paper .... **2.00+**
Baltimore & Ohio Railroad Stock, 1830's .... **40.00+**
Ohio Railroads, 1800's .... **10.00+**
Coca-Cola Stock .... **25.00+**
Civil War Bonds .... **25.00+**
Ben Hur Motor Car Co. .... **35.00+**
Packard Motor Car Co. .... **75.00+**
Moulton Mining, 1886 .... **35.00+**
Gold Placer Mining Co., 1881 .... **20.00+**
Alden Type Setting & Distributing .... **50.00+**

American Express, 1800's	**60.00+**
Ohio Industrial Stocks	**2.00+**

America West Archives is buying most types of old stock certificates and bonds from the United States dating from the 1850's through the 1930's. We are especially interested in mining, railroad, and energy stocks, as well as other industries. We are not interested in stocks and bonds from outside of the U.S. nor are we interested in 'blank' or unissued stocks. We prefer that the certificates are in good condition with no damage and will buy one piece or 1,000 pieces. We have not listed examples of what we can pay, as some certificates have little or no value while others may be rare and worth $100.00 or more, depending upon age, condition, attractiveness, and region of origin. Send photocopies if possible for a quick reply.

American West Archives
P.O. Box 100
Cedar City, UT 84720

I am looking to buy stock certificates. Please see the brief listing below for certificates in mint condition, and contact me if you have certificates to sell.

Irvin Gendler
11222 Davenport St.
Omaha, NE 68154
(402) 330-2656

We Pay

Levi Strauss	**100.00**
Circus	**50.00**
Carnivals	**50.00**
Amusement Parks	**Write**
Funeral Parlors	**Write**

STONEWARE

I am interested in buying stoneware jugs and jars that are brushwork-decorated or have cobalt stenciling on gray ground. Pieces need to be in good condition without cracks or chips.

345

Sachs Antiques
2433 Nicholson Rd.
Sewickley, PA 15143

We Pay

Gallon Jars, stenciled .... **75.00+**
Gallon Jugs, stenciled .... **100.00+**
10-Gallon Jars, stenciled.. **250.00+**
20-Gallon Jars, stenciled.. **400.00+**
Gallon Jars, brushwork .... **150.00+**
Gallon Jugs, brushwork.. **175.00+**
10-Gallon Jars, brushwork .... **250.00+**
20-Gallon Jars, brushwork .... **500.00+**
Gallon Pitchers, brushwork... **200.00+**
Milk Pans, brushwork... **150.00+**
Any Others .... **Write**

In the 1890's it was very popular for liquor dealers, merchants, and saloons to advertise their liquor or saloon on stoneware whiskey jugs. At that time it only cost a few pennies extra to get the potter to stencil the customer's advertisement under the glaze before the jug was being fired.

I am interested in buying undamaged **advertising whiskey jugs from Arkansas, Texas, Louisiana, and Mississippi.** We are also interested in miniature jugs or other jugs with saloon names from other states. We pay a minimum of $30.00 up to several hundred dollars.

Dempse B. McMullen
P.O. Box 402
Natchez, MS 39120
(601) 446-9037

STRING HOLDERS

I am interested in buying chalk or china string holders. I collect figurals such as faces of people and animals as well as other wall-hanging forms. I especially like Black Mammy or butler holders.

Jean D. Derian
745 Westbrook Dr.
N Tonawanda, NY 14120
(716) 693-5157

We Pay

Animal, People, Etc. **25.00-35.00**
Black Face.. **up to 100.00**

TEA LEAF

During the second half of the nineteenth century, English potters began shipping large quantities of Tea Leaf ironstone to the United States American housewives were looking for a change from the plain white ironstone they had used for years. The new copper-luster sprig decoration was the change they had been awaiting. Anthony Shaw, who is credited with creating the new design, was soon joined by nearly twenty different firms in producing this inexpensive everyday china. Several prominent English potters were

347

Alfred Meakin, Anthony Shaw, Henry Burgess, Powell and Bishop, A.J. Wilkinson, and Thomas Furnival.

When collecting Tea Leaf ironstone, it is important to find pieces which are not stained, chipped, or cracked. The prices which are quoted are for mint examples of marked English Tea Leaf ironstone. If you have fine pieces of English Tea Leaf ironstone for sale, I hope to hear from you.

Tom Harrison
P.O. Box 374
Brimfield, IL 61517
(309) 446-3229

We Pay

Bowl, 8"	15.00
Covered Casserole	40.00
Cup & Saucer	30.00
Gravy Boat	25.00
Dinner Plate	5.00
Platter	10.00
Relish Dish	15.00
Sugar Bowl w/Lid	25.00
Teapot	55.00
Tureen, Lid, Ladle	150.00

TEA STRAINERS

I collect tin tea strainers with advertising written around the edge. I will pay from $5.00 to $7.50 each, depending upon condition and rarity.

Jim Goldsmith
8012 SE Thirteenth
Portland, OR 97202
(503) 233-7334

TELEPHONES

As a charter member of A.T.C.A. (Antique Telephone Collector's Association), I'm a collector of early telephones and telephone-related items such as wall phones, candlestick phones, colored cradle phones, coin phones, phone parts, and porcelain telephone signs. Please describe items and price when replying.

A.W. Merrell, Jr.
3121 SE Bedford Dr.
Stuart, FL 34997
(407) 283-4312

TELEVISIONS

I buy vintage televisions from the 1920's to the 1970's. Look for early mechanical TVs from 1920 to 1935 with a round perforated wheel in front of a neon light (or light socket). It may have a magnifing glass in front of the cabinet. Names to look for include Baird, Jenkins, ICA, Daven, Western, and Empire State. 1930's electronic televisions have 5" to 14" screens, with only 1, 3, or 5 channels. Look for any Don Lee or Peck, RCA TT5 and their TRK and RR series, DuMont Models 180–195, General Electric push-button TV's, and Andrea, Westinghouse, Zenith, and Philco mirror-in-lid sets, etc.

I also buy 1940's wooden cabinet televisons with small screens and unusual cabinets plus unique-looking TVs from 1950 to 1975. Sets need not work, but cabinet condition is important. A photo helps, and all letters with SASE enclosed will be answered. I will travel to pick up important items.

Harry Poster
P.O. Box 1883
S Hackensak, NJ 07606

We Pay

Any Mechanical TV, 1920's-1930's **1,000.00-10,000.00**
Any Electronic 1935-1942 Television................................. **1,000.00-12,000.00**
Andrea I-F-5 or KTE-5 Kit TV .... **2,000.00+**
General Electric HM-225, 5-Channel TV .... **3,500.00+**
1930's TV Catalogs & Dealer Information **50.00-150.00**
Pilot TV-37, 3" portable, circa 1947 .... **100.00+**
RCA 621-TS, 7" wooden .... **350.00+**
DuMont 'Clifton,' RA-102 Console.. **450.00+**
1950's Color TV w/9"-19" Screen................................. **500.00-1,500.00**
Color Wheels & Adapters for B&W TV's.................... **500.00-1,000.00**
Philco Predictas & Other Unusual Sets......................... **100.00-800.00**

Vintage televisions are needed for a private museum. Regardless of where you live, transportation of sets can be arranged. The sets do not have to work and should not be plugged in — serious damage may result without preliminary servicing. I also purchase other sets not listed below.

Donald D. Hauff
P.O. Box 16351
Minneapolis, MN 55416

Pre-1938 Scanning Disk Sets   **We Pay**

Baird, Daven, Delft, Freed, Globe, Hartman, ICA, Jenkins, Pioneer, See-All,
Trav-ler, or Western .... **up to 2,500.00**

1938–1942 Electronic Sets (all have 5 or fewer channels)   **We Pay**

Andrea .... **up to 4,000.00**
Belmont.. **up to 2,500.00**
Don Lee .... **up to 1,500.00**
DuMont .... **up to 2,000.00**
Garod.. **up to 1,00.00**
General Electric .... **up to 3,000.00**
Meissner.. **up to 750.00**
Peck.. **up to 750.00**
Philco.. **up to 2,000.00**
Pilot.. **up to 1,500.00**
RCA .... **up to 4,000.00**
Stewart Warner.. **up to 1,500.00**
Stromberg Carlson .... **up to 2,000.00**
Westinghouse .... **up to 3,500.00**
Zenith.. **up to 3,000.00**

1946–1949 Electronic Sets   **We Pay**

Sets w/3" or 7" Picture Tubes... **up to 200.00**

THERMOMETERS

I collect a specialized type of **advertising thermometer in plastic, shaped like old gasoline station pole signs.** Almost 7" tall, these thermometers, imbedded under the gasoline sign in the support column, often had the dealer/distributor's name and location stamped on the base and often had a small paper calendar attached to the base. These were given away by gasoline stations as a premium/gift item in the late 1950's through the mid-1960's. I am seeking regional and local gasoline brand thermometers such as those listed below. No national or more common brands such as Esso, Texaco, Mobil, etc. are wanted. Let me hear from you if you have one; I'll respond immediately. Prices paid range from $10.00 to $20.00 each.

APCO	Hudson	Sunoco
Ashland	Husky	Tenneco

Barnsdall	Keystone	Total
Bay	Martin	United
CALSO	M-F-A	76 (Union 76)
Clark	Pan-Am	UTOCO
Deep Rock	Humble	Vickers
Derby	Shamrock	White Rose
ENCO	Signal	Zenith
Fleet-Wing	SOC	Zephyr
Frontier	Speed-Wing	
FS (Farm Service)	Spur	

Peter Capell
1838 W Grace St.
Chicago, IL 60613-2724

TOASTERS

I am a private collector interested in purchasing vintage electric toasters made from 1908 through 1940. I am interested in old and unusual models that are in very good condition without cracks or corrosion and with all parts intact. Prices listed are for toasters in excellent condition. I am also interested in other unusual models not listed below.

Joe Lukach
7111 Deframe Ct.
Arvada, CO 80004
(303) 422-8970

We Pay

Armstrong Automatic Toaster	30.00
Bersted #78	30.00
Bigelow Electric	25.00
Birtman 1-Slice	45.00
Cadillac Electric	35.00
Cookenette	35.00
Cutler Hammer	30.00
Dalton Electric Heater	45.00
D.A. Rogers Self Timing	75.00
Delco	35.00
Thomas A. Edison Edicraft	45.00
Electric Specialties Okeco	30.00
Electro Mfg. Co. Automatic Toaster	50.00
Excelsior Twin Reversible	70.00
Hewitt	35.00
Landers, Frary, & Clark E-3941	20.00
Landers, Frary, & Clark E-1941	20.00
Landers, Frary, & Clark E-1942	35.00
Landers, Frary, & Clark E-943	90.00
Landers, Frary, & Clark E-9410	65.00
Landers, Frary, & Clark E-7732	45.00
Landers, Frary, & Clark E-2122	40.00
Manning Bowman No. 1209 to No. 1223	25.00
Manning Bowman w/Toast Rack	45.00
Mattatuck Commander #101	50.00
Mecky	100.00
Mesco	60.00
Millar	40.00
Pan Electric	100.00-300.00
Paragon	35.00
Pelouse	65.00
Perm-Way Electric	40.00
Phelps Mfg. Co. Cozy Toaster	65.00
Plant & Co. Double Ray	40.00
Porcelier	100.00
Radion Helion	50.00

Simplex T-215 .... **50.00**
Sprite Automatic 4-Slice **50.00**
Steelcraft **30.00**
Superior Electric, Super Lectric 55 .... **30.00**
Toast-O-Lator Models A to H **40.00-100.00**
Trimble **35.00**
Truit **35.00**
Wicks **50.00**
White Beauty **35.00**

TOBACCIANA

I buy **wooden cigar boxes that generally date before 1920**. Boxes can be made in many shapes and sizes such as log cabins, bottles, cheese boxes, etc. Fine condition boxes from before 1920 with colorful and interesting labels are priced below. I also want **cigar tins with colorful labels from before 1940**. Prices paid are based mainly on condition. All boxes made prior to 1880 are highly desired and will be priced accordingly. A photocopy of the inside box label usually provides me with enough information to give firm prices.

Henry F. Neis
621 Main St. Terrace
Eudora, KS 66025
(913) 542-2244

Boxes w/Labels Featuring   **We Pay**

Cartoon Characters .... **10.00+**

Indians, Blacks, or Chinese .... **15.00+**
Book-Shaped (very common) .... **2.00+**
Sports Figures & Athletic Events... **20.00+**
Nudes or Semi-Nudes.. **20.00+**
Trains, Old Cars, Airplanes, or Boats... **5.00+**
Christmas.. **5.00+**
Health Claims... **25.00+**
Uncle Sam .... **15.00+**
Gambling or Political... **15.00+**
Cigar Tins w/Colorful Labels.. **80.00+**

I am looking for cigarette collectibles, particularly **old advertising items, promotional material, flat 50's tins, round tins, pre-1940 items, but no cigar items**. Listed below are examples of items and prices paid.

Dennis R. Adams
13624 Stacey Dr.
Hudson, FL 34667
(813) 862-2990

We Pay

Advertising Ash Trays.. **5.00+**
Cigarette Lighters .... **5.00+**
Tin Signs .... **30.00+**
Flat 50's Tins.. **15.00+**
Paper Signs, pre-1930's... **25.00+**
Unique Promotional Items... **50.00+**
Trade Cards .... **3.00+**

I am a collector buying **wooden cigar boxes**. I am especially interested in buying boxes or related items from the factories of the mountain states, Nebraska, and Kansas. I also want boxes from other western states and the midwestern state of Ohio, or any others with tropical or humorous designs. In describing a box, I need the factory number and state from the bottom of the box and the series number or date from the tax stamp (if available). A photocopy of the inner lid label is the best way to describe the design. Of course, price depends on condition. Trades are possible. All inquiries including SASE will be answered.

Chuck Tuthill
1421 Clayton St. #1
Denver, CO 80206

We Pay

Miners Pick, Colorado... **75.00**
State Seal of Nebraska... **50.00**
Lincoln County Booster, Wyoming... **65.00**
Ordinary Designs from States.. **5.00+**
Indians (except Rocky Ford).. **10.00+**
Famous Actors, Patriots, Etc... **10.00+**

I want to buy **tobacco tins**. Those with paper labels are not wanted. Prices listed are for mint condition tins.

Clayton D. Zeller
1115 26th Ave. S #4
Grand Forks, ND 58201
(701) 772-4995

We Pay

Penns Pail, 7" x 5" **20.00**
Old Rover Pail, 7" x 5" **55.00**
Sweet Mist Pail, 7" x 4".. **40.00**
Brotherhood Lunch Box, 6" x 5" x 4" **20.00**
Central Union Lunch Box, 8" x 6" x 4"... **25.00**
Dixie Queen Lunch Box, 6" x 5" x 4"... **60.00**
Fashion Lunch Box, 6" x 5" x 4".. **25.00**
Friends Lunch Pail, 6" x 5" x 4"... **55.00**
George Washington Lunch Box, 6" x 5" x 4" **15.00**
Gail & Axe Navy Lunch Box, 6" x 5" x 4"... **25.00**
New Bachelor Vertical Box, 5" x 4" x 2"... **30.00**
New Bachelor, round, 6" x 3" **50.00**
Red Feather, round, 6" x 4".. **15.00**
Scottie Vertical Box, 5" x 4" x 4".. **55.00**
Two Orphans, round, 6" x 4".. **45.00**
Frishmuth's Pail, 7" x 5" **30.00**
Old Partner Pail, 7" x 5".. **55.00**
Miners & Puddlers Pail, 7" x 5" **55.00**
Nigger Hair Pail, 7" x 5" **60.00**

Tiger Chewing Tobacco Cylindrical Container, 14" x 8"........................... **55.00**
Sweet Mist Cylindrical Container, 14" x 8" **40.00**
Possum Cylindrical Container, 6" x 4½" **30.00**
Stag Horizontal Box, 5" x 5" x 5" **30.00**
Union Leader Red Cut Pocket Tin, 4" x 2" **20.00**
Sterling Cylindrical Container, 14" x 8"... **25.00**
Old Glory, round, 5" x 5" **20.00**
Old Seneca, round, 6" x 3" **55.00**
Popper's Ace Vertical Box, 7" x 5" x 5" **50.00**
Owl Brand Vertical Box, 6" x 2" x 2" **25.00**
Oxford Gems Horizontal Box, 6" x 5" x 4" **25.00**
Pippins Vertical Box, 5" x 2" x 2".. **20.00**
North Pole Lunch Box, 4" x 6" x 3" **45.00**
Warnick & Brown Lunch Box, 6" x 5" x 4" **25.00**
Winner Lunch Box, 6" x 5" x 4" **45.00**
Cylindrical Admiral, 6" x 3½".. **25.00**
Cylindrical Archer, 4" x 3".. **10.00**
Cylindrical Big Ben, 6" x 5" **15.00**
Cylindrical Boston, 6" x 3"... **15.00**
Cylindrical Brotherhood, 6" x 4" **65.00**
Cylindrical City Club, 6" x 3" **55.00**
Cylindrical Central Union, 6" x 3"... **50.00**
Cylindrical Country Life, 4" x 2½"... **15.00**
Cylindrical Daily Mail, 5" x 3"... **15.00**
Cylindrical Culture, 6" x 3".. **25.00**
Cylindrical Flycasters, 3½" x 4"... **40.00**
Cylindrical Eight Brothers, 6" x 3" **15.00**
Cylindrical Dixie Queen, 6" x 3" **45.00**
Cylindrical Forest & Stream, 5" x 3"... **45.00**
Cylindrical Fountain, 7" x 4".. **50.00**
Cylindrical Hi Plane, 6" x 3".. **25.00**
Cylindrical Handmade, 6" x 3"... **50.00**

TOKENS

Tokens and related items are of interest to me as a collector. Tokens are usually made of metal but may be made of paper, fiber, wood, or even in the form of advertising 'Good For' pocket mirrors. I want **metal composition tokens** only. No amusement, sales tax, transportation, telephone, or OPA tokens are wanted. Tokens may have some wear but no damage. Please write first before shipping. Your postage will be reimbursed. You will be sent a check for your material the same day it is received. Listed below are some of the tokens I seek. Send any other old unidentified tokens not listed here with your price or request my offer.

Norman K. Knaak
Rt. 3, Box 132-A-5
Purvis, MS 39475

We Pay

Any Type 'Good For' Token From Mississippi	**50¢**
Other States 'Good For' Tokens w/City & State on Token, aluminum	**25¢**
Other States 'Good For' Tokens w/City & State on Token, brass	**35¢**
Tokens From any State, composed of 2 metals	**50¢**
Dairy-Related Tokens	**40¢**
Tokens, dated 1832–1844, large	**3.00**
Tokens, dated 1861–1865, penny-sized	**3.00**
Advertising 'Good For' Mirrors, average or better condition	**35.00**
Military Civil War Dog Tags	**50.00**

Since 1932 when first introduced at Tenino, Washington, wood has been used as money, souvenirs for celebrations, and advertising for many different businesses. I am primarily interested in wooden souvenirs of celebrations by various governmental units such as for a 150th anniversary of a city, town, or state or wood used as money during the depression era. When responding, a copy of both sides of the wood (copy machines usually make excellent copies), quantity available, and price you desire is very helpful. Multiple pieces are welcomed.

Norman R. Boughton
1356 Buffalo Rd.
Rochester, NY 14624

Flats (must be unbroken)   **We Pay**

Tenino, WA (25¢ to $1.00)	**25.00-60.00**
Tenino, WA Tax Token	**2.00**
Other Flats	**1.00-20.00**

Rounds   **We Pay**

Celebration	**25¢-15.00**

McDonald's	**25¢**
Dairy Queen	**25¢**
Dunkin' Donuts	**25¢**
Sambo's (must show city of issue)	**35¢**

For twenty years, Presidential Coin & Antique Co. has been a leader in the token and medal collecting field. Our Americana auctions and mail order business requires that we purchase a wide variety of these items. We are most (but not exclusively) interested in:

Civil War, Hard Times, and Politicals: buttons, ribbons, pre-1940 medals (especially those by well-known sculptors), Indian peace medals (particularly silver), pre-1900 medals struck by the U.S. mint.
Old Transportation Tokens, Official Inaugural Medals, World's Fair or Expo: also related memorabilia, award medals (particularly of agricultural or mechanical societies), etc.

We will gladly make fair offers on any of the above or other similar items you have. It is easiest to do this if we can see the item. We will refund your postage on anything you send us which we do not buy.

H. Joseph Levine
Presidential Coin & Antique Co.
6550-I Little River Turnpike
Alexandria, VA 22312

TOYS

If it says **G Man**, I'm interested! I collect all G Man items from the height of their popularity (1930's) to present day FBI pieces. I have access to a number of collectors with similar interests and will purchase your item for my advanced collection or common pieces for other collectors. Please send photocopy or description with price. Sample prices are given below. I especially want a 1939 NY World's Fair G Man badge.

Richard A. Guttler
42 Circle Dr.
Syosset, NY 11791
(516) 935-7218

We Pay

Marx G Man Pursuit Wind-Up Car	**200.00+**
Melvin Purvis Girl's Division Secret Operator's Badge	**20.00+**
Melvin Purvis Captain's Secret Operator's Badge	**25.00+**
Cars: Wind-Up, Friction, Etc.	**35.00+**
Common & Unusual Badges	**10.00+**
Boxed Games & Play Sets	**25.00+**
Other Premiums	**20.00+**

We are buying **all collectible toys, toy boxes, and incomplete or damaged toys** for restoration. Write and describe finish, size, missing or broken parts. Price or ask for a quote.

Robert J. Cufr
3319 County Rd. L
Swanton, OH 43558

Tin Character Wind-Up   **We Pay**

Complete & Working **75.00-600.00**

Broken Springs or Missing Parts **20.00-360.00**
Popeye or Bluto Dippy Dumper Cart or Boxes **150.00-400.00**
Celluloid Popeye & Bluto Figures (for above) **25.00-75.00**
Howdy Doody Band, Clock-a-Doodle, or Band Figures **35.00-500.00**

Battery-Operated (excellent condition; not working, no rust)	**We Pay**

Robots, tin **25.00-500.00**
Robots, part tin... **10.00-75.00**
Character (Popeye, Mickey, etc.).. **75.00-200.00**
Monsters or Gorillas **25.00-150.00**
People or Animals **5.00-50.00**
Any Above w/Rust in Battery Box or Parts Missing......................... **5.00-100.00**
Original Boxes for Battery or Tin Wind-Up..................................... **10.00-50.00**
All Above Complete & Working... **Write**

I am always buying old **toys from the 1860's to the 1960's**. Toys made in the U.S.A., Japan, Germany, England, and France that are made of paper on wood, celluloid, cast iron, tin, pot metal, plastic, etc. are wanted. Remember that condition is everything! The better the condition, the more I will pay.

Chris Savino
P.O. Box 419
Breesport, NY 14816
(607) 739-3106

	We Pay

Disney Toys from 1928 through 1960's **50.00-5,000.00**
Toy Robots, tin or plastic .... **100.00-4,000.00+**
Motorcycles & Autos .... **100.00-2,500.00+**
Comic Character Toys .... **100.00-5,000.00+**
Pressed Steel Trucks... **250.00-1,000.00+**
Pre-War Japan Toys .... **500.00-2,500.00+**

We are serious buyers of **German, Japanese, and old U.S. tin toys** in good condition.

Dora Lerch
P.O. Box 586
N White Plains, NY 10603

We Pay

Cars, Jeeps, Buses, Tanks... **20.00-500.00**
Other Wind-Up Toys **50.00-500.00**

I am buying any **1960's monster and science fiction-related** toys from such TV shows as Land of the Giants, Lost in Space, Munsters, Addams Family, Twilight Zone, Outer Limits, Green Hornet, etc. I am also looking for **Universal Studios monster toys** — especially those advertised in *Famous Monsters* magazine.

Roland Coover, Jr.
1537 E Strasburg Rd.
W Chester, PA 19380

We Pay

Board Games .... **20.00+**
Puzzles .... **10.00+**
Model Kits... **25.00+**
Lost in Space Items... **25.00+**
Colorforms... **10.00+**
Halloween Costumes .... **20.00+**
Coloring Books.. **5.00+**
Gum Cards.. **1.00+**
Remco Munster or Addams Family Dolls in Original Boxes................ **200.00+**

I have clients with immediate needs for certain items. I will pay the amounts shown for the first copy I receive of each of the following items listed below. I am also looking for **1950's American brick sets and 1950's Tinkertoy sets,** either partial or complete, in any condition.

Andrew Egendorf
P.O. Box 646
Weston, MA 02193
(617) 647-1025

Monopoly Game Board, copyright between 1951 & 1954, fine condition. **50.00**
Magic Slate, from Swayze board game, very good condition.................... **25.00**
Crayola Box, 64-crayon size, mid-1960's, fine condition.......................... **50.00**
Chinese Checkers, 1950–1954, very good condition................................. **50.00**
Chutes & Ladders, 1940–1954, very good condition **50.00**
1955 Quiz Book for Go to the Head of the Class, very good condition **25.00**
Geniac, good (labels & box must be fine) **250.00**
Shipping, fine condition... **1,000.00**

I am buying antique toys. I primarily collect tin wind-up toys but am also interested in friction and battery-operated toys. **Toys made prior to 1965** in good to mint-in-box condition are preferred. Listed below are some of the manufacturers that I am seeking.

Scott T. Smiles
848 SE Atlantic Dr.
Lantana, FL 33462-4702
(407) 582-4947

We Pay

Marx .... **100.00+**
Chein .... **50.00+**
Wolverine .... **75.00+**
Unique Art .... **100.00+**
Strauss .... **150.00+**
Lehmann .... **250.00+**
Martin .... **250.00+**
U.S. Zone Germany... **75.00+**
Occupied Japan .... **50.00+**
Made in Japan .... **50.00+**
Made in Germany.. **125.00+**
Made in France .... **100.00+**
Made in Spain .... **75.00+**
Made in Great Britain .... **50.00+**
Made in Italy .... **75.00+**

I seek any toy that is old and unusual but have a special interest in **toy reed organs**. Small plastic electric reed organs with keyboards made in the 1940's through the early 1960's are wanted. One specific reed organ, the Tru-Note Pipe Organ, was made by the Hit Products Corporation of South Norwalk, Connecticut. I will pay market price for any of these organs. Listed below is a sampling of toy organs wanted.

E.L. Chaney
906 4th Ave.
Jacksonville, AL 36265

We Pay

Chein Melody Player w/Paper Rolls	**115.00+**
Toonerville Player Piano w/Disks	**35.00+**
Crank Reed Organs (cathedral shaped & lithographed)	**85.00+**
Concert Roller Organ Pinned Cobs	**5.00+**

We are interested in buying **old tin wind-up character or character-related toys**. Any toy in fine condition by Marx, Strauss, Lehmann, Marklin, Nifty, Animate Toy, Chein, Unique Art, Wolverine, along with other companies will be considered. We also buy **robots, rare metal lunch boxes, Schoenhut animals, Buddy-L trucks, and Smith-Miller toys**. Toys in their original boxes are particularly desirable. Please send a photo with a brief description of the toy and its condition along with your price.

Midstates
1706 AV G-301
Sterling, IL 61081
(815) 625-4848

We Pay

Lost in Space Lunch Box, domed	**200.00**
Robbie Robot, Yoneyawa, 1950's	**500.00**
Popeye the Pilot Wind-Up Plane, Marx	**300.00**
Smitty on a Scooter, Marx	**500.00**
Merry Makers Band, Marx	**500.00**
Roy Rogers Gun & Holster Set	**150.00**
Sparkplug Wooden Toy, Schoenhut	**200.00**
Shirley Temple Doll, 1940's	**200.00**
Popeye Rowboat, Hoge	**500.00**

Mickey on Horse, celluloid, 1930's **800.00**
Felix Wooden Pull Car, Borgfeldt, 1925 .... **200.00**
Amos & Andy Fresh Air Taxi **400.00**
Ocean Liner, Fleischmann, 1930 .... **500.00**
Humphrey Mobile, Wyandotte, 1940's **80.00**

I am interested in a **variety of toys for my personal collection**. Tin lithographed comic toys (mint-in-box only), especially Marx Amos Walker with moving eyes and Atomic Robot Man, are wanted. All tin lithographed transportation toys such as zeppelins, motorcycles, ships, automotive or aeronautical items are wanted. Tin-plated foreign trains are the only type of train that is sought. **Fortuneteller machines with figures** are another interest.

P.N. Constantine
833 Troy St.
Elmont, NY 11003
(516) 561-9217

We Pay

Pulver Gum Machines (with animated figures) .... **600.00+**
Flash Gordon or Buck Rogers Paper Items .... **100.00+**
Andy Gump Sheet Music .... **30.00+**
Amos & Andy Stand-Up Paper Figures .... **100.00+**

I will buy all Auburn rubber items as well as **hard rubber vehicles** by other manufacturers such as Sun, Barr, Goodrich, etc. — one item or an entire collection. Also collected are **all types of toy soldiers made before 1960**, including but not limited to dimestore, tin, rubber, U.S. or foreign composition, plastic, etc. Prices paid depend upon condition.

Robert Jossart
4251 Willowbrook Rd.
De Pere, WI 54115

A wide variety of toys and toy-related items are wanted. Listed below are only a sampling of items with prices paid. Other trains by Lionel, American Flyer, Bing, Ives, Hornby, etc. are wanted as well as any toy motorcycles, airplanes, boats, cars, and trucks. Toys made by Schuco, Dinky, Marx, Smith-Miller, Structo, Marklin, Hubley, etc. are also sought. Anything marked Sky King, Tom Mix, Captain Midnight, Terry and the Pirates, Hopalong Cassidy, Roy Rogers, and Gene Autry is of interest. Related areas of collecting are pre-1926 post cards, old toy robots from the 1950's, any aviation memorabilia, Black Americana, old stereo cameras, old fountain pens, old 10¢ comic books, and old aviation, motorcycle, or toy magazines and catalogs.

Richard Gronowski
140 N Garfield Ave.
Traverse City, MI 49684
(616) 941-2111

We Pay

Racing Cars, old gas-powered, 1930's–1950's, each .... **up to 200.00**
Model Airplane Motors, old spark ignition, each...................................... **35.00**
Toy Outboard Boat Motors, metal, each **35.00**
Lionel Locomotives 5344, 700E, or 773, each **200.00**
Lionel Locomotives 726, 736, 746, or 2332, each................................... **100.00**
Aviator Wings, sterling silver, 3", each.. **20.00**
Matchbox Toys w/Gray Wheels, each... **3.00**
Christmas Catalogs (pre-1976) Sears, Spiegels, Wards, Penneys, Etc., each.. **5.00**

I am buying **character toys and related items** (clothing, household items, etc.). I prefer items from the 1930's through the 1980's and have a special interest in the 1950's through 1960's period. Listed below are some of the things I am seeking.

Terri L. Marids
1104 Shirlee Ave.
Ponca City, OK 74601
(405) 762-5174

We Pay

Remco Dolls (Munsters, Addams Family, Beatles, etc.)........................... **15.00+**
Other Manufacturer Character Dolls... **10.00+**
Louis Marx, Marx, or Linemar Toys or Games .... **15.00+**
Children's Metal Litho Lunch Boxes or Thermoses............................... **10.00+**
Cowboy Personality Items (Hopalong Cassidy, Lone Ranger, etc.).......... **10.00+**
Hanna Barbera Cartoon Character Items... **5.00+**
Any Elvis Presley Item (pre-1977 preferred) .... **5.00+**

Robots .... **20.00+**
Hartland Plastics Inc. Items (baseball or western plastic toys) .... **20.00+**
Breyer Molding Co. (plastic horses) .... **5.00+**
Advertising Toys .... **5.00+**
Wind-Up Toys .... **10.00+**
Battery-Operated Toys .... **10.00+**

————————————

Toy and model school busses are wanted by collector. The yellow school bus is 51 years old. Busses were first painted School Bus Yellow and National Glossy Black in 1939. Prior to that, there was no standard color, just what the community desired. Many were painted red, white, and blue — our national colors. Painting school busses in the school's colors was also a popular practice.

Each morning and afternoon during the school year, hundreds of thousands of busses transport millions of American children to and from school. The school bus and commercial air flight remain two of the safest methods of travel in the United States today.

I collect toy and model school busses, old or new. If you have busses you wish to sell or trade, let us get together. Please state your asking price with the first correspondence.

Kenn Norris
P.O. Box 4830
Sanderson, TX 79848-4830

————————————

I am collecting **cap guns and rifles** in very good to mint condition and will pay a fair price depending on the make of gun and its condition (only very good to mint-in-box items are wanted). Specific makes and models are listed here.

Nichols (near-mint to mint-in-box items):
Stallion 45, steel blue
Stallion 36, gold & turquoise grips
Pony, Pinto, Cowman, Cowtike, Cowpuncher
Colt Special
Fury 500 Machine Gun
Shell-Firing Derringer

Kilgore (very good to mint, no box or card needed)
Long Tom, cast iron

American, cast iron
Roy Rogers, cast iron
Big Horn, orange grips, cast iron

Others
George Schmidt Pathfinder
Wyatt Earp Buntline Special, Actoy
Wyatt Earp Long Barrel, Hubley

Dave Case
12652 SR 120
Middlebury, IN 46540
(219) 825-9848 (5 pm to 9:30 pm)

I am interested in buying **all wind-up toys or battery-operated toys that are defective**. The older, the better the toy, and remember that broken is OK. Prices paid will depend on the extent of defects of toys. I am interested in quantity. Call the Toy Doctor!

Leo E. Rishty, Toy Doctor
77 Alan Loop
Staten Island, NY 10304
(718) 727-9477

TRADE SIGNS

I am buying trade signs that date from before 1960. Items that are wood, embossed tin, or porcelain and from commercial establishments are preferred. Listed below are some of the items I am seeking. Also wanted is anything old or unusual; single items, whole or partial collections are wanted.

W. Baxter
River Rd., R.R. #2
Titusville, NJ 08560

We Pay

Coca-Cola .... **25.00+**

Soda, Water, Juice.. **25.00+**
Beer, Whiskey, Spirits .... **25.00+**
Hardware... **25.00+**
Grocery .... **25.00+**
Neon, all types .... **25.00+**
Bank.. **25.00+**
General Store.. **25.00+**
Tobacco .... **25.00+**
Farm Signs.. **50.00+**
Posters .... **5.00+**

TRAMP ART

I am buying wooden tramp art articles such as boxes, letter holders, picture frames, dollhouses, furniture, etc. These were made during the turn of the century and into the 1920's from cigar boxes cut into strips. The strip edges were notched with a knife, and then the strips were layered to make a design or the whole item. Please send a photo or very good description along with your price.

M.L. Matzke
5022 Tongen Ave. NW
Rochester, MN 55901

TRIBAL ART

A study of the art forms of any people must essentially take into consideration the cultural background from which art springs. Therefore, the Museum of Classical Antiquities and Primitive Arts (MOCAPA) is interested in acquisitions of tribal art from the following areas: American Indian, Africa, New Guinea, Taino, Indonesia, etc. We are not searching for pieces that were created for airport sale, tourist, or export. The works of art must have been used by their makers for religious, social, or ceremonial rites. Our business transactions are handled in a professional, judicious, and discreet manner.

MOCAPA
P.O. Box 2162
Medford Lakes, NJ 08055

We Pay

Fetish Figures.. 35.00+
Masks... 45.00+
Weapons.. 45.00+
Household Objects... 25.00+
Statues... 35.00+
Beaded Bags .... 35.00+
Beaded Moccasins... 50.00+
Hide Clothing.. 90.00+
Baskets... 25.00+
Textiles.. 40.00+
Bows.. 45.00+
Shields... 60.00+

TROLLS

I am looking for certain troll dolls which are listed below. They must be in excellent condition. Tags and original packages are a plus. Trolls must be from the 1960's and have been manufactured by Wishnik, Uneeda, Thomas Dam (Dam Things Est.), Royal Design of Florida, or Scandia House Enterprises (S.H.E.). No Nyform, Norfins, or 'Made in Japan' trolls, please. These trolls must have long, thick hair (mohair) with no skin showing. Trolls should be dressed in original outfits. Photos are helpful for verification of condition to determine price but not necessary.

Roger M. Inouye
192 E Pasadena St.
Poma, CA 91767
(714) 623-4798

We Pay

3" Troll.. **8.00+**
6" Troll (Especially: Dam Playboy Bunny, Cheerleader, Astronaut, Viking, Wave).. **15.00+**
8" Troll (Especially: Dam Hula Girl, Wave, Santa Claus, Playboy Bunny, Indian, Astronaut, Robin Hood, Poker Player, Tailed. (Not interested in Pirates, rain coats, plain girls & boys in felt jumpers)... **20.00+**
9" or 10" Troll... **20.00+**

11" or 13" Troll (Especially wanted: Dam Black, Playboy Bunny, Santa Claus, Astronaut, Wave, Hobo, Sailor, Marine) .... **55.00+**
Troll Mountain.. **15.00+**
Troll Manor .... **15.00+**
Troll Bat Cave w/Bat Mobile .... **15.00+**
Original Clothes (complete outfit)... **5.00+**
Small Dam Animals (Especially: Elephant, Horse, Cow, Monkey, Tailed, Mermaid).. **20.00+**
Large Dam Animals (Especially: Monkey, Horse, Turtle, Cow, Pig, Alligator, Donkey, Lion with gray or white hair)... **50.00+**

They are fat-bellied and fuzzy-haired. They are companions and good luck charms. They are troll dolls and they have invaded my life. My first one was bought in a five-and-dime store in the middle 1960's. How was I to know then that they would become my obsession.

They come in all sizes from less than one inch to over eighteen inches. There are animal trolls, celebrity trolls, monster trolls, and a wide range of troll accessories. I am looking for all trolls and troll-related items in any condition. I will buy one troll or a whole collection of them. I buy any and every kind of troll-related item, too. I also buy items that are not listed, as these are just a fraction of what is available. Remember, that one poor-condition troll you have could be the one I am looking for.

Debbie Brown
541 S St. Clair St.
Painesville, OH 44077

We Pay

Trolls 1.00-75.00
Troll Houses.. 3.00-25.00
Charms .... **up to 5.00**
Animals 3.00-50.00
Coloring Books .... **up to 10.00**
Bicycle Handle Bar Covers.. **up to 10.00**

TYPEWRITER RIBBON TINS

I will buy most tin typewriter ribbon boxes. They date from 1900 through the 1970's and were usually round or square. Tins should be in good condition with no rust, dents, or fading. Value is based on age, condition, rarity, and graphic appeal. Excellent single items or collections may be sent to me on approval; you may send photocopies of the tops or telephone me for a quick answer.

Hoby Van Deusen
28 The Green
Watertown, CT 06795
(203) 945-3456

We Pay

Tins w/Indian, Black, or Typewriter.. **8.00+**
Tins w/Airplane, Ship, or Birds.. **4.00+**
Tins w/Common Subjects (or only lettering)... **2.00+**

    I am buying small (approximately 2½") typewriter ribbon tins. Most of these are round, but occasionally I find a square one. They must be in good condition with no rust. Colorful tins with figures, scenes, etc. are most desirable. Please send a description or photo.

Jane Stewart
1947 E 6075 South
Ogden, UT 84403

We Pay

Plain w/Writing.. **2.00**
Scenes, Figures, or Embossed... **3.00**

    I buy typewriter ribbon tins, regardless of condition. I also buy the cardboard boxes that packaged ribbon tins, if they are in at least good condition. Most of the tins in my collection were bought for under $5.00, but I can pay more for a unique tin.

    I want to someday have the largest collection of ribbon tins in the country, but I'll need your help to accomplish this goal. So please root around in your attic or basement, and send me your tins. They'll be out of your house and in mine — and we'll both be happy! Please send a description and your lowest price. To save time, ship your tins to me, and I'll make you a fair offer. Please pack tins carefully, as they are fragile.

Ken Stephens
12 Lloyd Ave.
Florence, KY 41042
(606) 371-5907

TYPEWRITERS

First attempts to build a typewriter date back to the beginning of the eighteenth century, but the first practical machine was invented by an American, Christopher L. Sholes, in 1867. Production did not begin until 1873 when E. Remington & Sons bought the rights and produced this legendary machine called 'The Sholes & Glidden Typewriter' to help fill excess industrial capacity. (They had made their fortune on guns during the Civil War.)

Around 1880, dozens of ingenious inventors came up with all sorts of odd mechanisms for writing machines. Only very few were successful. Some of them tried to simplify machines by reducing parts through substituting the keyboard and type-bar mechanism with single-type wheels or bars holding all the types. Then around 1895 Underwood started producing a revolutionary machine whose basic design became the standard for the entire industry.

I am very eager to buy any unusual typewriter. I do not buy standard machines such as Underwood, Royal, L.C. Smith, etc. Please contact me for a free complete list of 180 different models of machines wanted.

Peter Frei
P.O. Box 500
Brimfield, MA 01010-0500
(800) 942-8968

We Pay

Arnold	4,000.00+
Blickensderfer Models 5, 6, 7, 8, or 9	50.00+
Bennett	80.00+
Burns	2,500.00+
Brady & Warner	10,000.00+
Crandall	3,800.00+
Crary	5,500.00+
Duplex	3,200.00+

Essex	9,000.00+
Franklin	300.00+
Hammond (wooden keys)	500.00+
Hammond (3-row, straight keyboard)	70.00+
International (double keyboard)	6,500.00+
Thurber	10,000.00+
Morris	7,000.00+
Niagara	3,900.00+
Odell	350.00+
Oliver	20.00+
Prouty	6,700.00+
Rapid	3,400.00+
Sholes & Glidden	4,500.00+
Thomas	10,000.00+
Waverly	6,200.00+
World	250.00+

Collectible typewriters are generally those which pre-date 1920 and have mechanisms which differ from the conventional format. Look for machines which do not have four rows of keys, front-striking type bars, and a ribbon for inking. This would include machines with odd shapes, single-element printing mechanisms, odd keyboards — and even those with no keyboards.

Condition is very important to typewriter collectors, and the prices shown are for machines in truly excellent, fully-functional condition. The list which follows is incomplete, as hundreds of different typewriters were made before 1920. If you have a question, don't hesitate to contact me.

Darryl Rehr
11433 Rochester Ave. #303
Los Angeles, CA 90025
(213) 477-5229

We Pay

American	100.00
Automatic	500.00
Blickensderfer Electric	1,500.00
Brooks	500.00
Chicago	100.00
Coffman	500.00
Columbia	300.00
Crandall	300.00
Commercial Visible	300.00

Crown	300.00
Daugherty	150.00
Duplex	150.00
Edison Mimeograph	1,000.00
Emerson	100.00
Fay-Sho, bronze	200.00
Ford	500.00
Fitch	1,500.00
Franklin	75.00
Garbell	75.00
Hammond #1	150.00
Jackson	500.00
Index Visible	500.00
International	500.00
Keystone	200.00
Lambert	200.00
Merritt	100.00
Morris	300.00
McCool	500.00
National, curved	350.00
Niagara	1,200.00
Pittsburgh, #1-11	100.00
Postal	125.00
Pullman	125.00
Rapid	500.00
Rem-Sho, bronze	200.00
Sholes Visible	500.00
Sholes & Glidden	5,000.00
Sterling	200.00
Victor	300.00
Williams	200.00
World	250.00

The first production-line typewriters were manufactured by Remington in 1874. These clumsy behemoths had many features adapted from the company's sewing machines, including foot-treadle carriage returns. Sales were very slow since these machines worked poorly, printed on capitals which struck underneath the platen (out of sight), and — worse yet — the contraptions sold for $125.00. Beginning in the early 1800's, scores of machines weighing five pounds or less that typed just as well began to compete at prices ranging from $10.00 to $20.00. Most of the little machines used pointers or indicators to select letters that were printed on a paper index and typed from molded, rubber strips rather than by using typebars. These small typewriters are today referred to as indicators or index machines, while the big

machines patterned after the Remington are called blind writers. I buy
unusual early machines which appear to be in good condition with little rust
at the prices listed below. I will also negotiate to purchase broken specimens
of rarer typewriters and machines not listed.

Mike Brooks
7335 Skyline
Oakland, CA 94611
(415) 339-1751

We Pay

American, square index	100.00
American Visible	200.00
Automatic	1,000.00
Baltimore	100.00
Bennington	500.00
Blickensderfer Electric	2,500.00
Boston, index	500.00
Brooks	1,000.00
Burns	700.00
Cahill	1,200.00
Carpenter	500.00
Cash	500.00
Century, index	300.00
Champion, index	300.00
Cleveland	100.00
Coffman, index	700.00
Conde	100.00
Conover	125.00
Crandall New Model	700.00
Crary	600.00
Crown, index	500.00
Darling	100.00
Daugherty	100.00
Daw & Tait	500.00
Dennis Duplex	200.00
Dollar	100.00
Eagle	100.00
Edison	1,500.00
Edland	500.00
English	100.00
Eureka	150.00
Farmer	500.00
Fitch	2,000.00
Ford	500.00
Gardner	500.00

Hall, index	200.00
Hamilton	200.00
Hartford	100.00
Horton	1,500.00
Index Visible	300.00
International	600.00
Jackson	500.00
Jewett	100.00
Keystone	125.00
Lambert	200.00
Lasar	500.00
Liliput, index	100.00
Martin	150.00
Maskelyne	500.00
McCool	600.00
McLoughlin	300.00
Mercury	200.00
Merritt	150.00
National, curved front	500.00
Niagara	1,500.00
Norths	400.00
Odell	100.00
Pearl	500.00
Pocket	200.00
Rem-Sho	125.00
Sun, index	300.00
Travis	300.00
Victor, index	500.00

_____

Antique typewriters are wanted. Listed below are some company names. Please <u>contact</u> me about any old typewriter you may have. I also collect **typewriter ribbon tins and other typing collectibles.**

American	Merritt
Bennett	Mignon
Blickensderfer Electric	Monarch
Brooks	Muson
Burnett	Molle
Caligraph	Moon-Hopkins
Chicago	National
Century	North
Champion	Odell
Columbia Bar-Lock	Oliver 1-2-3-4-6-10-11
Conover	Pearl

Crandall
Crown
Daugherty
Densmore
Edison
Elliot Fisher
Emerson
Fay Sholes
Fitch
Fox
Ford
Franklin
Hall
Hammond Curved Keyboard
Hartford
International
Jackson
Jewett
Junior
Keystone
Lambert
McCool

Peerless
Peoples
Pittsburgh
Postal
Prouty
Rapid
Reliance
Rem Blick
Rem Sholes
Remington 1-2-3-4-5-8-9
Salter
The Shimer
Sholes
Sholes & Glidden
Sun
Victor
Virotype
Williams
World
Yost
Ye Ess

Conrad & Terry Hamil
615 Grandridge
Grandview, WA 98930
(509) 882-3617

We Pay

Typewriters Not in Our Collection .... **500.00+**
Typewriter Ribbon Tins... **2.00+**
Other Typewriter Collectibles .... **2.00+**

U.S. MARINE CORPS

U.S. Marine Corps memorabilia is wanted by collector. I want to buy items such as recruiting posters, books, photos, sheet music, belt buckles, cigarette lighters, steins and mugs, toy soldiers, trucks, planes, documents and autographs, art work, post cards, trench art, bronzes, novelties, and John Phillip Sousa items.

Dick Weisler
53-07 213th St.
Bayside, NY 11364
(718) 428-9829 (home)
(718) 626-7110 (office)

UTAH

I will pay top price for your items related to Utah and/or its people and heritage including but not limited to Mormonism, anti-Mormonism, Utah Indians, cowboys, railroads, county, state, and historical events involving Utah. Old and unusual items are highly sought after but more recent items are also desirable, if they pertain to Utah history. Permanent interests are books, pamphlets, literature, state and country histories, photographs, post cards, maps, stereoscopic slides, toys, souvenirs of Utah's sights and monuments, crocks and liquor jugs or bottles marked Utah or U.T. (Utah Territory).

Donald L. Miller
781 W 300 S
Heber, UT 84032
(801) 654-4382

We Pay

Utah Liquor Crock Jugs	50.00+
U.T. Bottles	20.00+
Books of Mormon	up to 5,000.00
Post Cards	50¢+
Photographs	10.00+
Pre-1900 Books, Latter Day Saints	5.00+
Pre-1900 Books, Anti-Mormon	20.00+
Pre-1900 Books, County Histories	15.00+

VACUUM CLEANERS

The British claim to have invented the vacuum cleaner, but there is no place on earth where domestic work was less popular than in the U.S.! It was no surprise that the first U.S. patent was granted more than thirty years before Cecil Booth's English patent in 1901. Despite the fact that the most important part for a successful vacuum cleaner, a small electric motor, was not available, all kinds of weird mechanisms were invented. Most of those early devices worked on a suction principle but were driven by either a hand or foot bellows. As you might well imagine, these early cleaning machines did more for the musculature of the user than the rugs on the floor.

I am eager to buy all kinds of early cleaning machines. In particular, hand-powered vacuum cleaners, mechanical carpet beaters, pre-1880 carpet sweepers, and pre-1915 electric vacuum cleaners. I do not want the following brands: Doty, Fenny, Good House Keeper, Hoover, Reeves, or Regina.

Sandra Edenhofer
P.O. Box 500
Brimfield, MA 01010-0500
(800) 942-8968

We Pay

Agan, Whitehead & Hoag Co.	250.00+
Cornell	250.00+
Hydra Vacuum Cleaner, Vulcan Metals Co. (water driven)	300.00+
Ideal, The American Vacuum Cleaner Co. (electric)	200.00+
Magic	150.00+
Mechanical Carpet Beaters	1,000.00+
Rocking Chair Vacuum Cleaner	2,500.00+
Settee	450.00+
Suction Sweeper Co., patent June 2, 1908 (electric)	1,000.00
Skinner 1906 (electric)	800.00+
U.S.	250.00+
Water Witch (water driven)	1,400.00+
Western Electric (electric)	100.00+

VIEW-MASTER REELS AND PACKETS

View-Master, the invention of William Gruber, was first introduced to the public at the 1939–1940 New York World's Fair and at the same time at the Golden Gate Exposition in California. Since then the company has produced thousands of reels and packets on subjects as diverse as life itself. The product has been owned by five different companies: the original Sawyer's View-Master, G.A.F. (in the middle 1960's), View-Master International (in 1981), Ideal Toy, and (most recently) Tyco Toy Company.

Unfortunately, since G.A.F, neither View-Master International, Ideal, nor Tyco Toy have had any intention of making View-Master anything but a toy item, selling only cartoons. This, of course, has made the early non-cartoon single reels and the three-reel packets desirable items. Sawyer's items are especially becoming collectible, as they produced the best quality and made this hobby a fascinating 3-D experience. They even made two cameras for the general public which enabled them to take their own 'personal' reels in 3-D; then they designed a projector so that people could show their pictures in full-color 3-D on a silver screen.

I am a collector and dealer and can pay well for good items in nice condition. Condition is important, but please let me know what you have. The prices listed below are what I will pay for items in near mint or mint condition.

Walter Sigg
P.O. Box 208
Smartswood, NJ 07877
(201) 383-2437

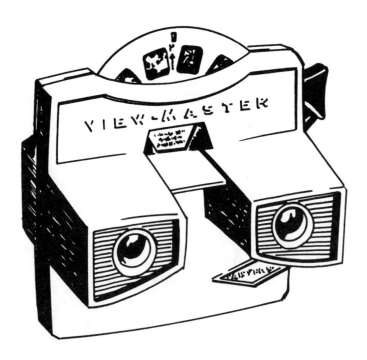

We Pay

Gold-Center Reels in Gold Envelopes	10.00
Blue-Baked Reels	2.50-10.00
Early Sawyer's Single Reels (white)	25¢-5.00
3-D Movie Preview Reels	25.00

Commercial Reels **5.00-50.00**
Scenic Packets (Sawyers and G.A.F.)................................. **1.00-25.00**
TV & Movie Packets (Sawyer's & G.A.F.)........................... **1.00-25.00**
Belgium-Made Packets **4.00-35.00**
Mushroom Set.. **100.00**
Mushroom Set w/Book **150.00**
Mushroom Set w/Case **200.00**
Blue Model 'B' & Other Rare Viewers..................................... **100.00+**
'Personal' or 'Mark II' Cameras w/Case................................ **100.00**
'Stereo-Matic 500' Projector **200.00**
Film Cutter for View-Master Cameras.................................. **100.00**
Close-Up Lenses for 'Personal' Camera................................ **100.00**
Tru-Vue 3-D Film Strips.. **1.00-20.00**
Other 3-D Items .... **Call or Write**

WATCH FOBS

I am buying advertising watch fobs. I prefer strap-type fobs but also buy chain or charm-type fobs. Prices range from $15.00 up to $100.00. If I already have the fob offered or I am not interested, I will sell your fob on consignment for 10%. I will pay a finder's fee on any collection that I buy. Send SASE for list of fobs and prices paid. All correspondence that includes a SASE will be answered. A photocopy or tracing of your fob is very helpful. Also bought are **advertising stickpins and WWI or WWII (foreign and American) military wings.** I will try to answer any questions.

Greg Cooney
R.R. 3
Wellington, KS 67152
(316) 326-5241

Wanted: strap-type advertising watch fobs. There are thousands of different ones. I've only listed six below to show examples of what I'll pay. Send a rubbing or photocopy of your fob for an offer.

David Hong
2625-146th Ave. SE
Bellevue, WA 98007

We Pay

John Deere, blue	100.00
John Deere, green	100.00
John Deere, black	150.00
John Deere, red, white, & blue	150.00
Holt (early Caterpillar)	175.00
Automobile	25.00-75.00

Watch fobs are becoming popular collectibles. I collect watch fobs advertising old road or farm machinery or related items. I also collect fobs advertising fur, traps, powder, and gun companies. I'll pay $25.00 and up depending on age and condition.

John Cline
609 N East St.
Carlisle, PA 17013
(717) 249-4253

WELLER POTTERY

From a humble beginning in 1873, Samuel Weller moved his pottery to Zanesville, Ohio, in 1882 to begin a long and prosperous career which would place his company among the elite potteries in America. Equipped with great imagination and a talented staff of artists, the Weller Pottery created many diverse lines including Louwelsa, Dickens, Hudson, Sicard, and L'Art Nouveau. They also produced many floral patterns, utility wares, garden ornaments, and novelty items.

I am interested in purchasing any piece of Weller pottery in mint condition. Please send a color photo and/or a full description of any item you wish to sell for a prompt reply. Thank you.

Tom Harrison
P.O. Box 374
Brimfield, IL 61517
(309)446-3229

We Pay

Ardsley Fan Vase, 8".. **25.00+**
Cameo Basket, 7".. **15.00+**

Coppertone Vase w/Handles, 10"... 35.00+
Dickens Vase, golfer, 7"... 175.00
Dickens Mug, Indian, 6".. 225.00
Etna Mug, 5" 30.00
Forest Pitcher, 5" 50.00
Forest Vase, 8".. 30.00
Glendale Vase, 7" 50.00
L'Art Nouveau Vase, 8".. 40.00
Louwelsa Vase, 7" 65.00
Sicard Vase, 6".. 125.00
Silvertone Vase, 9" 50.00

Weller is probably the most beautiful pottery in the U.S. Well, it is to me. Roseville has lovely floral lines and interesting pieces, but there is something mysterious and primitive about the older Weller pieces. I don't see much Weller in my area; I'm hoping you can help me. I prefer not to buy some of the newer patterns such as Wild Rose, Blossom, or Cameo. But I do like Roba and Bouquet. If you have a piece of pottery, please call or write telling me what you have. I try to pay fair prices for the pieces I buy. If you don't think you've been offered reasonable prices for your Weller pottery, I hope you will call me and give me a try. I will try to beat any offer you have been made.

Leslie K. Ray
2000 Robyn Rd.
Springdale, AR 72764
(501) 750-2012

WESTERN COLLECTIBLES

I'm interested in buying all working cowboy items from the 1800's through the 1950's. I will buy gauntlet gloves, early cowboy hats and boots, clothing, bits, horse tack, quirts, Colt revolvers, Winchester rifles, cowboy photos, saddle catalogs, and advertising for cowboy-related items. Prices quoted are for items in good condition. I will pay premium prices for items in excellent condition but will consider items in any condition. Because of the popularity of western collectibles, some items can be very valuable. I can't quote prices for all the items I'm collecting but will be glad to make you an offer on almost any western item.

Paul Jensen
P.O. Box 256
Poncha Springs, CO 81242
(719) 539-6729

We Pay

Chaps, Batwing	**75.00+**
Chaps, Batwing w/Studs	**100.00-150.00+**
Chaps, Shotgun	**125.00-175.00+**
Chaps, Angora or Wooly	**150.00-350.00+**
Double-Loop Holster	**25.00-75.00+**
Cartridge or Money Belt	**25.00-75.00+**
Saddle Bags	**35.00-100.00+**
Pommel Bags	**100.00+**
Wrist Cuffs	**20.00-50.00+**
Spur Leathers	**5.00-45.00+**
Rifle Scabbards	**10.00-50.00+**
Rawhide Ropes	**25.00-75.00+**
Buermann Spurs, Star brand, steel	**50.00+**
Buermann Spurs, Star brand, bronze	**75.00-100.00+**
Buermann Spurs, Star brand, silver inlay	**100.00-150.00+**
North & Judd Spurs, Anchor brand	**35.00-100.00+**
McChesney Lady-Leg Spurs	**35.00-100.00+**
Crockett Spurs, early	**75.00-175.00+**
Mexican Chihuahua Spurs	**25.00-50.00+**
Wide-Brim Stetson Hats, early	**50.00-100.00+**
Brand Books from Western States	**10.00-30.00+**

I am interested in buying for my collection pre-1950's western saddles, western gear, spurs, bits, branding irons, Navajo blankets, saddle catalogs, stockman supply catalogs, and other horse publications. Examples are given below.

Mrs. Paulette Johnson
4966 Hickory Shores Blvd.
Gulf Breeze, FL 32561-9209

We Pay

Spurs	20.00+
Bits	10.00+
Catalogs, pre-1960	3.00+
Branding Irons	15.00+
Saddle Watch Fobs	10.00+
Saddles	75.00+

I collect all types of pre-1930 cowboy or western-related paraphernalia, including spurs, advertising, hats, belts, guns and gun belts, badges, horsehair items, bits, chaps, etc. Send photo and price with first letter, or call.

The Fan Man, Inc.
4614 Travis
Dallas, TX 75205
(214) 559-4440

WRISTWATCHES

I collect high-grade mechanical wristwatches (no quartz, please) from 1920 to present. I am particularly interested in watches that do more than just tell time (for example, chimers, moon phases, calendars, stop watch buttons, bezels, military shrapnel covers, etc.). Plain styles are fine, but fancy is better. Small is okay, but large is best. Ladies' watches are acceptable, but men's watches are preferred.

Condition is important. Watches in good to excellent condition are worth more than watches in poor or 'worn' condition. A sample listing with prices I pay are listed below. If you have watches to sell, please send a photocopy of your watches (please, use a separate photo copy for each watch) along with any descriptive information, such as metal finishes, markings, colors, etc., and the approximate ages of the watches, if known.

Glen Bowen
2240 N Park Drive
Kingwood, TX 77339

Brand	We Pay
Agassiz	100.00-1,000.00
Audemars Piguet	100.00-500.00
Baume-Mercier	100.00-1,000.00
Breguet	100.00-1,000.00
Breitling	50.00-150.00
Buche-Girod	100.00-500.00
Bucherer	100.00-500.00
Bulova	20.00-100.00
Cartier	100.00-1,000.00
Chopard	100.00-300.00
Concord	100.00-1,000.00
Corum	50.00-500.00
Ditisheim	100.00-300.00
Girard Perregaux	50.00-500.00
Gruen	20.00-150.00
Gubelin	100.00-1,000.00
Hamilton	20.00-75.00
Illinois	20.00-50.00
International Schaffhausen	100.00-1,000.00

Wristwatches

Le Coultre	50.00-200.00
Jules Jurgensen	50.00-150.00
Longines	20.00-50.00
Lucien-Piccard	100.00-500.00
Madtthey-Tissot	100.00-300.00
Mido	100.00-300.00
Movado	20.00-100.00
Ollendorf	50.00-300.00
Omega	100.00-300.00
Patek Phillipe	500.00-10,000.00
Piaget	150.00-500.00
Rolex	100.00-5,000.00
Tiffany	500.00-3,000.00
Tissot	50.00-200.00
Touchon	50.00-250.00
Ulysse Nardin	50.00-500.00
Universal Geneve	20.00-100.00
Vacheron Constantin	500.00-10,000.00
Waltham	20.00-100.00
Wittnauer	25.00-100.00
Zenith	25.00-100.00
Zodiac	25.00-100.00

They say: The 'first' watch made was in the year 1500 A.D. The minute hand did not appear until 1687 A.D. Watches with movable figures began in 1790 A.D. There are 195,000 watches sold per day.

We say: Dig out those watches and turn them into money. They need not be working or in good shape. Our policy is to return your watch that day if you don't like our offer. In all these years, we are proud to say that we haven't returned one watch! Examples of prices are listed below. Depending on condition, gold, diamonds, etc., prices may be much more.

James Lindon
5267 W Cholla St.
Glendale, AZ 85304
(602) 878-4288

Brand	We Pay
Audemars Piquet	350.00
Benrus	20.00
Breitling	100.00
Bucherer	20.00

Bulova	20.00
Cyma	20.00
Ebel	30.00
Gruen	30.00
Hamilton	30.00
Heuer	40.00
Hyde Park	20.00
Illinois	30.00
Le Coultre	100.00
Longines	50.00
Mido	30.00
Movado	80.00
Omega	50.00
Patek Phillippe	1,200.00
Rolex	300.00
Tiffany	100.00
Ulysse Nardin	80.00
Universal Geneva	100.00
Vacheron Constantin	1,000.00
Wittnauer	30.00
Any Character Watches	Call or Write

I am buying gold-filled and 14K wristwatches, working or not. I pay for Bulova, Rolex, Gruen, Waltham, Elgin, Vacheron Constantin, Tissot, Hamilton, Longines, and other quality watches. I buy watches others often refuse to buy. I also buy pocket watches made by these companies. Character watches, such as Donald Duck, Tom Mix, Howdy Doody, Mickey Mouse, and others, are wanted. As I repair all these watches, broken watches are wanted for parts. I buy items pertaining to clocks and watches: engraving machines, watchmakers' lathes and lathe chucks, crystal cutting machines and wheels, cleaning machines, hand tools, supplies and parts, and any other related item.

Send a letter describing the item as well as possible. Let me know if it is silver, gold-filled, 14K or 18K gold, if possible. A photocopy or photo is almost essential in helping to determine price. Prices vary according to condition, etc. I have been buying watch and clock-related merchandise since 1948 and will pay you by personal check or postal money order — your choice. All inquires enclosing SASE will be answered. Estimated price offerings are listed below.

Herbert M. S. Sheldon
Clock-Watch Repairs
P.O. Box 474, Great Kills
Staten Island, NY 10308

We Pay

Alarm Clock, Ansonia, Peep-O-Day .... 50.00+
Mechanical Bird Clock, Kroeber .... 600.00+
Porky Pig Watch, Ingraham .... 20.00+
Betty Boop Watch, Ingraham.. 50.00+
Pocket Watch, Edward Howard USA, Wolf Teeth Model....................... 700.00
Stop Watch, NY Standard Co., Dan Patch Model..................................... 85.00+
Repeater Pocket Watch, Longines, Leroy, or Tiffany .... 1,000.00+
Wristwatch, Movado, 15-Jewel, Polyplan (1910), 18K White Gold.... 1,000.00+
Wristwatch, Gruen, 14K, Duo-Dial, 1935 Model..................................... 600.00+
Wristwatches, Piaget, Patek-Philippe, or Rolex .... **up to 5,000.00**
Watchmaker Lathe w/Lathe Fixtures.. 100.00+
Jeweler Engraving Machine (small or large)............................... 50.00-300.00+

Wanted to buy are working or non-working wristwatches. Send a complete description or your phone number so that I may call you. Listed below are minimum prices paid; prices may be much more.

David Hong
2625-146th Ave. SE
Bellevue, WA 98007

Brand

We Pay

Rolex, stainless steel case 300.00
Rolex, 14K gold case 1,500.00
Le Coultre, 17 jewel, triple date, moon phase, gold-filled 600.00
Le Coultre, 17 jewel, triple date, moon phase, 18K gold..................... 2,500.00
Breitling, 17 jewel, Navatimer, stainless steel 300.00
Breitling, 17 jewel, Navatimer, 18K gold 1,500.00
Longines, 17 jewel, extra large movable bezel & center dial, nickel..... 1,500.00
Longines, 17 jewel, extra large movable bezel & center dial, silver...... 3,000.00
Longines, 17 jewel, extra large movable bezel & center dial, 18K gold .. 12,000.00

WORLD'S FAIR AND EXPOSITIONS

I am buying **1893 Columbian Exposition items, especially tickets and trade cards** — whether a single piece or an entire collection. I'm looking for admission tickets which are backstamped either compliments or specimen. If you have any of these items send your asking price. All letters will recieve a reply. Other items of interest are listed below.

Ted Targosz
11687 Virgil
Redford, MI 48239-1448

Tickets   We Pay

Good Only on Day of Sale .... 7.00+
Adult Chicago Day w/Stub.. 10.00+
Child Chicago Day w/Stub .... 12.00+
Any Transportation (steamship, etc.)... 10.00+
Any Ride .... 10.00+
Any Amusement (Hagenbeck, etc.).. 10.00+
Java Village w/Stub (25¢, $7.00, $9.00, or $15.00).............................. 10.00+
Any Exhibition (Wild East Show, etc.) .... 10.00+
Any Food (German Village Restaurant, etc.) .... 8.00+

Other Items   We Pay

Any Token (5¢, 10¢, 25¢, 50¢, $1.00, $2.00, or $5.00)............................... 8.00+

Passes (workman, press, etc.) .... **8.00+**
Trade Cards (send short description) .... **6.00+**

─────────────────────────

I am a cash buyer, no checks — U.S. money orders only! **Items from the 1893 Columbian Exposition up to today are wanted**. Prices paid range up to $1,000.00. Uniforms and badges are most wanted. Send an accurate description of your merchandise, note its condition (very important in determining value), and state your asking price. No problem. If you're fair, I'll pay. We'll both be satisfied — guaranteed, or no deal!

Bob Richardson
38600 5th Ave.
Zephyrhills, FL 33540
(813) 783-9342

─────────────────────────

I am a strong, active buyer of **souvenirs and collectibles from the 1876 Centennial Exhibition of Philadelphia**. I will buy a single item or a whole collection. Because I am a collector (not a dealer) I can pay you more for your items. I spend hundreds of dollars monthly on my collection. In addition to the list below, I will also buy other interesting items.

Paul S. Frank
2823 NE 57th Ave.
Portland, OR 97213
(503) 284-6859

We Pay

Coins, Medals, Tokens, Badges **5.00-100.00**
Buttons, Studs .... **3.00+**
Trade Cards **5.00-30.00**
Cabinet View Cards **3.00-7.00**
Stereopticon Cards .... **5.00+**
Flags, Kerchiefs .... **25.00-100.00+**
Fans .... **40.00+**
Books, Guidebooks .... **5.00-100.00+**
Prints .... **10.00-125.00+**

Stamp Covers .... 20.00-60.00+
Maps... 10.00-50.00+
Stevengraphs, Ribbons, Bookmarks 20.00-90.00
Pamphlets, Foldouts, Flyers, Advertising .... 5.00-20.00+
Posters, Broadsides... 20.00-200.00+
Games, Toys, Children's Blocks... 25.00-100.00
Centennial Pocket Watch.. 150.00+
Letters w/Centennial on Letterhead................................... 5.00-50.00+
Any Miscellaneous Paper.. 5.00+
Stock Certificate, U.S. Centennial Exhibition..................... 250.00+
Centennial Scrapbooks .... 35.00+

I am buying all types of items related to **Canada's 1967 Centennial Expo-sition**. I am putting together a major collection of Expo 67 and related materi-als. Also wanted are all items dated 1967 from different cities and provinces in Canada. I will pay top dollar for the right item — one piece or a collection! Please describe items and name your price. All letters will be answered.

Ron Marcetti
24949 St. Christopher
Mt. Clemens, MI 48045

We Pay

Medals .... 5.00+
Tokens .... 5.00+
Wooden Nickels.. 1.00+
Elongated Coins .... 1.00+
Watch Fobs.. 5.00+
Key Chains .... 3.00+
Paper Money .... 2.00+
Trade Dollars... 5.00+
Pins.. 1.00+
Dog Tags .... 1.00+
Parking Tokens .... 2.00+
Sports Medals.. 3.00+
Transportation Tokens.. 3.00+
Organization Medals & Pins .... 2.00+
Award Medals.. 5.00+

YOSEMITE NATIONAL PARK MEMORABILIA

Early photographs and memorabilia of Yosemite National Park, California, are wanted (such as artifacts, paper, documents, ephemera, etc.). Purchase prices depend on condition, subject, and desirability.

William L. Thompson
P.O. Box 4333
Carlsbad, CA 92008

OTHER INTERESTED BUYERS OF MISCELLANEOUS ITEMS

In this section of the book we have listed some 250 buyers of miscellaneous items and related material. When corresponding with these collectors, be sure to enclose a self-addressed stamped envelope if you want a reply. Do not send lists of items for appraisal. If you wish to sell your material, quote the price that you want or send a list of items you think they might be interested in and ask them to make you an offer. If you want the list back, be sure to send a SASE large enough for the listing to be returned.

ADS
(Cream of Wheat)
Carol J. Beattie
3374 Ver Bunker Ave.
Port Edwards, WI 54469

ADVERTISING
(signs)
William C. & Jerrod R. Danielson
18 Smith Acres
Northport, AL 35476

(beer signs w/moving scenery)
Kevin Sloan
1145 W Sloan
Burt, MI 48417

(advertising stoneware)
Clark Benne
P.O. Box 73
Bradshaw, NE 68319
(402) 736-4410

(gasoline or oil-related signs)
George Rapoza
14346 Sandy Ct.
Sonora, CA 95370
(209) 532-1309

(porcelain/enamel signs)
Robert Newman
10809 Charnock Rd.
Los Angeles, CA 90034-6608
(213) 559-0539

(straight razor porcelain signs)
Russ Palmieri
27 Pepper Rd.
Towaco, NJ 07082

ALASKA
(pre-1959 items)
Bob Faro
7729 Country Creek Dr.
Longmont, CO 80503
(303) 652-2805

ALCOHOLICS ANONYMOUS
(1939–1954)
Paul Melzer Fine Books
P.O. Box 1143
Redlands, CA 92373
(714) 792-7299

AMERICAN FOSTORIA
(punch bowl w/base)
Kim Battle, Classics
215½ Winchester
Tyler, TX 75701
(214) 561-0126

ANIMAL DISHES & COVERS
(by Beaver Falls Fint Co-Op)
Ja Dee Antiques
P.O. Box 149
New Brighton, PA 15066
(412) 846-8737

ART GLASS
William C. & Jerrod R. Danielson
18 Smith Acres
Northport, AL 35476

(lamps)
Armand Miranda
126 Reldyes Ave.
Leonia, NJ 07605
(201) 592-6384

ART POTTERY
Armand Miranda
126 Reldyes Ave.
Leonia, NJ 07605
(201) 592-6384

Scott H. Nelson
P.O. Box 6081
Santa Fe, NM 87502
(505) 986-1176

Cliff Thornhill
186 Kit Carson Way
Vallejo, CA 94589

ARTS & CRAFTS
Keith Browne
P.O. Box 1592
Rockford, IL 61104
(815) 398-7137

ARTWORK
(prints, paintings, art)
Henry Barnet
516 Maverick Circle
Spartanburg, SC 29302

ATLASES
(before 1880)
Dennis Clare
818 Duboce Ave.
San Francisco, CA 94117
(415) 552-0437

Kathleen Manning
209 Corbett
San Francisco, CA 94114
(415) 621-3565

AUTOGRAPHS
(letters, documents, manuscripts)
Paul Melzer Fine Books
P.O. Box 1143
Redlands, CA 92373
(714) 792-7299

AUTOMOBILIA
(especially CA chauffeur badges)
Peter Van Rossem
58056 El Dorado Dr.
Yucca Valley, CA 92284
(619) 365-6424

(radiator emblems)
George Rapoza
14346 Sandy Ct.
Sonora, CA 95370
(209) 532-1309

AUTUMN LEAF
Brent Dilworth
87 E Alice
Blackfoot, ID 83221
(208) 785-7109

AVIATION
(military & civilian to 1950)
19th Century Company
P.O. Box 5151
Lincoln, NE 68505

BANKING
(Eastman College Bank money)
Elongated Coin Museum
228 Vassar Rd.
Poughkeepsie, NY 12603

BANKS
(still)
Marvin S. Weinstein
405 Nova Albion Way
San Rafael, CA 94903
(415) 479-9246

BAR ACCESSORIES
(carved, wooden)
27 Bleecker St.
New York, NY 10012
(212) 505-2455

BARBER EQUIPMENT
William C. & Jerrod R. Danielson
18 Smith Acres
Northport, AL 35476

BASEBALL MEMORABILIA
(Negro league)
Bob Faro
7729 Country Creek Dr.
Longmont, CO 80503
(303) 652-2804

BJORNHOLM POTTERY
Harriet James
227 N Fillmore St.
Arlington, VA 22201

BLACK MEMORABILIA
Betty Yates
P.O. Box 759
Greeneville, TN 37744

Walter David
833 Troy St.
Elmont, NY 11003

William C. & Jerrod R. Danielson
18 Smith Acres
Northport, AL 35476

Allen Liffman
27 Bleecker St.
New York, NY 10012
(212) 505-2455

The Red Ribbon Antiques
101 W Main St.
Greenfield, IN 46140
(317) 462-5211

(no kitchen or paper items)
Meta Bleier
3204 Portofino Point, K-1
Coconut Creek, FL 33066

BLUE RIDGE POTTERY
(Southern Potteries, all patterns)
Treasure Hunt
416 Walnut St.
Hattiesburg, MS 39401

Kathryn B. Colrard
315 Hogan Rd.
Rossville, GA 30741
(404) 861-6757

BLUE WILLOW
Brent Dilworth
87 E Alice
Blackfoot, ID 83221
(208) 785-7109

BOOKS
(worldwide post office publications)
Dr. Frank R. Scheer, Curator
Railway Mail Service Library
12 E Rosemont Ave.
Alexandria, VA 22301-2325

(antiques & collectibles)
Marilyn Hardy
817 E Milwaukee St.
Janesville, WI 53545
(608) 752-7366

(antiquarian & autographed)
AL-PAC
H.C. 1, Box 7120
Yucca Valley, Ca 92284-9489
(619) 366-2071

(antiques & collectibles)
The Reference Rack
P.O. Box 445
Orefield, PA 18069
(215) 395-0004

(art)
Book Beat, attn: Cary Loren
26010 Greenfield Rd.
Oak Park, MI 48237
(313) 968-1190

(religious, all denominations)
Lillian Kaiser
419 Cedar St.
Santa Cruz, CA 95060-4304

(card games & playing cards)
Bill Sachen
927 Grand Ave.
Waukegan, IL 60085
(708) 662-7204

(by Jan Westcott)
Laura Steenhoek
Pella, IA 50219
(515) 628-4647 or (515) 628-4769

(any old paper items)
Joel Cotton
225 Trenton St.
W Monroe, LA 71292
(318) 322-6479

Sandi Wakefield
Rte. 6, Box 439
Smithville, TN 37166
(615) 597-1270

Lenora's Fine Antiques
5802 Morningside Dr.
Richmond, VA 23226
(804) 282-3904

BOSSON HEADS
(any signed pieces)
Bruce Bleier
73 Riverdale Rd.
Valley Stream, NY 11581
(516) 791-4353

BOTTLES
William C. & Jerrod R. Danielson
18 Smith Acres
Northport, AL 35476

Ken Schwartz
P.O. Box 956
Redding, CA 96099
(916) 243-2521

Tom Zachary Sr.
2996 Pangborn Rd.
Decatur, GA 30033
(404) 939-2307

Krol's Rock City
Star Rt. 2, Box 15A
Deming, NM 88030

BREYER HORSES
Gretchen & Wildrose
5816 Steeplewood Dr.
N Richland Hills, TX 76180
(817) 581-4477

BRUSH MC COY
(Zuniart & Florastone)
Dream Merchant Antiques
Rte. 1, Box 482
Beaufort, NC 28516
(919) 728-7447

BUTTER MOLDS & STAMPS
(also butter rollers)
Dan Bercu
Rte. 4, Box 707
Marion, IL 62969

BUTTONS
(for apparel)
B.A. Steele Jr.
1922 N Byrkit St.
Mishawaka, IN 46545
(219) 259-7323

CAKE KNIVES
(depression glass)
Robert Carrell
PSC Box 2678
APO Miami, FL 34004
(507) 82-3728 (Panama)

CAKE TOP DECORATIONS
(bride & groom)
Joan Benke
804 E High
Jefferson City, MO 65101
(314) 636-5509

CALCULATORS
Darryl Rehr
11433 Rochester Ave. #303
Los Angeles, CA 90025
(213) 477-5229

CAMARK POTTERY
Joel Cotton
225 Trenton St.
W Monroe, LA 71292
(318) 322-6479

CAMBRIDGE GLASS
T. Hirshberg
2181 Bancroft Way
Berkeley, CA 94704
(425) 845-3653

CANES
(glass batons)
Janice R. Lachance
302 Lamond Pl.
Alexandria, VA 22314

CARNIVAL GLASS
Rose Barash
7200 SW 6th St.
Miami, FL 33144
(305) 261-0640

CAT COLLECTIBLES
Pam Wiggins
10701 Sabo #202
Houston, TX 77089
(713) 944-7520

MARC CHAGALL
Paul Melzer Fine Books
P.O. Box 1143
Redlands, CA 92373
(714) 792-7299

CHARACTER COLLECTIBLES
(original Fleischer Studio/King Features)
Sharon Greenberg
740 Leggett Pl.
Whitestone, NY 11357
(212) 790-4719

CHICKEN WATERER
(glass)
C.E. Jones
Rte. 7, Box 2083
Palestine, TX 75801
(214) 723-3865

CHILDREN'S DISHES
Elissa Cusumano
15943 E Lantana Ln.
Fountain Hills, AZ 85268
(602) 837-0588

CHINA
(souvenir American, pre-1920)
Gary Crabtree
P.O. Box 3843
San Bernardino, CA 92413

CIGARETTE LIGHTERS
Les Druyan
311 E 38th St.
New York, NY 10016
(212) 599-6530

CIVIL WAR MEMORABILIA
Betty Yates
P.O. Box 759
Greeneville, TN 37744

Mark R. Bates
P.O. Box 646
Christiansburg, VA 24073
(703) 382-1078

CLICKERS
Danny Turner
P.O. Box 210992
Nashville, TN 37221
(615) 952-3699

COCA-COLA
Betty Yates
P.O. Box 759
Greeneville, TN 37744

(mint condition only)
Rick Newman
4813 E Hot Springs Ave.
Las Vegas, NV 89110
(702) 438-9100

Robert Newman
10809 Charnock Rd.
Los Angeles, CA 90034-6606
(213) 559-0539

COIN-OPERATED MACHINES
William C. & Jerrod R. Danielson
18 Smith Acres
Northport, AL 35476

Tom Neidinger
12012 Birdseye Terrace
Germantown, MD 20874
(301) 540-9598

Richard M. Bueschel
414 N Prospect Manor Ave.
Mt. Prospect, IL 60056
(708) 253-0791

COOKBOOKS
Grover Corey Sr.
R.R. #7, Box 900
Laurel Hill Rd.
Pineville, KY 40977
(606) 337-3439

(also leaflets)
Lori Hughes
253 Magda Way
Pacheco, CA 94553
(415) 687-1029

COOKIE JARS
(also odd tops & bottoms)
Mercedes Di Renzo
Chicago, IL 60613
(312) 472-1500

(unusual)
The Red Ribbon Antiques
101 W Main St.
Greenfield, IN 46140
(317) 462-5211

(Twin Winton)
Connie C. Christman
4116 Petersville Rd. NE
Bremerton, WA 98310
(206) 377-7850

COORS ART POTTERY
Louis L. Scher
P.O. Box 8668
Asheville, NC 28814
(704) 258-3308

COMIC BOOKS
Andrew Egendorf
P.O. Box 646
Weston, MA 02193
(617) 647-1025

COWBOY
Rex Arrowsmith
P.O. Box 2700
Santa Fe, NM 87504
(505) 982-0225

CRACKER JACK PRIZES
Joan Benke
804 E High
Jefferson City, MO 65101
(314) 636-5509

CUT GLASS
(Zipper pattern master salt dip)
Lowell Pasley
718 Carter
Farmington, MO 63640
(314) 756-3653

DANBURY MINT
(Sailing Ship Tankard Series)
Calvin J. Meider
P.O. Box 1602
Dubuque, IA 52001
(319) 557-1722

DECANTERS
Tom M. Blake
3400 W 111th St., Suite 301
Chicago, IL 60655
(312) 881-4159

DENTAL
William C. & Jerrod R. Danielson
18 Smith Acres
Northport, AL 35476

DEPRESSION GLASS
Betty Yates
P.O. Box 759
Greeneville, TN 37744

(green Cherry Blossom)
Linda Holycross
R.R. 3 Box 32
Veedersburg, IN 47987

Joan Somerville
25 N Main St.
Cedar City, UT 84720
(801) 586-3530

D.F. Yates
229 Forkner Dr.
Decatur, GA 30030

April Tvorak
P.O. Box 126
Canon City, CO 81215
(719) 269-3552

(all patterns)
Jean Williamson
298 Dogwood Ln. NW
Lawrenceville, GA 30245
(404) 963-7290

Orchard Sash/Okerleen Stout
Rte. 2, Box 54
Leoma, TN 38468
(615) 852-2905

(pink only)
Cathy Gorbunoff
678 Arrowsmith Ct.
Walnut Creek, CA 94598

DINNERWARE
(by American companies)
April Tvorak
P.O. Box 126
Canon City, CO 81215
(719) 269-3552

DOLLS
(Annalee Mobilitee)
Susan Cleff
P.O. Box 121
Streamwood, IL 60107

(Barbie before 1965)
Jean Williamson
298 Dogwood Ln., NW
Lawrenceville, GA 30245
(404) 963-7290

Dorothy Tancraetor
Box 306, 34 S Main St.
Mullica Hill, NJ 08062
(609) 478-6137

(also dollhouses)
Beverly A. Hutton
416 Live Oak Ln.
Boynton Beach, FL 33436

(hard plastic, ca 1930-1960)
Nancy Willner
1309 SW 22nd St.
Boynton Beach, FL 33426
(407) 369-8874

(also parts & children's dishes)
Norma Bennett
R.R. 1
Winner, SD 57580
(605) 842-0821

Gay Baron
13030 S Pacific Coast Hwy.
Redondo Beach, CA 90277
(213) 540-8212

DOOR KNOCKERS
Marlene Music
718 13th St. N
Great Falls, MT 59401
(406) 452-0671

DOROTHY C. THORPE
Lee Rosengren
2817 E Valley Blvd. 6H
W Covina, CA 91792
(818) 964-0768

DR. PEPPER ITEMS
Sam D. Hitchcock
1314 E Chestnut Exp.
Springfield, MO 65802
(417) 862-9302

DUCKS UNLIMITED
(pin-back buttons, 1930's–1950's)
M.L. Matzke
5022 Tongen Ave. NW
Rochester, MN 55901

EGG TIMERS
'Ourglass Antiques
P.O. Box 21054
Denver, CO 80221
(303) 429-4167

EGGS
(all except real)
Debbie Bercu
Rte. 4, Box 707
Marion, IL 62959

ELONGATED COINS
Elongated Coin Museum
228 Vassar Rd.
Poughkeepsie, NY 12603

EYE CUPS
(glass)
Donn Fagans
8 Knowlton Dr.
Marlton, NJ 08053
(609) 983-8841

FANS
Veronica Trainer
P.O. Box 409011
Cleveland, OH 44140
(216) 871-8584

FASHION
Mary Anderson
419 W Main
Grass Valley, CA 95945
(916) 273-2694

FIGURINES
(Brother Juniper)
Joy De Nagel
132 E Somerset Ave.
Tonawanda, NY 14150
(716) 836-3841

(nautical by Gorham)
Julious Bunn
2000 Lynn Rd.
Greensboro, NC 27405

FIRE KING DISHES
(any jadite)
Linda Holycross
R.R. 3 Box 21
Veedersburg, IN 47987

FOLK ART
(American & multicultural)
Eva M. Boicourt
Galerie de Boicourt
980 Chester
Birmingham, MI 48009
(313) 540-0166

FROGS
Catt Yeats
The Old Lund Store
HC 72 Box 2255
Lund, ID 83217

GASOLINE/PETROLIANA
Peter Capell
1838 W Grace St.
Chicago, IL 60613-2724

GEORGE OHR ART POTTERY
Marcie Phillips
P.O. Box 284
Montezuma, GA 31063
(912) 472-8638 or (912) 472-7525

GERMAN WORLD WAR II
Reddick Enterprises
P.O. Box 314
Denison, TX 75020
(903) 463-1366

GLASS
Tom Zachary Sr.
2996 Pangborn Rd.
Decatur, GA 30033
(404) 939-2307

GOOFUS GLASS
Krol's Rock City
Star Rt. 2, Box 15A
Deming, NM 88030

HATPIN HOLDERS
Lillian Baker, Founder
Int'l Club of Collector for Hatpins
& Hatpin Holders
15237 Chanera Ave.
Gardena, CA 90249

Ken Schwartz
Box 956
Redding, CA 96099
(916) 243-2521

HATPINS
Lillian Baker, Founder
Int'l Club for Collectors of Hatpins
& Hatpin Holders
15237 Chanera Ave.
Gardena, CA 90249

Ken Schwartz
Box 956
Redding, CA 96099
(916) 243-2521

HEISEY
(Greek Key)
Robert Carrell
PSC Box 2678
APO MIAMI, FL 34004
(507) 82-3728 (Panama)

HOLIDAYS
(Annalee Mobilitee dolls & animals)
Susan Cleff
P.O. Box 121
Streamwood, IL 60107

(especially Christmas)
Linda & Jeff Dykes
5 Valley Pl.
Upper Montclair, NJ 07043
(201) 746-5206

HONEY/BUMBLE BEES
(not cutesie; on vases, etc.)
Walt Raschick
Rte. 1, Box 153
Luck, WI 54853
(715) 327-8696

HOPALONG CASSIDY
Rachel Lachance
15 Woodside Ave.
Saco, ME 04072

HOUR GLASSES
'Ourglass Antiques
P.O. Box 21054
Denver, CO 80221
(303) 429-4167

HUMMELS
Eva Flynn
Box 4111
Thousand Oaks, CA 91359
(805) 495-0386

IMPERIAL GLASS
Annetta M. Bosselman
3103 Brentwood Circle
Grand Island, NE 68801
(308) 382-6384

INDIAN ARTIFACTS
Joan Somerville
25 N Main St.
Cedar City, UT 84720
(801) 586-3530

Reddick Enterprises
P.O. Box 314
Denison, TX 75020
(903) 463-1366

(American artworks)
Marcie Phillips
P.O. Box 284
Montezuma, GA 31063
(912) 472-8638 or (912) 472-7525

(Ioway Indian cultural materials)
19th Century Company
P.O. Box 5151
Lincoln, NE 68505

INKWELLS
Robert E. Boal
503 E Alder St.
Oakland, MD 21550
(301) 334-9501

INSULATORS
Krol's Rock City
Star Rt. 2, Box 15A
Deming, NM 88030

IRONS
Frank Pugliese
7510 Mountain Laurel Rd.
Boonsboro, MD 21713
(301) 293-7994

JEWELRY
(costume)
Pam Wiggins
10701 Sabo #202
Houston, TX 77089
(713) 944-7520

Scott F. Nussbaum Antiques
484 Ave. C
Bayonne, NJ 07002
(201) 436-7110

(by Georg Jensen)
Dee Jay Strope
P.O. Box 190
Mt. Holly, VA 22524
(804) 472-2141

(from 1800 to 1950)
Carol Braniff
603 13th Ave.
Devils Lake, ND 58301
(701) 662-2367

KALEIDOSCOPES
(pre-1940)
Marilyn Baseman
Main St.
S Egremont, MA 01258
(413) 528-3556

KEYS
(marked R.R. Switch Lock Key)
E.L. Burbage
P.O. Box 143
Ocean View, DE 19970
(302) 593-6537

KITCHEN COLLECTIBLES
Glen L. Green
Rte. 2, Box 71
Ochlocknee, GA 31773

LAMPS
(1930's–1950's)
Lenora's Fine Antiques
5802 Morningside Dr.
Richmond, VA 23226
(804) 282-3904

(rotating picture lamps)
Kevin Speaks
1145 W Sloan
Burt, MI 75020

(TV w/planters & clocks)
Dick's Antiques
c/o Coastal Empire Distributors
P.O. Box 1533
Brunswick, GA 31520
(912) 267-0333

(catalogs, glass shades)
Kathy Kelly
1621 Princess Ave.
Pittsburgh, PA 15216
(412) 561-3379

(lamp bases also)
William J. Gushue
318 Mill St.
Bristol, PA 19007
(215) 785-2395

LINENS
Marilyn Baseman
Main St.
S Egremont, MA 01258
(413) 528-3556

(also needlework)
Lori Hughes
253 Magda Way
Pacheco, CA 94553
(415) 687-1029

LOCKS
(obsolete postal)
Dr. Frank Scheer, Curator
Railway Mail Service Library
12 E Rosemont Ave.
Alexandria, VA 22301-2325

LUGGAGE
(Louis Vuitton, Mark Cross, Hermes)
Marilyn Baseman
Main St.
S Egremont, MA 01258
(413) 528-3556

MAJOLICA
William C. & Jerrod R. Danielson
18 Smith Acres
Northport, AL 35476

MAPS
(before 1880)
Dennis Clare
818 Duboce Ave.
San Francisco, CA 94117
(415) 552-0437

MARBLES
Danny Turner
P.O. Box 210992
Nashville, TN 37221
(615) 952-3699

Alecia MacMaster
Box 236
Williston, ND 58801
(701) 572-9633

MATCH COVERS
(collections in albums or boxes)
Bill Retskin
3417 Clayborne Ave.
Alexandria, VA 22306-1410

MATCH SAFES
B. Axler
P.O. Box 1288
Ansonia St.
New York, NY 10023
(212) 593-3570

MC COY POTTERY
Dick's Antiques
c/o Coastal Empire Distrbutors
P.O. Box 1533
Brunswick, GA 31520
(912) 267-0333

Rose Barash
7200 SW 6th St.
Miami, FL 33144
(305) 261-0640

MEDALS
David Smies
P.O. Box 522
Manhattan, KS 66502

Frank Pugliese
7510 Mountain Laurel Rd.
Boonsboro, MD 21713
(301) 293-7994

MILLEFIORI
Harriet James
227 N Fillmore St.
Arlington, VA 22201

MINIATURE IVORY PORTRAITS
Harriet R. Luster
Rt. 1, Box 177
Carson Creek Rd.
Limestone, TN 37681
(615) 257-3334

MISCELLANEOUS
(collector items in quantity)
Mark R. Bates
P.O. Box 646
Christiansburg, VA 24073

(unique, unusual old items for auctions)
Bear & Associates
718 Broadview Dr.
Green Bay, WI 54301
(414) 336-7672

MOLDS
(any cast iron, lead, or pewter)
Mrs. Harvey Markley
611 W Beardsley Ave.
Elkhart, IN 46514

MUSIC BOXES
(complete, broken, or parts)
Jack Brown
193 Roselawn NE
Warren, OH 44483
(216) 394-3201

NAPKIN RINGS
(figural, silverplate)
Deborah Golden
Rte. 2, Box 2365A
Grayling, MI 49738

NAUTICAL
(ships in bottles, ship prints)
Walter David
833 Troy St.
Elmont, NY 11003

(all types)
Julious Bunn
2000 Lynn Rd.
Greensboro, NC 27405

NEWSPAPERS
Kathleen Manning
209 Corbett
San Francisco, CA 94114
(415) 621-3565

NIPPON
Betty Yates
P.O. Box 759
Greeneville, TN 37744

(vases)
Julius Calloway
Audubon Station, P.O. Box 401
New York, NY 10032
(212) 928-5967

(mint condition only)
Kim Battle/Classics
215½ Winchester
Tyler, TX 75701

(undamaged items only)
Connie C. Christman
4116 Petersville Rd. NE
Bremerton, WA 98310
(206) 377-7850

(#1103 & #1106 w/green mark)
Harriet Meyer
82 Radburn Dr.
Hauppauge, NY 11788

NODDERS
Meta Bleier
3204 Portofino Point, K-1
Coconut Creek, FL 33066

OCCULT ARTIFACTS
Sandi Wakefield
Rte. 6, Box 439
Smithville, TN 37166
(615) 597-1270

OCCUPIED JAPAN
Bill Ogden
The Glass Pack Rat
3050 Colorado Ave.
Grand Junction, CO 81504

Mary Ann Lyttle
410 NE 51st St.
Ft. Lauderdale, FL 33334
(305) 776-7716

ORIENTAL RUGS
Heart Antiques
Great River Plaza
1821 2nd Ave.
Rock Island, IL 61201
(309) 788-5454

OYSTER PLATES
Meta Bleier
3204 Portofino Point, K-1
Coconut Creek, FL 33066

PACIFIC POTTERY DINNERWARE
(bright colors only)
Peter Van Rossem
58056 El Dorado Dr.
Yucca Valley, CA 92284
(619) 365-6424

PAPER
Elissa Cusumano
15943 E Lantana Ln.
Fountain Hills, AZ 85268
(602) 837-0588

PAPER DOLLS
Gretchen & Wildrose
5816 Steeplewood Dr.
N Richland Hills, TX 76180
(817) 581-4477

PATENT MEDICINE MEMORABILIA
William C. & Jerrod R. Danielson
18 Smith Acres
Northport, AL 35476

PENCIL SHARPENERS
(children's figural)
John R. Reece
1426 Turnesa Dr.
Titusville, FL 32780
(407) 383-9951

PERFUME BOTTLES
William C. & Jerrod R. Danielson
18 Smith Acres
Northport, AL 35476

(commercial French)
Cynthia Greenfield
12309 Featherwood Dr. #34
Silver Spring, MD 20904
(301) 622-5473

(crystal/sterling Victorian to 1950)
M. & H. Haas
Delray Beach, FL 33484
(407) 498-1083

PFALTZGRAFF
(cookie jars & art pottery, 1932–1937)
Louis L. Scher
P.O. Box 8668
Asheville, NC 28814
(704) 258-3308

PHOENIX GLASS
(geese motif, or blue color)
Joy De Nagel
132 E Somerset Ave.
Tonawanda, NY 14150
(716) 836-3841

PIANO ROLLS
Marlene Music
718 13th St. N
Great Falls, MT 59401
(406) 452-0671

PHOTOGRAPHICA
Another World
P.O. Box 507
Dillsboro, NC 28725
(704) 586-6572 or (704) 293-5197

Richard M. Bueschel
414 N Prospect Manor Ave.
Mt. Prospect, IL 60056
(708) 253-0791

(stereopticon)
Neal Nelson
302 E Becker
Willmar, MN 56201
(612) 235-7037

(photographs)
Book Beat, attn: Cary Loren
26010 Greenfield Rd.
Oak Park, MI 48237
(313) 968-1190

(cameras, stereoviews, etc.)
Treasure Hunt
416 Walnut St.
Hattiesburg, MS 39401

PLAYING CARDS
Bill Sachen
927 Grand Ave.
Waukegan, IL 60085
(708) 662-7204

PLATES
B. Axler
P.O. Box 1288
Ansonia St.
New York, NY 10023
(212) 593-3570

(pre-1960 Bing & Grondall
& Royal Copenhagen)
Eva Flynn
Box 4111
Thousand Oaks, CA 91359
(805) 495-0386

POLITICAL BUTTONS
Donn Fagans
8 Knowlton Dr.
Marlton, NJ 08053
(609) 983-8841

H. Joseph Levine
Presidential Coin & Antique Co.
6550-I Little River Turnpike
Alexandria, VA 22312

POPPYTRAIL CHINA
Orchard Sash/Okerleen Stout
Rte. 2, Box 54
Leoma, TN 38468
(615) 852-2905

POST CARDS
(all states & topics)
Another World
P.O. Box 507
Dillsboro, NC 28725
(704) 586-6572 or (704) 293-5197

(only before 1925)
William J. Gushue
318 Mill St.
Bristol, PA 19007
(215) 785-2395

(bank buildings or interiors)
Elongated Coin Museum
228 Vassar Rd.
Poughkeepsie, NY 12603

B.A. Steele Jr.
1922 N Byrkit St.
Mishawaka, IN 46545
(219) 259-7323

Joyce McLaughlin
1403 N Union St.
Fostoria, OH 44830
(419) 435-1262

POSTAL SCALES
(small English)
Irvine Gendler
11222 Davenport St.
Omaha, NE 68154
(402) 330-2656

PREMIUMS
(Junior G Man)
Richard A. Guttler
Syosset, NY 11791
(516) 935-7218

PUB JUGS
Dave Perry
420 W. Wrightwood
Chicago, IL 60614
(312) 528-8503

QUINN-BARRY COFFEE
Sam D. Hitchcock
1314 E Chestnut Exp.
Springfield, MO 65802
(417) 862-9302

RACING OUTBOARD MOTORS
Kevin Fife
2603 Ady Rd.
Forest Hill, MD 21050
(301) 879-6031

RAILROADIANA
(buy & trade)
E.L. Burbage
P.O. Box 143
Ocean View, DE 19970
(302) 539-6537

REAL ESTATE
(historical properties)
Mark R. Bates
P.O. Box 646
Christiansburg, VA 24073
(703) 382-1078

RECORDS
Ken Oilschlager
132 Parksitore W
Columbia, SC 29223
(803) 736-7315

RED WING
(advertising stoneware)
Clark Benne
P.O. Box 73
Bradshaw, NE 68319
(402) 736-4410

ROLLING PINS
(ceramic or glass)
Joan McGee
Rt. 2, Box 36
Mountain Home, AR 72653
(501) 491-5161

ROOSTERS
Charles H. Michler
3348 County Hwy. C
Rhinelander, WI 54501
(715) 369-0635

ROYAL DOULTON
L.C. Neuburger
Indian Tree Farm
Barryville, NY 12719
(914) 557-8141

(figurines)
Eva Flynn
Box 4111
Thousand Oaks, CA 91359
(805) 495-0386

ROYCROFT
T. Hirshberg
2181 Bancroft Way
Berkeley, CA 94704
(415) 845-3653

SALT & PEPPER SHAKERS
Mercedes Di Renzo
3831 N Lincoln Ave.
Chicago, IL 60613
(312) 472-1500

(people or bear figurals, pre-1970)
Nancy Willner
1309 SW 22nd St.
Boynton Beach, FL 33426
(407) 369-8874

SCANDINAVIAN ANTIQUES
Charles H. Michler
3348 County Hwy. C
Rhinelander, WI 54501
(715) 369-0635

SEWING
Mary Anderson
419 W Main
Grass Valley, CA 95945
(916) 273-2694

(tools)
Dee Jay Strope
P.O. Box 190
Mt. Holly, VA 22524
(804) 472-2141

SHIRLEY TEMPLE
Dora Lerch
P.O. Box 586
N White Plains, NY 10603

SLOT MACHINES
(complete, broken or parts)
Jack Brown
193 Roselawn NE
Warren, OH 44483
(216) 394-3201

SOFT DRINK ITEMS
William C. & Jerrod R. Danielson
18 Smith Acres
Northport, AL 35476

SOUVENIR PLATES
(U.S. Capitol, Washington, D.C.)
Janice R. Lachance
302 Lamond Pl.
Alexandria, VA 22314

SOUVENIR SPOONS
(unusual sterling)
Deborah Golden
Rte. 2, Box 2365A
Grayling, MI 49738

SPINNING OR FLAX WHEELS
(complete or incomplete)
Ja Dee Antiques
P.O. Box 149
New Brighton, PA 15066
(412) 846-8737

SPITTOONS
(metal figurals w/movement only)
Earl MacSorley
823 Indian Hill Rd.
Orange, CT 06477
(203) 387-1793

STEIFF ANIMALS
(especially teddy bears)
Linda & Jeff Dykes
5 Valley Pl.
Upper Montclair, NJ 07043
(201) 746-5206

STEINS
(Mettlach w/lids)
Walt Raschick
Rte. 1, Box 153
Luck, WI 54853
(715) 327-8696

Tom M. Blake
3400 W 111th St., Suite 301
Chicago, IL 60655
(312) 881-4159

STEUBENVILLE POTTERY
(Adam Antique pattern)
Jeanne Linquist
8 Fairoaks Ct.
San Mateo, CA 94403
(415) 573-9735

STERLING SILVER
William C. & Jerrod R. Danielson
18 Smith Acres
Northport, AL 35476

STORE ITEMS & MERCHANDISE
Glen L. Green
Rte. 2, Box 71
Ochlocknee, GA 31773
(912) 574-5529

STRING HOLDERS
(wall-hanging type)
John R. Reece
1426 Turnesa Dr.
Titusville, FL 32780
(407) 383-9951

SWANKY SWIGS
Cathy Gorbunoff
678 Arrowsmith Ct.
Walnut Creek, CA 94598

TATTOO-RELATED PARAPHERNALIA
Les Druyan
311 E 38th St.
New York, NY 10016
(212) 599-6530

TELEPHONES
(Chicago Supply Pay Phone)
Mrs. Harvey Markley
611 W Beardsley Ave.
Elkhart, IN 46514

TEXAS COLLECTIBLES
Pam Wiggins
10701 Sabo #202
Houston, TX 77089
(713) 944-7520

TEXTILES
Eva M. Boicourt
Galerie de Boicourt
980 Chester
Birmingham, MI 48009
(313) 540-0166

TIFFANY SILVER
(flatware, hollowware, jewelry)
M. & H. Haas
10A Burgundy
Delray Beach, FL 33484
(407) 498-1083

TIFFIN GLASS
Joyce McLaughlin
1403 N Union St.
Fostoria, OH 44830
(419) 435-1262

TOBACCO TINS
Rick Newman
4813 E Hot Springs Ave.
Las Vegas, NY 89110
(702) 438-9100

TOKENS
David Smies
P.O. Box 522
Manhattan, KS 66502

Frank Pugliese
7510 Mountain Laurel Rd.
Boonsboro, MD 21713
(301) 293-7994

TOYS
(G.I. Joe & action figures)
Paul Ivy
2300 McCullough St.
Austin, TX 78703

(personality)
Richard Gronowski
140 N Garfield Ave.
Traverse City, MI 49684
(616) 941-2111

E.L. Chaney
906 4th Ave.
Jacksonville, AL 36265
(205) 435-5701

Ken Oilschlager
132 Parksitore W
Columbia, SC 29223
(803) 736-7315

Grover Corey Sr.
R.R. #7, Box 900
Laurel Hill Rd.
Pineville, KY 40977
(606) 337-3439

C.E. Jones
Rte. 7, Box 2083
Palestine, TX 75801
(214) 723-3865

Dorothy Tancraetor
Box 306, 34 S Main St.
Mullica Hill, NJ 08062
(609) 478-6137

Andrew Egendorf
P.O. Box 646
Weston, MA 02193
(617) 647-1025

Gay Baron
1303 S Pacific Coast Hwy.
Redondo Beach, CA 90277
(213) 540-8212

(to 1960's)
Philip Stellmacher
3535 E Calle del Prado
Tucson, AZ 85716
(602) 325-3509

(Marx electric trains)
Bill Ogden
The Glass Pack Rat
3050 Colorado Ave.
Grand Junction, CO 81504

(space toys)
Donald Sheldon
P.O. Box 3313
Trenton, NJ 08619
(609) 588-5403

TRAINS
(toy by Lionel)
Neal Nelson
302 E Becker
Willmar, MN 56201
(612) 235-7037

UMBRELLA HANDLES
Meta Bleier
3204 Portofino Point, K-1
Coconut Creek, FL 33066

VIEW-MASTER REELS
D.F. Yates
229 Forkner Dr.
Decatur, GA 30030

WALKING STICKS
Kimball Sterling
204 E Main
Jonesborough, TN 37604

WATCHES
Scott F. Nussbaum Antiques
484 Ave. C
Bayonne, NJ 07002
(201) 436-7110

WATT POTTERY
Kathryn B. Colrard
315 Hogan Rd.
Rossville, GA 30741
(404) 861-6757

WELLER
Cliff Thornhill
186 Kit Carson Way
Vallejo, CA 94589

WESTMORELAND
Annetta M. Bosselman
3103 Brentwood Circle
Grand Island, NE 68801
(308) 382-6384

WICKER
(anything circa 1800's-1930's)
Marilyn Ringel
211 Guinea Woods Rd.
Old Westbury, NY 11568

WOODEN-BACKED PICTURES
(3½" x 4½")
M. & T. Schoeffler
124 Terrace St.
Arlington, TX 76012

WORLD'S FAIR & EXPOSITIONS
(elongated coins)
Doug Fairbanks, Sr.
5937 Beadle Dr.
Jamesville, NY 13078

(Paris Expo of 1900)
A.J. Petersen
2722 John Day
Kennewick, WA 99336
(509) 783-8732

H. Joseph Levine
Presidential Coin & Antique Co.
6550-I Little River Turnpike
Alexandria, VA 22312

Index

Schroeder's Antiques Price Guide

Schroeder's Antiques Price Guide has become THE household name in the antiques and collectibles field. Our team of editors work year around with more than 200 contributors to bring you our #1 best-selling book on antiques and collectibles.

With more than 50,000 items identified and priced, *Schroeder's* is a must for the collector and dealer alike. If it merits the interest of today's collector, you'll find it in *Schroeder's*. Each subject is represented with histories and background information. In addition, hundreds of sharp original photos are used each year to illustrate not only the rare and unusual, but the everyday "fun-type" collectibles as well – not postage stamp pictures, but large close-up shots that show important details clearly.

Our editors compile a new book each year. Never do we merely change prices. Each category is thoroughly checked to spot inconsistencies, listings that may not be entirely reflective of actual market dealings, and lines too vague to be of merit. Only the best of the lot remains for publication. You'll find *Schroeder's Antiques Price Guide* the one to buy for factual information and quality.

8½x11", 608 Pages   **$12.95**

COLLECTOR BOOKS
A Division of Schroeder Publishing Co., Inc.